This journal is abstracted or indexed in *Linguistics & Language Behavior Abstracts; Pascal; Psychological Abstracts; PsycINFO; PsycLIT; Social Planning/Policy & Development Abstracts; Sociological Abstracts.*

Microform copies of this journal are available through Bell & Howell Information and Learning, P.O. Box 1346, Ann Arbor, MI 48106–1346.

Personality and Social Psychology Review is an official publication of the Society for Personality and Social Psychology. Members of the Society receive the journal free of additional charge as a benefit of membership. For further information, contact Harry Reis, Executive Officer, SPSP, Department of Psychology, University of Rochester, Meliora 355, Rochester, NY 14627. E-mail: spsp@scp.rochester.edu.

First published 2000 by Lawrence Erlbaum Associates, Inc

Published 2015 by Psychology Press
711 Third Avenue, New York, NY 10017

and by Psychology Press
27 Church Road, Hove, East Sussex, BN3 2FA

Psychology Press is an imprint of the Taylor & Francis Group, an informa business

ISBN 13: 978-0-8058-9768-5 (pbk)

PERSONALITY AND SOCIAL PSYCHOLOGY REVIEW
An Official Journal of the
Society for Personality and Social Psychology, Inc.

Volume 4, Number 1   2000

SPECIAL ISSUE: PERSONALITY AND SOCIAL PSYCHOLOGY AT THE INTER-
FACE: NEW DIRECTIONS FOR INTERDISCIPLINARY RESEARCH

EDITORS' FOREWORD

ARTICLES

Personality and Social Psychology Review
2000, Vol. 4, No. 1, 2

FOREWORD

Personality and Social Psychology at the Interface: New Directions for Interdisciplinary Research

As the gateway to a new millennium, the year 2000 is destined to be a memorable one. For personality and social psychologists in particular, the year will be remembered as the occasion of the first stand-alone convention of the Society for Personality and Social Psychology. This issue of *Personality and Social Psychology Review* was planned to coincide with and complement the inaugural convention by providing a view of the past, present, and future of our field as an interdisciplinary endeavor.

As a broad field of inquiry, personality and social psychology by its very definition stands at the interface—linking the biology and development of the individual with the systems of interpersonal relationships, social structure, and culture within which the person is formed and functions. The history of the field has been marked by periods of relative insularity and inward focus and periods of relative expansiveness and outward focus. The last few years of the 20th century marked the beginning of a major shift in the direction of renewed interest in personality and social psychology as a central node in an interdisciplinary network with rich connections to other subdisciplines of psychology and to the life sciences and social sciences more broadly. The contributions to this special issue of this journal represent our effort to capture some of these exciting new directions at the various points of interface with other fields of inquiry.

The authors invited to contribute to this volume were among those whose own work exemplified the kinds of interdisciplinary outreach that we envision for the field. Collectively, the articles in this issue illustrate the vital contributions that can be made by pursuing the reciprocal connections between personality and social psychology and psychobiology (cf. Berntson & Cacioppo; Ryff), developmental psychology (Thorne), comparative psychology and evolutionary biology (Berntson & Cacioppo; Fiske), clinical and health psychology (Snyder, Tennen, Affleck, & Cheavens; Ryff; Thorne), communication studies (McKenna & Bargh), organizational studies and systems theory (McGrath, Arrow, & Berdahl), and cultural anthropology (Fiske). From the immune system to the Internet, the common thread is the critical role of individual personality and interpersonal relationships. What comes across clearly in all of these illustrations is the point that personality and social psychology is not in danger of losing its identity as a field by entering into cross-disciplinary collaborations and endeavors. To the contrary, such efforts are likely to ensure that our own field of specialization will not only thrive but perhaps reclaim ground that has been surrendered to other disciplines.

In developing their articles for this issue, the contributors were encouraged to be expansive and inspirational—to consider what can, may, and should be accomplished if personality and social psychologists take seriously the opportunities for working at the interface. The articles in this issue live up to this challenge, and the result is a set of articles that not only reflect our collective past and present but also set an agenda for our collective future.

Marilynn B. Brewer
David A. Kenny
Julie K. Norem

Personality and Social Psychology Review
2000, Vol. 4, No. 1, 3–15

Psychobiology and Social Psychology: Past, Present, and Future

Gary G. Berntson
Department of Psychology
Ohio State University

John T. Cacioppo
Department of Psychology
University of Chicago

Social psychology and psychobiology have a rich historical connection, although over the last half century these two disciplines have seemingly become estranged. To a significant extent, that alienation arose from an archaic and nonviable model of behavioral biology that retarded the development of both disciplines. With the emergence of modern biological perspectives, this impediment no longer limits fruitful collaborations among social psychologists and psychobiologists. Indeed, some of the most exciting contemporary developments are emerging from the areas of social neuroscience, cognitive neuroscience, and behavioral neuroscience. We review the history of links between social psychology and psychobiology, the factors that led to the segregation of these subdisciplines, and the modern biological perspectives that provide the basis for reintegration of these disciplines.

Social psychology and psychobiology share a richly intertwined, if not always harmonious, history. The Darwinian revolution had immense impact on psychology, as it focused attention on the biological origins of behavior and emphasized the continuity between the human and the animal mind. This perspective fostered a view of psychology as a biological science, despite its deep historical roots in philosophy, and promoted a natural conceptual evolution toward biological models of psychological processes (Cofer & Appley, 1964). Darwin himself became a pioneer in that development, with the publication of *Expression of the Emotions in Man and Animals* (Darwin, 1872/1998).

Among the benefactors of the Darwinian era were the instinct theorists, who were now emboldened by a solid evolutionary substrate for their views on the nature and origins of "purposive" behavior. Instincts were central to the thinking of many early psychologists, including notables such as James (1890). Evolutionary perspectives and instinct theories contributed to the emergence of the fields of behavioral genetics and a branch of psychobiology (comparative psychology) that sought to elucidate laws and principles of behavior, largely through animal studies. In the first

social psychology textbook, *An Introduction to Social Psychology,* McDougall (1908) outlined a theory of personality, with instincts and their associated "emotions" at the central core.

Instinct theories, however, came under increasing and often blistering attacks. Among other failings was their teleological focus, their devolution into massive instinct "lists," and their failure to mature into predictive, explanatory, and hypothesis-generating theoretical systems. Sharp criticisms came from social psychologists, as in F. H. Allport's (1924) *Social Psychology* and Bernard's (1924) volume *Instincts: A Study in Social Psychology.* The assault on instincts was not limited to social psychologists. Equally strident voices emanated, for example, from clinical psychology in Dunlap's (1919) *Journal of Abnormal Psychology* article "Are there any instincts?" and from comparative psychology in Kuo's (1924) *Psychological Review* piece, "A psychology without heredity."

Clearly, the instinct adventure was a failure for social psychology, but it was also a failure for psychobiology and for psychology in general. Although instinct models flourished in the post-Darwinian era, with its focus on biology and evolution, it would be a misattribution to ascribe the ultimate fall of instinct theories to their biological focus. The demise of instinct theories was not the failure of the biological perspective, but the failure of an inappropriate and ill-conceived biological model. Both social psychology and psychobiology were betrayed by the prevailing instinct theories, and both needed to seek

Preparation of this article was supported in part by a grant from the MacArthur Foundation, and by National Heart, Lung, and Blood Institute Grant HL 54428.

Requests for reprints should be sent to Gary G. Berntson, Department of Psychology, Ohio State University, Columbus, OH 43210. E-mail: berntson.2@osu.edu.

alternative paradigms, models, and theoretical schemas.

Among the early critics of the instinct concept were Watson and Morgan (1917), who argued that genetically endowed "instincts" could at best account for a very limited range of behavior. Later, Watson (1924) developed and formalized his concepts in his first volume *Behaviorism.* The early work of Thorndike (1898, 1927) on learning and *The Law of Effect,* and that of Pavlov (1927) on conditioning processes, together with Watson's views on behaviorism, would forever remodel psychological thinking. Although McDougall (1908) recognized the important role of experience in shaping the expression of instincts, there now emerged the specter of a generalized learning mechanism that could liberate the organism from the otherwise immutable dictates of heredity. According to this view, although learning processes may be indirectly dependent on genetically endowed motivational mechanisms, the direction and form of learned behaviors were not so constrained.

Behaviorism and the emphasis on learning assumed preeminence in experimental psychology for several decades. Great empirical and conceptual strides were made during this era. The Hull–Spence model of drive, reinforcement, and learning (e.g., see Spence, 1960) dominated much of the field of psychobiology. Comparative psychologists were busy with attempts to enumerate the laws and principles governing learning, and the emerging field of "physiological psychology" often focused on the neural mechanisms of learning (Beach, Hebb, Morgan, & Nissen, 1960; Hebb, 1949), or the brain mechanisms underlying the putative drives that motivate or reinforce that learning (Hebb, 1955; Stellar, 1954).

Social psychology was also heavily influenced by the prevailing emphasis on learning processes. The emergence of social learning theories during this era (Dollard, Doob, Miller, Mowrer, & Sears, 1939; Dollard & Miller, 1950; Miller & Dollard, 1941) had not only historical significance but also continues to have an impact on research and concepts in social psychology (Bjoerkqvist, 1997; Liao & Cai, 1995; Miller, Shoda, & Hurley, 1996; Smith & DeCoster, 1998). The synergism between social psychology and psychobiology was illustrated by the publication of the first edition of *A Handbook of Social Psychology* (Murchison, 1935), which included 8 (of 22) chapters on animal models of social behavior. Among these was a chapter on nonhuman primates, authored by Yerkes and Yerkes, who would later be instrumental in establishing the federally funded Yerkes Regional Primate Research Center in Atlanta, where social psychological studies of primates have continued.

There was a sense during that period that a comprehensive, meaningful social science would require an integration of social psychology and psychobiology. Considering the scientific status of the social sciences relative to that of the physical sciences, Murchison (1935), in the preface to the first social psychology handbook, beseeched serious students of social psychology to

> reflect concerning the problems of social mechanics that are basic enough to require identification and analysis before progress can even begin in this field. Whatever those mechanisms may be, they are certain to be essential components of *all social behavior in all social bodies in all social situations whatever* [italics added]. The social scientist must discover those mechanisms, or there will never be a social law. (p. IX)

Although both psychobiology and social psychology benefitted from research and theory on learning, and from interactions between the disciplines, both were also hampered by what increasingly had become the straightjacket of behaviorism. Especially pernicious was the radical behaviorism of Skinner (see Evans, 1968), who eschewed scientific explanations of behavior that appeal to something going on in another universe, such as the mind or the nervous system. Although Skinner may have emerged from the psychobiological tradition, his extremist form of behaviorism excluded meaningful accounts of behavior in the terms of biology (except in a trivial sense). It also failed to admit many emerging concepts and theories from social and cognitive psychology.

In his presidential address to the first annual meeting of the American Psychological Association (APA) Division of Personality and Social Psychology, G. W. Allport (1947) railed against what he termed "motorized psychology"—a mechanistic psychology that would deny the influence of factors like attitudes or intentions. Many social psychologists followed suit. Again, however, the rejection of radical behaviorism should not be equated with a rejection of the biological perspective. Indeed, psychobiologists also rejected this extremist behaviorism, because it denies a fundamental tenant of psychobiology—that there is substantial benefit to the study of behavior from approaches that extend across subdisciplinary domains or levels of analysis. These include the social as well as the neuropsychological, neurochemical, and neurophysiological levels.

A phoenix is rising, however, from the ashes of historical behavioral biology. It is based not on a biological paradigm that happens to be transiently in vogue at the moment, but on a progressively emerging contemporary psychobiology that is richly grounded in, and calibrated by, the constraints of cross-disciplinary data, concepts, and perspectives. Of equal importance, given this interdisciplinary grounding, modern psychobiology now has the scientific authority to significantly impact on other disciplines and levels of analysis. There were, of course, growing pains in the emergence of modern behavioral neuroscience from its roots in historical psychobiology. At times, the methods, empirical data, and concepts of psychology seemed incompatible or at least inharmonious with the developing neuroscience perspective. At an early point in the 1970s and 1980s, many psychobiologists rejected their psychological heritage, and sought identification with disciplines such as physiology, pharmacology, or neurochemistry. Other psychobiologists with greater prescience were instrumental in establishing the interdisciplinary Society for Neuroscience (in 1970), which is the premier association for behavioral neuroscience that today has more than 25,000 members. This initiative resulted in gradually increasing communication and integration across levels of analysis, whereby conceptual and methodological barriers that once stood as disciplinary fortresses now seem archaic and regressive.

This multilevel interdisciplinary perspective, which seeks to integrate information derived from levels of analysis ranging from psychology to molecular biology, is now increasingly embraced by the rapidly developing fields of behavioral neuroscience, cognitive neuroscience, behavioral medicine, behavior genetics, psychoneuroimmunology, and social neuroscience. In fact, it is the thesis of this article that the explosive developments in these fields is causally, rather than serendipitously, related to the recognition of the value of multilevel analyses and the biological perspective.

Modern Behavioral Biology

So what is the new biological paradigm or perspective that has fostered the recent explosive developments in both behavioral neuroscience and social neuroscience? There are many factors, but by far the most important is the recognition that evolution not only endowed us with primitive functions like reflexes and a sex drive, but it sculpted the awesome information processing capacities of the highest levels of the brain. Although the conceptual domain of some early evolutionary social psychological theories may have stopped at the limbic system, evolution did not. All behaviors are not invariably adaptive, either in terms of our immediate survival or in the proliferation of our genes. Likely related to the multiplicity of unforeseen adaptive challenges that terrestrial organisms may encounter, natural selection continued to craft complex neural systems that can defy primitive genetic imperatives. For an organism to be generally adaptive it must be eminently flexible, and evolution has seen to it. As cogently articulated by the cognitive neuroscientist Pinker (1997) in his book, *How the Mind Works,* "The

ultimate goal of natural selection is to propagate genes, but that does not mean that the ultimate goal of people is to propagate genes" (p. 24). He later elaborated:

> Well into my procreating years I am, so far, voluntarily childless, having squandered my biological resources reading and writing, doing research, helping out friends and students. ... By Darwinian standards I am a horrible mistake, a pathetic loser. ... But I am happy to be that way, and if my genes don't like it, they can go jump in the lake. (p. 52)

The new behavioral biology is fundamentally different from the old, not just because it is now endowed with a technical armamentarium that permits probing of the lowest levels of neuronal molecular biology (although these developments are far from irrelevant). It is not merely because an interdisciplinary approach can increase the probability of federal funding (in fact, the opposite is sometimes the case), nor is it attributable to an abject denial of our scientific heritage—in fact, appropriately conceptualized instinct models may offer meaningful accounts of some aspects of behavior. Rather, modern behavioral biology is distinct because it recognizes that natural selection and evolution progressed beyond the limbic system, and continue to mold the highest level cortical substrates that underlie cognitive operations. In contrast to the justifiable wrath of G. W. Allport (1947) concerning motorized psychology and the extant biological models of the time, the vision of contemporary behavioral biology is increasingly focused on the manner in which the mind is realized in the brain. Modern behavioral neuroscience is as interested in constructs such as attention and cognition as it is in issues such as why people seek food and water.[1]

The notable 19th-century neurologist Jackson (1884/1958), in an essay on "Evolution and dissolution of the nervous system," emphasized the hierarchical structure of the brain and the rerepresentation of functions at multiple levels within this neural hierarchy. Implicit in his message was the fact that information is processed at multiple levels of organization within the nervous system, but it would be almost 100 years before this concept was comprehensively embraced by behavioral biology. Primitive protective responses to

---

[1]This is documented by a Medline search. The APA *Journal of Comparative and Physiological Psychology* (*JCCP*) became *Behavioral Neuroscience* (*BN*) in 1983. In the *JCCP* years (from 1965–1982), the number of articles retrieved by the keyword *attention* was only about 25% of the number retrieved by *hunger* or *thirst*, and the number retrieved by *social* was about 80% of the latter. During the 1980s period of *BN*, those proportions had shifted considerably, as either *attention* or *social* now retrieved about 160% of the number retrieved by *hunger* or *thirst*. That trajectory continues into the 1990s period of *BN*, over which the keywords *attention* or *social* each retrieved about 700% more articles than did *hunger* or *thirst*.

aversive stimuli are organized at the level of the spinal cord, as is apparent in flexor (pain) withdrawal reflexes to noxious stimuli that can be seen even after spinal transections. These primitive protective reactions are expanded and embellished at higher levels of the nervous system (see Berntson, Boysen, & Cacioppo, 1993). The evolutionary development of higher neural systems, such as the limbic system, endowed organisms with an expanded behavioral repertoire, including escape reactions, aggressive responses, and even the ability to anticipate and avoid aversive encounters. However, it was not until the emergence and elaboration of the cerebral cortical mantle that the ultimate protective strategies were fully developed in humans. These include not only the ability to anticipate potential danger but also to weigh alternative tactics for dealing with it, including the establishment of social organizations such as governments and militaries.

Social and cognitive mechanisms are not localized to a single neural level, but are represented at multiple levels of the nervous system. At progressively higher levels of organization, there is a general expansion in the range and relational complexity of contextual controls and in the breadth and flexibility of discriminative and adaptive responses (Berntson et al., 1993). Higher level systems confer greater behavioral variability and adaptive flexibility, but do not eliminate lower behavioral mechanisms. Thus, evolutionary forces have more rigidly canalized some aspects of behavior, such as those organized at subcortical levels, but have also forged higher level interacting neural systems. A behavioral biology or evolutionary social psychology that restricts its focus to these more primitive levels is necessarily incomplete.

Adaptive flexibility has costs, however, given the finite information processing capacity of neural tissue. Greater flexibility implies a less rigid relation between inputs and outputs, a greater range of information that must be processed, a slower serial-like mode of processing, and an increased susceptibility to miscalculation. Consequently, the evolutionary layering of higher processing levels onto lower substrates has considerable adaptive advantage, in that lower and more efficient processing levels may continue to be utilized, and may be sufficient in some circumstances. Pain withdrawal reflexes are fast, and rarely lie. A pain stimulus is an obligatory condition for the rapid invocation of the flexor withdrawal reflex. Given the hierarchical organization of the nervous system, however, an invoked reflex does not necessarily manifest in a reflexive response. Information is processed at multiple levels of the neuraxis, and reactions to that information may be quite divergent across levels. Priority in the control of behavior may shift among these levels. Practiced drivers on a familiar thoroughfare may be largely unaware of the control behavior they exercise in driving, which can be mediated by relatively low-level automated processing mechanisms. However, in unfamiliar or treacherous terrain, such as a narrow and winding mountain road, every control action may become thoughtful and deliberate. Similarly, although people have powerful pain withdrawal reflexes, they can be overridden by higher level processes under some circumstances (e.g., if a child was caught in a fire).

An Illustration of Multiple Levels of Processing

Higher level neural systems do not always dominate, however, and the multiple levels of neural processing may even come into conflict. In a project (Boysen & Berntson, 1995) designed to study the possible use of deception in chimpanzees, an initial stage entailed training the animals in a simple choice selection task between two quantities of candies. Animals were presented with two discrete candy arrays, and their task was to select one of the choice options. A reversed reward contingency was imposed, such that the animals were reinforced with the nonselected array, whereas the selected array was given to a passive observer animal. Consequently, the animal could optimize payoff by selecting the smaller candy array, and thus receive the larger reward. This was a simple task, or so it seemed, that would be mastered in a few trials. In fact, even after hundreds of trials of differential reinforcement, the animals could not be trained to reliably select the smaller of the two candy arrays (Boysen & Berntson, 1995).

This was a startling result, as the chimpanzees in this study (Boysen & Berntson, 1995) were among the most highly trained and cognitively sophisticated nonhuman animals in the world. They were accomplished in the use of numeric symbols (Arabic numerals) both receptively and expressively, and could demonstrate logical reasoning in a transitive inference task. Seemingly, this was one of the most elementary tasks in which they had engaged. Nevertheless, trial after trial, they continued to select the larger candy array, thereby receiving the smaller reward, and no improvement in performance was apparent even with extended training.

We asked why such intelligent animals could not learn to optimize performance in such a simple task. That was the wrong question, and that became apparent with further analysis of performance. Overall, the animals tended to select the larger candy array, and this tendency increased as the numerical disparity between the array choices increased. That is, their performance became even less optimal under the very conditions in which they stood to benefit the most by selecting the smaller array. Was this a violation of the basic principles of reinforcement? A learning failure?

The answer to those questions is no. Arabic numerals were then substituted (mounted on a placard) for the candy arrays. The same reversed reward contingency was in effect, with the animals receiving the number of candies corresponding to the nonselected numeral as a reward. Under these conditions, performance became more optimal on the very first trial (Boysen, Berntson, Hannan, & Cacioppo, 1996). Animals now reliably selected the smaller Arabic numeral and thus received the larger reward. Moreover, opposite the pattern with candy arrays, performance became more optimal with larger numeric disparities between the choice stimuli, consistent with the greater payoff differential. It appears that the animals had indeed learned the rules of the game, but were unable to implement that implicit knowledge with candy arrays as choice stimuli. When candy arrays were again introduced, performance plummeted, and when Arabic numerals were reintroduced as stimuli, performance was again immediately optimized.

These findings (Boysen et al., 1996) imply a powerful interfering response bias in this task, perhaps related to the perceptual features of the candy arrays. The task interference appears to be related to a primitive disposition to select a larger quantity of food, which would likely have adaptive value in the evolutionary history of the species. In the contrived environment of the experimental psychologist, however, such a disposition can lead to suboptimal choices. Although this primitive disposition may have introduced an interfering bias in response selection, it did not preclude higher level processing and learning of the reward contingencies, as that learning was expressed immediately on introduction of the Arabic numerals.

These results (Boysen et al., 1996) can be understood within the framework of the multiple levels of processing within the nervous system. The findings illustrate that multiple processing levels, although generally coordinated, may under some conditions lead to very different behavioral conclusions. These results suggest that an important function of symbols is that they can come to represent selective abstract features of their referents (e.g., numerosity), without the perceptual imperatives that may have been endowed on those referents by evolution. That is, higher level cognitive processing of information may serve as a powerful liberating force from the dictates of a more primitive evolutionary biology. Indeed, this was likely an important factor in the emergence of human intellect, culture, and civilization.

Relevance to Social Psychology

Multiple levels of processing, implied by the hierarchical structure of the nervous system, likely underlie important aspects of social psychology. The Elaboration Likelihood Model (Petty & Cacioppo, 1986) asserts that there are distinct routes to persuasion, some being more peripheral (based on factors such as context, authority, etc.) and others more central or rationally based. The conditions under which the peripheral route predominates are those in which inadequate knowledge is available, or higher level cognitive processing is otherwise diminished. In humans, mere exposure to novel stimuli has been shown to alter evaluative judgments of those stimuli in subsequent tests (Zajonc, 1968). Similarly, simple somatomotor posturing can bias evaluative judgments of stimuli in the absence of preexisting knowledge, a condition that favors the peripheral processing route (Cacioppo, Priester, & Berntson, 1993; Priester, Cacioppo, & Petty, 1996). However, the effectiveness of peripheral routes is greatly reduced for stimuli that have an existing associative meaning (Cacioppo, Marshall-Goodell, Tassinary, & Petty, 1992). The powerful interference observed in chimpanzees, despite knowledge of the payoff rules, suggests that one consequence of continued phylogenetic development of cognitive mechanisms is an enhanced ability of higher level mechanisms to overcome more primitive dispositional biases. The availability of animal models that parallel human cognitive and behavioral processes can provide an important link between social psychological phenomena and their underlying neurobehaviorial mechanisms.

Although we carry a primitive evolutionary undercarriage that is generally but not always adaptive, the real psychological significance of evolution is that it has progressively endowed organisms with the cognitive machinery that allows more elaborate and flexible processing of information. This can be a tremendously liberating force from the fixed dictates of primitive dispositions arising from our genetic heritage, allowing for the regulation, shaping, and integration of more primitive levels of organization. Although conflicts may develop across levels of organization under certain circumstances, generally there is a synergism rather than an antagonism among levels, and between biological and cultural determinants of social behavior.

A feature of the antiquated behavioral biology of the past is that it failed to progress conceptually beyond the level of the limbic system. In contrast, contemporary behavioral neuroscience fully recognizes the multiplicity of processing levels, and embraces those aspects of cognition and behavior that derive from the highest levels of neural organization. These are the levels that underlie the most complex psychological processes, and are most closely related to what may be termed the *mind.* The behavioral biology of the past, which was appropriately rejected by social psychologists, was a mindless biology. In contrast, contemporary behavioral neuroscience is highly mindful. It is clear that what we have learned about the physiology of thirst and body water balance offers few insights into the drinking behavior of an alcoholic in a bar. For this understanding, we will need a knowledge base ranging from the genetic and neurochemical predispositions to the rewarding effects of alcohol, to the cognitive and sociocultural factors that dispose toward alcohol usage. In short, a multilevel approach will be necessary to unravel this vexing social problem. Given the hierarchical structure of the brain, and the multiple levels of processing, biological determinants are no longer equated with fixed, innate mechanisms.

Principles of Multilevel Analyses

The central tenet of the emerging discipline of social neuroscience is simple: Social psychology and psychobiology will mutually benefit by greater integration among our subdisciplines. Both lower and higher levels of neural organization can contribute to psychological processes, and a crucial focus for the future is how moderator variables come to determine the relative contributions of these levels of processing in a given context. This knowledge can transform generalizability failures into comprehensive theoretical integrations. Does this raise the specter that social psychology will be overwhelmed, supplanted, or otherwise rendered subservient to psychobiology? The dirty little secret of reductionism is that, in the recorded history of science, there has never been a discipline that has been obliterated by reduction to a lower level of analysis. The emergence of subatomic physics did not render biochemistry obsolete. To the contrary, it offered the basic conceptual framework within which biochemistry and neurochemistry have flourished.

Cross-disciplinary constraints from one level of analysis to another come not only from lower strata in the reductionist hierarchy. As previously discussed, early instinct theories were felled in large part by social psychologists, and radical behaviorism buckled under the assault of the cognitive revolution. The intellectual sword of multilevel analysis cuts both ways. It is not the subjugation of one discipline or level of analysis to another, as higher level analyses often provide the fundamental subject matter and guiding concepts for lower level disciplines. Rather, multilevel analysis affords a mutual calibration among disciplines that enriches both. This entails a reciprocal anchoring of disciplines in the knowledge base of the other, and offers insights that can dramatically enhance progress of each of the subfields. Disciplinary or subdisciplinary isolation poses a real threat to the survival of a field. At best, such isolationism is inefficient, often requiring the rediscovery of basic principles that have been well-established in other disciplines. This applies to lower as well as higher levels of analysis. Although genes may rigidly encode their specific gene product, the behavioral effect of gene expression may be far less fixed. Indeed, behavioral geneticists increasingly recognize that

> for behaviors with smaller genetic effects (such as those likely to characterize most of the effects of a gene knockout), there can be important influences of environmental conditions specific to individual laboratories, and specific behavioral effects should not be uncritically attributed to genetic manipulations such as targeted gene deletions. (Crabbe, Wahlsten, & Dudek, 1999, p. 1672)

Principle of Multiple Determinism

It is increasingly apparent that problems and issues in genetics as well as psychology will not be fully understood by studies restricted to a single level of analysis, regardless of the specific level selected (Anderson, 1998; Cacioppo & Berntson, 1992). A process or event at one level of organization may have antecedents and determinants both within and across organizational levels, as encapsulated in what has been termed the *principle of multiple determinism* (Cacioppo & Berntson, 1992). In prairie voles, oxytocin, vasopressin, adrenal glucocorticoids, and other hormones, along with experiential factors, exert important influences on mate selection, the establishment of monogamous relationships, and on parenting behavior (Carter & Altemus, 1997; Carter, DeVris, & Getz, 1995). Similar hormonal–behavioral relations have been documented in other mammalian species (Insel, 1997; Nelson & Panksepp, 1998). In view of the elaborations of higher level processing mechanisms in humans, it is not surprising that sociocultural and interpersonal factors assume greater significance in mate selection and maternal–infant attachments. Nevertheless, it is increasingly recognized that, in addition to the obvious role of gonadal hormones in sexual function and potency, a broader range of hormonal influences may modulate attraction and affiliation, as well as maternal–infant and paternal–infant attachments in humans (Flemming, Ruble, Krieger, & Wong, 1997; McCarthy & Altemus, 1997; Nelson & Panksepp, 1998; Rosenblatt, 1994). These relations do not represent the obligatory dictates of a one-way biological mandate on behavior. In fact, hormonal status is known to be modulated by psychological states and processes. We will return to this reciprocal pattern of modulation between psychological and biological determinants.

Neither social psychologists nor psychobiologists can, or should, directly concern themselves with all possible levels of analysis. A corollary to the principle of multiple determinism is that mapping relations across levels of organization becomes more complex as the number of intervening levels increases. Although it is certainly worthwhile to adopt a broad scientific perspective, specific research programs would probably achieve maximal benefit by attention to more proximate levels of analysis (both higher and lower). If this perspective was embraced generally by those pursuing distinct levels of analysis, it may be sufficient to ensure the ultimate integration among disciplines.

As previously considered, disciplines are not obliterated by reduction to a lower level of analysis, as there are efficiencies in higher level organizations of information. The essential features of Beethoven's Ninth Symphony may be captured by the sequential digital data on a compact disc (CD), and examination of that data set may be sufficient to identify the piece. It may be faster, easier, and likely more enjoyable to simply play it out. Similarly, although a horse race may be characterized by specifying all relevant, temporally unfolding synaptic interactions and neuromuscular events of each of the participant horses, it would not be a particularly parsimonious account, and probably not nearly as much fun as watching the race, or even listening to the energetic narrative of a race announcer. This is not to say that a mapping across levels would be worthless. Indeed, it would be invaluable. Of the bewildering number of cellular events underlying the performance of the horses, a subset will relate to psychological concepts such as motivation, and the myriad social interactions among the horses as well as between the horses and their jockeys. Understanding this subset would undoubtedly yield insights into the psychological states and processes, and the neurological mechanisms and dynamics that make for a good horse race.

Principle of Nonadditive Determinism

As important as is the issue of efficiency, there is another reason why higher levels of analysis will always be with us. That is that the properties of more basic elements at lower levels of organization may only become apparent when these elements interact with others at a higher level of organization. Although the whole may not be greater than the sum of its parts, the properties of its parts may only, or more readily, be knowable by the properties of the whole. This has been articulated as the *principle of nonadditive determinism* (Cacioppo & Berntson, 1992). Although the essential features of Beethoven's Ninth Symphony may be fully captured by the sequential digital data on a CD, the esthetic impact of that data is more efficiently processed

by auditory perceptual mechanisms. There is no magic involved, as the perceptual qualities relate to specific temporal patterns of the data, but identification of the relevant patterns that correspond to specific perceptual qualities could not be derived readily from the digital data stream alone.

An illustration of this principle comes from recent studies on the impact of social stress on immune function. In a study (Padgett & Sheridan, 1999) of the effects of social reorganization on immune processes in mice, the social structure of a mouse colony was disrupted by introduction of an unfamiliar mouse. Two social reorganization cycles were given before and two after the animals were inoculated intranasally with an influenza virus. In a socially stable control group, about 8% of the animals died of the resulting infection. In the social stress group, however, about 70% of the animals died—from the flu. Despite comparable hypothalamic–pituitary–adrenal (HPA) activation, as evidenced by similar corticosteroid levels, the social stressor had a substantially greater impact on immune function than did a standard physical stressor (restraint stress), which was associated with only a 15% mortality rate. Similarly, herpes simplex was found to be reactivated by social stress in mice, whereas physical stressors such as restraint and shock were largely ineffective (Padgett et al., 1998). In these cases, psychosocial stresses were translated into physiological signals that modulated the expression and pathological impact of virally transmitted host–pathogen genes.

Such effects are not limited to animals. Parallel findings of stress effects on susceptibility to viral infections and other markers of immune function have also been reported for humans, with social stressors being particularly potent (Cohen et al., 1998; Cohen, Tyrrell, & Smith, 1991; Glaser, Kiecolt-Glaser, Malarkey, & Sheridan, 1998; Kiecolt-Glaser, Malarkey, Cacioppo, & Glaser, 1994). A meta-analytic review (Uchino, Cacioppo, & Kiecolt-Glaser, 1996) of the extant human literature revealed that perceived social isolation is associated with a variety of altered physiological functions, such as blood pressure regulation, catecholamine levels, and immune reactions. A causal link in these relations was suggested by findings of improved physiological functioning after interventions that served to reduce social isolation (Uchino et al., 1996). The role of psychological variables in these relations is indicated by the fact that subjective indexes of social isolation are often better predictors of stress and health than objective indexes (Seeman, 1996; Uchino et al., 1996). These examples demonstrate the potent influence of social relations on physiological and immunological function, and illustrate how the order in physiological, pharmacological, or immunological data may not be fully understandable from the vantage of a single level of analysis. Rather, comprehensive accounts of psychophysiological relations will likely require multiple analyses across distinct levels of functional organization.

Principle of Reciprocal Determinism

A final principle that characterizes the relations among levels of organization is the *principle of reciprocal determinism*, which asserts that there can be mutual influences among higher and lower levels of organization in the determination of behavior. As considered earlier, social stressors can lead to activation of the HPA axis and other signaling pathways that impact on physiological and immune functions. In rats, a low-reactive HPA system produces an adult who is low in stress reactivity and is attentive to offspring, showing increased levels of licking and grooming of the pups (Liu et al., 1997). The latter are important for the offspring to develop into low-reactive adults, who in turn attend to and frequently lick and groom their own pups (Liu et al.). Similarly, genotypic high-reactive infant monkeys develop into high-reactive adults (e.g., high HPA reactivity to stress, aggressive, and maladaptive social behaviors) when raised by their biological mothers or surrogate mothers who are also highly reactive (Suomi, 1999). When raised by low-reactive mothers, however, these same infants develop into low-reactive adults (Suomi, 1999). Patterns of parental care can modulate genetic actions and shape glucocorticoid binding in the hippocampus and cortex, leading to altered stress reactivity and social behavior in adulthood (Meaney et al., 1996; Meaney, Sapolsky, & McEwen, 1985). Genetic constitution clearly impacts on physiology, but what appears to be a genetic influence on physiological function may well be mediated by a behavioral variable. Such influences are not limited to animals, as the early loss of a parent, poor quality family relationships in humans, or both, have been reported to be associated with higher blood pressure and enhanced HPA reactivity in infancy (Hertsgaard, Gunnar, Erickson, & Nachmias, 1995) and adulthood (Luecken, 1998).

Summary

The principles articulated previously emphasize the important contributions to the scientific enterprise of multiple levels of analysis. They further illustrate the reasons why a one-way reductionism is an empty enterprise, rather than a threat to social psychology. However, we should seek a reductionism that allows a closer mapping of constructs from differing levels of analysis, and permits a representation of higher level constructs in the vocabulary and models of lower levels of analysis. This is what science ultimately demands. By the same token, the terms and constructs of lower levels of analysis will be equally vitalized and enriched by knowledge gleaned from higher levels of analysis, and this is increasingly recognized in contemporary behavioral neuroscience. The emphasis on interdisciplinary approaches and multilevel analyses is not a fad. It is the future. A discipline that fails to embrace this perspective threatens its very survival, and is in jeopardy of an isolationism that can only diminish itself as well as the broader scientific community. Multilevel analyses cannot be coerced, and if they were, they would not likely be productive. There is a continuing need for analyses restricted to a single level. Rather, what is important is a multilevel perspective that will ultimately foster multilevel analyses as the scientific problem dictates, and as interdisciplinary collaborative opportunities present themselves.

Contemporary Social Neuroscience Perspective

A fundamental organizational feature of the nervous system lies in the basic hierarchical structure of multiple processing levels. Not a strict hierarchy in the formal sense, but a more complex set of interacting levels, with parallel and serial processing components, and both ascending and descending communication between proximate and remote levels—what has been referred to as a heterarchy (see Berntson, Boysen, & Cacioppo, 1993). This heterarchical organization is not limited to sensorimotor processes or primitive reflex organizations, but also extends to the highest levels of neurobehavioral and cognitive functions. Although there are distinguishable levels and components of this system, they are highly interactive. Consequently, an understanding of a target level of functional organization, as gleaned from a single level of analysis, may be accurate but is likely to be incomplete. Sources of variance in behavior and cognition, arising from divergent levels of organization, would be relegated to the error term in disciplinary approaches that limit their vision exclusively to a single level of analysis.

For social psychologists, biological parameters should be viewed as theoretical elements, not merely dependent (or independent) variables. Available methods now permit not only the monitoring of biological systems in humans but also allow explicit manipulations of biological states. The latter range from simple noninvasive experimental procedures (e.g., postural change that can alter the balance of sympathetic and parasympathetic activity; Cacioppo et al., 1994), to pharmacological manipulations (e.g., autonomic blockades or HPA modulation; Berntson et al., 1994; Malarkey, Lipkus, & Cacioppo, 1995), to neuropsychological studies of naturally occurring brain insults (e.g., Kline & Kihlstrom, 1998). Although behavior is the ultimate product of neurobiological systems, the fact remains that psychological processes can have an impact on this biology. Indeed, the third principle articulated—the principle of reciprocal determinism—is particularly relevant, as it captures the mutually interacting influences among the varied levels of neurobehavioral organization. Of the multitude of reciprocal influences across levels of organization, an especially intriguing subset may be of particular interest to social neuroscience. This relates to bottom-up influences from lower level systems that can exert subtle biases on higher level processes, paralleling the top-down modulations of lower level systems by higher neural mechanisms.

Bottom-Up Influences

Multiple levels of processing, implied by the hierarchical structure of the nervous system, may help clarify aspects of social cognition and behavior. Although the evaluative disposition and associated interference displayed by chimpanzees in the candy selection task may have been inherent in chimps, acquired evaluative dispositions in humans can operate similarly. Evaluative predispositions (attitudes) can be formed in humans through classical conditioning (Cacioppo, Marshall-Goodell, et al., 1992). The experimental stimuli were neutral words and pronounceable nonwords that were matched in terms of structural features and participants' prior attitudes and affect. A differential conditioning procedure was used such that the word was paired with electric shock, the nonword was paired with shock, or the word and nonword were paired randomly with shock. A simulation experiment in which participants read descriptions of the conditioning procedures revealed that they expected (and believed the experimenter anticipated) simply that whatever stimulus was paired with electric shock would become disliked. In accord with latent inhibition, however, we posited that conditioning would be more apparent for nonwords than for words because of the preexposures to the former class of stimuli. Results confirmed that more negative attitudes were formed when nonwords were paired with shock than when words were paired with shock.

Research by LeDoux and colleagues (LeDoux, 1995) on conditioned fear reactions to acoustic stimuli, indicates that projections from the auditory thalamus to the amygdala bypass the cortex and constitute a sufficient subcortical mechanism for affective learning.

Although an adequate subcortical mechanism exists for simple conditioning, more complex contextual conditioning appears to be dependent on a cortical link (LeDoux, 1995). Similarly, visually masked fear stimuli can trigger autonomic reactivity in humans, despite the fact that the stimuli are not seen or recognized (Ohman, 1996). A more recent imaging study revealed that masked fear stimuli preferentially increase activity in thalamic–amygdala circuits, and decrease amygdala–cortical activity, relative to nonmasked stimuli that were consciously perceived (Morris, Ohman, & Dolan, 1999). These findings are consistent with the thesis that the acquisition and representation of affective (evaluative) dispositions can operate at multiple, interrelated levels of the neuraxis. Moreover, the lower level processing systems may exert important biases on higher attentional, cognitive, and affective reactions (Berntson, Sarter, & Cacioppo, 1998; Ohman, 1996).

These data are reminiscent of Nisbett and Wilson's (1977) and Gazzaniga and LeDoux's (1978) proposition that individuals can come to feel certain ways about stimuli and can even construct rationalizations for their feelings, although not really knowing why they come to feel as they do about people, objects, or events around them. The results of our simulation study indicated that people's declarative knowledge about classical conditioning led them to believe that whatever stimulus was associated with electric shock would also become disliked. Our results, however, conformed to animal studies showing that individuals felt more negatively about a novel stimulus than a familiar stimulus that was paired with electric shock. These data suggest a process by which individuals can come to feel differently toward stimuli in their world even though they do not comprehend the true basis for these differential feelings. Work on split-brain patients further suggests that people spontaneously confabulate to explain their feelings, with sometimes humorous results to the experimenter with all the facts. To the patient who is trying to construct a meaningful world from disparate parts, however, the confabulations are sensible and sober (Gazzaniga & LeDoux, 1978).

The evidence reviewed previously is consistent with the view that racial prejudice may rest in part on the conditioned evaluative predispositions that coexist with egalitarian beliefs, leaving people unwittingly of two minds about members of racial minorities. Thus, it may be verbal beliefs and evaluative attitude representations that are more likely to influence and predict behavioral intentions, but lower level (e.g., conditioned) evaluative predispositions that are more likely to influence a variety of affective and unintentional behaviors—the kinds of behaviors that have been shown to be most likely to reveal prejudice in contemporary research on stereotypy (cf. Clark & Squire, 1998). Contrary to the notion in modern racism that people are of one mind but two faces, work in social psychology and in the neurosciences raises the possibility that individuals who report being egalitarian but find themselves acting in a discriminatory fashion are speaking truthfully, in a sense, when they say that their actions were not premeditated or intentional. Their actions may not reflect what they see to be the behavioral implications of their beliefs. Symbolic representations provided a different glimpse into the minds of the chimps; similarly, words and rating scales may provide an accurate yet incomplete glimpse into human prejudices.

Bottom-Up Influences Arise Not Only From Lower Neural Systems

Since James's (1890) suggestion that strong emotions may represent the perceptual consequences of visceral afferent feedback, there has been a continuing history of research and theory on the role of visceral afference in affective reactions (for a review, see Cacioppo, Berntson, & Klein, 1992). Although studies on patients with spinal injuries have suggested that visceral feedback is not essential for emotional reactivity, this conclusion must be tempered by the fact that major visceral afferent systems remain intact in people with spinal injuries. Moreover, rather than constituting the sole basis for emotional reactions, a more likely role for visceral afference is in the priming of central systems underlying affective response (see Cacioppo et al., 1992). Recent research offers considerable support for the view that visceral afferent input can exert important modulatory influence over higher neural systems.

Invasion of the body by foreign microbes (or mitogens such as lipopolysaccaride) can trigger a neuroendocrine cascade that manifests in many common features of stress reactions (e.g., central catecholamine release, elevated corticosterone levels, anorexia, decreased activity, and hyperthermia). Recent findings suggest that this central stress-like response is mediated by a peripheral immune cytokine (lymphocyte secretion) that is transduced into a neuronal signal and conveyed to the brain via afferent fibers in the vagus nerve (Maier & Watkins, 1998; Watkins, Maier, & Goehler, 1995).

Additional data further indicate that vagal afferent activity can impact on the plasticity of central networks and can modulate memory in humans (Clark, Naritoku, Smith, Browning, & Jensen, 1999). Systemic administration of epinephrine has been shown to potentiate "emotional" memories in rats—an effect that is blocked by beta blockers (McGaugh, Cahill, & Roozendall, 1996; Williams & McGaugh, 1993). Sim-

ilar to the illness response, these memory affects appear to be mediated by a peripheral feedback signal carried by afferent vagal activity (Clark et al., 1999; Williams & McGough, 1993). Together, these findings suggest an important modulatory role for visceral afferent information on central information processing.

Further findings suggest that visceral afference may come to modulate and bias, more generally, the cognitive and attentional processing of behaviorally relevant stimuli (Berntson et al., 1998). The significance of this perspective is that it focuses on important biological influences on psychological processes that arise not from the inherent organizational features of higher level cognitive substrates, but from more subtle functional biases on these higher level processing substrates that arise from lower level influences. That is, feedback from peripheral biological states can bias the processing of higher level cognitive systems (see Berntson, Sarter, & Cacioppo, 1998). Indeed, there is now an emerging recognition of a symmetry in the reciprocal interplay among levels of organization, entailing both direct and indirect mutual interactions (top down and bottom up) that impact both biological and psychological processes. This interplay can neither be appreciated from the perspective of a primitive model of biology, nor from a social psychology that limits its focus exclusively to higher level processes.

Top-Down Influences Are Generally More Flexible

Important in the further integration of the biological and the social psychological perspectives will be the ability to relate constructs at one level of analysis to those of another. That does not entail a one-way process, as the scientific value of multilevel efforts accrues to both higher and lower levels of analysis. Illustrative of this issue is the traditional view of the sympathetic and parasympathetic branches of the autonomic nervous system being subject to reciprocal central control, with activation of one branch associated with inhibition of the other. This is a conception that arose from the early physiological literature, and continues to the present, although qualifications are increasingly recognized (see Berntson, Cacioppo, & Quigley, 1991). Malliani, Montano, and Pagani (1997) asserted that "in most physiological conditions, the activation of either (sympathetic or parasympathetic) outflow is accompanied by the inhibition of the other" (p. 343).

This opponent pattern of central autonomic control does characterize many lower level cardiovascular reflexes (e.g., baroreceptor reflexes), but is incomplete and noncomprehensive. As previously outlined, higher level systems are generally endowed with much greater flexibility than lower level mechanisms. Consequently, in behavioral contexts, activities of the two autonomic branches may show reciprocal, concordant (coactive), or independent changes. This represents an important expansion and calibration of biological conceptions of autonomic control, which arose to a large extent from the psychophysiological literature and is crucial in understanding psychophysiological relations. For example, heart rate acceleration to standard psychological stressors has been reported to predict immune reactions to stress (Manuck, Cohen, Rabin, & Muldoon, 1991). This predictive relation has not always been found, however, and the amount of variance accounted for may be modest. However, an increase in heart rate in behavioral contexts can arise from sympathetic activation, parasympathetic withdrawal, reciprocal sympathetic activation together with parasympathetic withdrawal, or even sympathetically dominant coactivation of both autonomic branches. These varied patterns may be related to distinct psychological states, and may have differential implications for immune function.

Whereas lower levels of neural organization are generally characterized by relatively fixed response patterns, higher levels foster a broader and more flexible range of responses. Lower level cardiovascular reflexes, such as the baroreceptor heart rate reflex, manifest in a relatively rigid reciprocal pattern of autonomic control, with little variation among individuals (Berntson et al., 1994; Cacioppo et al., 1994). In contrast, social stressors yield a more variable pattern of response, characterized by notable, but stable, individual differences (Berntson et al., 1994; see also Malarkey et al., 1995). This is important, because it is the sympathetic component of heart rate reactivity, rather than heart rate reactivity per se, that is most predictive of immune responses (Cacioppo, 1994). This feature of psychophysiological relations would not have been apparent without the inclusion of higher level analyses.

A parallel can be seen in social psychological studies on the Elaboration Likelihood Model, in which lower level influences (the peripheral route) can lead to relatively simple and mindless changes in attitudes when higher level processes are precluded. In contrast, more mindful influences on attitudes are apparent when conditions favor higher level processing (Cacioppo, Marshall-Goodell, et al., 1992; Petty & Cacioppo, 1986). These findings highlight an important focus for future research in multilevel analyses—the conditions that foster higher versus lower levels of processing in a given context.

Synergism Across Levels of Analysis

The conceptual synergism among levels of analysis is apparent in social psychological research. The docu-

mented dissociation between central substrates for positive and negative affect, for example, lends important support to the recent conception of the bivariate nature of affect in humans (Cacioppo & Berntson, 1994). Further information concerning the form of the activation functions of these bivariate affective substrates, derived from basic psychobiological studies in animals, suggested a quantitative refinement of the bivariate model that more effectively accounts for the variance in human affective response (Cacioppo, Gardner, & Berntson, 1999). Additional social neuroscience approaches, including measurements of cerebral electrical activity, provide added support for this view and offer important methods for further exploring the quantitative parameters of affective systems (e.g., Crites, Cacioppo, Gardner, & Bernston, 1995). These multilevel analyses have substantially broadened the conception of affective systems. Although there are many manifestations of affective response that can be subsumed by a bipolar affective dimension, the bivariate model is more comprehensive and corresponds more closely to the known organizational features of neurobehavioral systems, as well as the psychology of affective response.

Summary

In summary, there is much to be gained by multilevel analyses. This approach enriches not only the higher level disciplines but also the lower level disciplines. The modern biological perspective, with its recognition of higher cognitive processing mechanisms, offers a powerful set of analytical tools to social psychologists, including neuroimaging and neuropsychological approaches in human participants. This does not mean that all social psychologists should seek additional training in behavioral neuroscience. An equally viable approach, and one that is increasingly visible, is the development of interdisciplinary teams that can address social psychological as well as psychobiological issues from a multilevel perspective. Most important, however, is the recognition on the part of both social psychologists and psychobiologists, of the value of multilevel analyses.

References

Allport, F. H. (1924). *Social psychology.* Boston: Houghton Mifflin.

Allport, G. W. (1947). Scientific models and human morals. *Psychological Review, 54,* 182–192.

Anderson, N. B. (1998). Levels of analysis in health science: A framework for integrating sociobehavioral and biomedical research. *Annals of the New York Academy of Sciences, 840,* 563–576.

Beach, F. A., Hebb, D. O., Morgan, C. T., & Nissen, H. W. (1960). *The Neuropsychology of Lashley.* New York: McGraw Hill.

Bernard, C. (1924). *Instincts: A study in social psychology.* New York: Holt.

Berntson, G. G., Boysen, S. T., & Cacioppo, J. T. (1993). Neurobehavioral organization and the cardinal principle of evaluative bivalence. *Annals of the New York Academy of Sciences, 702,* 75–102.

Berntson, G. G., Cacioppo, J. T., Binkley, P. F., Uchino, B. N., Quigley, K. S., & Fieldstone, A. (1994). Autonomic cardiac control: Vol. 3. Psychological stress and cardiac response in autonomic space as revealed by pharmacological blockades. *Psychophysiology, 31,* 599–608.

Berntson, G. G., Cacioppo, J. T., & Quigley, K. S. (1991). Autonomic determinism: The modes of autonomic control, the doctrine of autonomic space, and the laws of autonomic constraint. *Psychological Review, 98,* 459–487.

Berntson, G. G., Sarter, M., & Cacioppo, J. T. (1998). Anxiety and cardiovascular reactivity: The basal forebrain cholinergic link. *Behavioural Brain Research, 94,* 225–248.

Bjoerkqvist, K. (1997). The inevitability of conflict, but not of violence: Theoretical considerations on conflict and aggression. In D. P. Fry & K. Bjoerkqvist (Eds.), *Cultural variation in conflict resolution: Alternatives to violence* (pp. 25–36). Mahwah, NJ: Lawrence Erlbaum Associates, Inc.

Boysen, S. T., & Berntson, G. G. (1995). Responses to quantity: Perceptual versus cognitive mechanisms in chimpanzees (Pan troglodytes). *Journal of Experimental Psychology: Animal Behavior Processes, 21,* 82–86.

Boysen, S. T., Berntson, G. G., Hannan, M. B., & Cacioppo, J. T. (1996). Quantity-based interference and symbolic representations in chimpanzees (Pan troglodytes). *Journal of Experimental Psychology: Animal Behavior Processes, 22,* 76–86.

Cacioppo, J. T. (1994). Social neuroscience: Autonomic, neuroendocrine, and immune responses to stress. *Psychophysiology, 31,* 113–128.

Cacioppo, J. T., & Berntson, G. G. (1992). Social psychological contributions to the decade of the brain: Doctrine of multilevel analysis. *American Psychologist, 47,* 1019–1028.

Cacioppo, J. T., & Berntson, G. G. (1994). Relationship between attitudes and evaluative space: A critical review with emphasis on the separability of positive and negative substrates. *Psychological Bulletin, 115,* 401–423.

Cacioppo, J. T., Berntson, G. G., Binkley, P. F., Quigley, K. S., Uchino, B. N., & Fieldstone, A. (1994). Autonomic cardiac control: Vol. 2. Basal response, noninvasive indices, and autonomic space as revealed by autonomic blockades. *Psychophysiology, 31,* 586–598.

Cacioppo, J. T., Berntson, G. G., & Klein, D. J. (1992). What is an emotion? The role of somatovisceral afference, with special emphasis on somatovisceral "illusions." *Review of Personality and Social Psychology, 14,* 63–98.

Cacioppo, J. T., Gardner, W. L., & Berntson, G. G. (1999). The affect system has parallel and integrative processing components: Form follows function. *Journal of Personality and Social Psychology, 76,* 839–855.

Cacioppo, J. T., Marshall-Goodell, B. S., Tassinary, L. G., & Petty, R. E. (1992). Rudimentary determinants of attitudes: Classical conditioning is more effective when prior knowledge about the attitude stimulus is low than high. *Journal of Experimental Social Psychology, 28,* 207–233.

Cacioppo, J. T., Priester, J. R., & Berntson, G. G. (1993). Rudimentary determinants of attitudes: Vol. 2. Arm flexion and extension have differential effects on attitudes. *Journal of Personality and Social Psychology, 65,* 5–17.

Carter, C. S., & Altemus, M. (1997). Integrative functions of lactational hormones in social behavior and stress management. *Annals of the New York Academy of Sciences, 15,* 164–174.

Carter, C. S., DeVris, A. C., & Getz, L. L. (1995). Physiological substrates of mammalian monogamy: The prairie vole model. *Neuroscience and Biobehavioral Reviews, 19,* 303–314.

Clark, K. B., Naritoku, D. K., Smith, D. C., Browning, R. A., & Jensen, R. A. (1999). Enhanced recognition memory following vagus nerve stimulation in human subjects. *Nature Neuroscience, 1,* 94–98.

Clark, R. E., & Squire, L. R. (1998). Classical conditioning and brain systems: The role of awareness. *Science, 280,* 77–81.

Cofer, C. N., & Appley, M. H. (1964). *Motivation: Theory and research.* New York: Wiley.

Cohen, S., Frank, E., Doyle, W. J., Skoner, D. P., Rabin, B. S., & Gwaltney, J. M. (1998). Types of stressors that increase susceptibility to the common cold in adults. *Health Psychology, 17,* 214–223.

Cohen, S., Tyrrell, D. A. J., & Smith, A. P. (1991). Psychological stress in humans and the susceptibility to the common cold. *New England Journal of Medicine, 325,* 606–612.

Crabbe, J. C., Wahlsten, D., & Dudek, B. C. (1999). Genetics of mouse behavior: Interactions with laboratory environment. *Science, 284,* 1670–1672.

Crites, S. L., Cacioppo, J. T., Gardner, W. L., & Berntson, G. G. (1995). Bioelectric echoes from evaluative categorization: Vol. 2. A late positive brain potential that varies as a function of attitude registration rather than attitude report. *Journal of Personality and Social Psychology, 68,* 997–1013.

Darwin, C. (1998). *Expression of the emotions in man and animals* (3rd ed.). New York: Oxford University Press. (Original work published 1872)

Dollard, J., Doob, L. W., Miller, N. E., Mowrer, O. H., & Sears, R. R. (1939). *Frustration and aggression.* New Haven, CT: Yale University Press.

Dollard, J., & Miller, N. E. (1950). *Personality and psychotherapy.* New York: McGraw-Hill.

Dunlap, K. (1919). Are there any instincts? *Journal of Abnormal Psychology, 14,* 35–50.

Evans, R. I. (1968). *B. F. Skinner; the man and his ideas.* New York: Dutton.

Flemming, A. S., Ruble, D., Krieger, H., & Wong, P. Y. (1997). Hormonal and experiential correlates of maternal responsiveness during pregnancy and the puerperium in human mothers. *Hormones and Behavior, 31,* 145–158.

Gazzaniga, M. S., & LeDoux, J. E. (1978). *The integrated mind.* New York: Plenum.

Glaser, R., Kiecolt-Glaser, J. K., Malarkey, W. B., & Sheridan, J. F. (1998). The influence of psychological stress on the immune response to vaccines. *Annals of the New York Academy of Sciences, 840,* 649–655.

Hebb, D. O. (1949). *The organization of behavior.* New York: Wiley.

Hebb, D. O. (1955). Drives and the C. N. S. (Conceptual nervous system). *Psychological Review, 62,* 243–254.

Hertsgaard, L., Gunnar, M., Erickson, M. F., & Nachmias, M. (1995). Adrenocortical responses to the strange situation in infants with disorganized/disoriented attachment relationships. *Child Development, 66,* 1100–1106.

Insel, T. R. (1997). A neurobiological basis of social attachment. *American Journal of Psychiatry, 154,* 726–735.

Jackson, J. H. (1958). Evolution and dissolution of the nervous system (Croonian Lectures). In J. Taylor (Ed.), *Selected writings of John Hughlings Jackson* (Vol. 2). New York: Basic Books. (Original work published 1884)

James, W. (1890). *The principles of psychology.* New York: Holt.

Kiecolt-Glaser, J. K., Malarkey, W. B., Cacioppo, J. T., & Glaser, R. (1994). Stressful personal relationships: Endocrine and immune function. In R. Glaser & J. K. Kiecolt-Glaser (Eds.), *Handbook of human stress and immunity* (pp. 321–339). San Diego, CA: Academic.

Kline, S. B., & Kihlstrom, J. F. (1998). On bridging the gap between social-personality psychology and neuropsychology. *Personality and Social Psychology Review, 2,* 228–242.

Kuo, K. Y. (1924). A psychology without heredity. *Psychological Review, 31,* 427–451.

LeDoux, J. E. (1995). Emotion: Clues from the brain. *Annual Review of Psychology, 46,* 209–235.

Liao, T. F., & Cai, Y. (1995). Socialization, life situations, and gender-role attitudes regarding the family among White American Women. *Sociological Perspectives, 38,* 241–260.

Liu, D., Diorio, J., Tannenbaum, B., Caldji, C., Francis, D., Freedman, A., Sharma, D., Pearson, D., Plotsky, P. M., & Meaney, M. J. (1997). Maternal care, hippocampal, glucocorticoid receptors, and hypothalamic–pituitary–adrenal responses to stress. *Science, 277,* 1659–1662.

Luecken, L. J. (1998). Childhood attachment and loss experiences affect adult cardiovascular and cortisol function. *Psychosomatic Medicine, 60,* 765–772.

Maier, S. F., & Watkins, L. R. (1998). Cytokines for psychologists: Implications of bidirectional immune-to-brain communication for understanding behavior, mood, and cognition. *Psychological Review, 105,* 83–107.

Malarkey, W. B., Lipkus, I. M., & Cacioppo, J. T. (1995). The dissociation of catecholamine and hypothalamic–pituitary–adrenal responses to daily stressors using dexamethasone. *Journal of Clinical Endocrinology and Metabolism, 80,* 2458–2463.

Malliani, A., Montano, N., & Pagani, M. (1997). Physiological background of heart rate variability. *Cardiac Electrophysiology Review, 3,* 343–346.

Manuck, S. B., Cohen, S., Rabin, B. S., & Muldoon, M. F. (1991). Individual differences in cellular immune responses to stress. *Psychological Science, 2,* 111–115.

McCarthy, M. M., & Altemus, M. (1997). Central nervous system actions of oxytocin and modulation of behavior in humans. *Molecular Medicine Today, 3,* 269–275.

McDougall, W. (1908). *An introduction to social psychology.* London: Methuen.

McGaugh, J. L., Cahill, L., & Roozendall, B. (1996). Involvement of the amygdala in memory storage: Interaction with other brain systems. *Proceedings of the National Academy of Sciences, 93,* 13508–13514.

Meaney, M. J., Bhatnagar, S., Larocque, S., McCormick, C. M., Shanks, N., Sharma, S., Smythe, J., Viau, V., & Plotsky, P. M. (1996). Early environment and the development of individual differences in the hypothalamic–pituitary–adrenal stress response. In C. R. Pfeffer (Ed.), *Severe stress and mental disturbance in children* (pp. 85–127). Washington, DC: American Psychiatric Press.

Meaney, M. J., Sapolsky, R. M., & McEwen, B. S. (1985). The development of the glucocorticoid receptor system in the rat limbic system: II. An autoradiographic study. *Developmental Brain Research, 18,* 159–164.

Miller, N. E., & Dollard, J. (1941). *Social learning and imitation.* New Haven, CT: Yale University Press.

Miller, S. M., Shoda, Y., & Hurley, K. (1996). Applying cognitive-social theory to health-protecting behavior: Breast self-examination in cancer screening. *Psychological Bulletin, 119,* 70–94.

Morris, J. S., Ohman, A., & Dolan, R. J. (1999) A subcortical pathway to the right amygdala mediating "unseen" fear. *Proceedings of the National Academy of Sciences, 96,* 1680–1685.

Murchison, C. (1935). *A handbook of social psychology.* Worchester, MA: Clark University Press.

Nelson, E. E., & Panksepp, J. (1998). Brain substrates of infant–mother attachment: Contributions of opiods, oxytocin, and norepinephrine. *Neuroscience and Biobehavioral Reviews, 22,* 437–452.

Nisbett, R. E., & Wilson, T. D. (1977). Telling more than we can know: Verbal reports on mental processes. *Psychological Review, 84,* 231–259.

Ohman, A. (1996). Preferential preattentive processing of threat in anxiety: Preparedness and attentional biases. In R.M. Rapee (Ed.), *Current controversies in the anxiety disorders* (pp. 253–290). New York: Guilford.

Padgett, D. A., & Sheridan, J. F. (1999). *Social stress, dominance, and increased mortality from an influenza viral infection.* Manuscript submitted for publication.

Padgett, D. A., Sheridan, J. F., Dorne, J., Berntson, G. G., Candelora, J., & Glaser, R. (1998). Social stress and the reactivation of latent herpes simplex virus–type 1. *Proceedings of the National Academy of Sciences, 95,* 7231–7235.

Pavlov, I. P. (1927). *Conditioned reflexes* (G. V. Anrep, Trans.). Oxford, England: Clarendon.

Petty, R. E., & Cacioppo, J. T. (1986). The elaboration likelihood model of persuasion. *Advances in Experimental Social Psychology, 19,* 123–205.

Pinker, S. (1997). *How the mind works.* New York: Norton.

Priester, J. R., Cacioppo, J. T., & Petty, R. E. (1996). The influence of motor processes on attitudes toward novel versus familiar semantic stimuli. *Personality and Social Psychology Bulletin, 22,* 442–447.

Rosenblatt, J. S. (1994). Psychobiology of maternal behavior: Contribution to the clinical understanding of maternal behavior among humans. *Acta Paediatrica Supplement, Vol. 397,* 3–8.

Seeman, T. E. (1996). Social ties and health: The benefits of social integration. *Annals of Epidemiology, 6,* 442–451.

Smith, E. R., & DeCoster, J. (1998). Knowledge acquisition, accessibility, and use in person perception and stereotyping: Simulation with a recurrent connectionist network. *Journal of Personality and Social Psychology, 74,* 21–35.

Spence, K. W. (1960). *Behavior theory and conditioning.* New Haven, CT: Yale University Press.

Stellar, E. (1954). The physiology of motivation. *Psychological Review, 61,* 5–22.

Suomi, S. (1999, June). *Jumpy monkeys.* Address presented at the annual meeting of the American Psychological Association, Denver, CO.

Thorndike, E. L. (1898). Animal intelligence: An experimental study of the associative processes in animals. *Psychological Review, 1*(Pt. 2).

Thorndike, E. L. (1927). The law of effect. *American Journal of Psychology, 29,* 212–222.

Uchino, B. N., Cacioppo, J. T., & Kiecolt-Glaser, J. K. (1996). The relationship between social support and physiological processes: A review with emphasis on underlying mechanisms and implications for health. *Psychological Bulletin, 119,* 488–531.

Watkins, L. R., Maier, S. F., & Goehler, L. E. (1995). Cytokine-to-brain communication: A review and analysis of alternative mechanisms. *Life Sciences, 57,* 1011–1026.

Watson, J. B. (1924). *Behaviorism.* New York: Norton.

Watson, J. B., & Morgan, J. B. B. (1917). Emotional reactions and psychological experimentation. *American Journal of Psychology, 28,* 163–174.

Williams, C. L., & McGaugh, J. L. (1993). Reversible lesions of the nucleus of the solitary tract attenuate the memory-modulating effects of posttraining epinephrine. *Behavioral Neuroscience, 107,* 955–962.

Zajonc, R. B. (1968). Attitudinal effects of mere exposure. *Journal of Personality and Social Psychology, 9,* 1–27.

Personality and Social Psychology Review
2000, Vol. 4, No. 1, 16–29

Social, Personality, Clinical, and Health Psychology Tributaries: The Merging of a Scholarly "River of Dreams"

C. R. Snyder
Department of Psychology
University of Kansas, Lawrence

Howard Tennen and Glenn Affleck
Department of Community Medicine
University of Connecticut Health Center

Jen Cheavens
Department of Psychology
University of Kansas, Lawrence

Results of a survey from the contents of six 1998 journals in social, clinical, personality, and health psychology allow one to conclude that interface research in these fields is grounded in theory, focuses more on understanding weaknesses than strengths, has personality variables playing major roles, and often involves correlation-based studies using related self-report variables. It is also suggested that promising future interface research would include the psychological predictors of medical outcomes, stress-related growth, enhancing psychotherapy outcomes, and the effects of social comparisons, as well as a methodological paradigm that involves the analyses of multilevel daily processes. The article closes with exhortations for enhancing the viability and potential impact of interface research.

In this review article, we attempt to look back over where we have been recently, to discern some order in our collective scholarly efforts, and to predict our future psychological ventures at the interface of social, clinical, personality, and health psychology. Our approach has two facets. First, we examine the contents of recent leading journals in these four specialty areas. Our purpose is to derive a sense of what is being published now on the interface. Accordingly, we describe that survey and the related findings. Second, we comment on where research at the interface of these areas of psychology is going.

Survey Study

Method and Results

One hundred articles taken from the specialty areas of clinical, health, social, and personality psychology were sampled. The journals included in the

sampling were: *Health Psychology* (*HP*), the *Journal of Consulting and Clinical Psychology* (*JCCP*), the *Journal of Experimental Social Psychology* (*JESP*), the *Journal of Personality* (*JP*), the *Journal of Social and Clinical Psychology* (*JSCP*), and the *Journal of Personality and Social Psychology: Personality and Individual Differences section* (*JPSP:PID*). Every volume of each journal from the 1998 calendar year was examined, with one fourth of the articles from each journal volume being randomly chosen. With this method, the journals are represented by different numbers of articles based on the number of articles published in each journal in 1998. Therefore, the sample included 7 *JSCP*, 7 *JESP*, 11 *JP*, 16 *HP*, 28 *JCCP*, and 31 *JPSP:PID* articles.

An advanced clinical psychology graduate student read the 100 articles twice, first completing the ratings, and second checking for accuracy. Tabulations were made for demographic information (number of participants, age, race, gender, and sample type), statistical and methodological information (number of variables, type of analyses, design, time interval, data collection method, and number of experiments within a study), and theoretical issues (subject area, level of theory, and manipulation type). Except for the demo-

Requests for reprints should be sent to C. R. Snyder, Graduate Training Program in Clinical Psychology, Department of Psychology, 305 Fraser Hall, University of Kansas, Lawrence, Kansas 66045–2462. E-mail: crsnyder@ukans.edu.

graphic variables, such as age and number of participants, the classification of the articles was primarily categorical and largely subjective.

The first tabulation examined area of focus. All articles were coded for the four fields of psychology that were the focus of the research design. An article was classified as clinical if it contained a variable that could be found in the *Diagnostic and Statistical Manual of Mental Disorders* (4th ed. [*DSM–IV*], American Psychiatric Association, 1994; e.g., eating disorders, depressed mood, phobias, etc.). An article was classified as health if the study used a medical diagnosis or physical illness as a variable or topic of interest (e.g., social stress and illness proneness); moreover, any studies that used preventative health behaviors that focused on health were included in this category (e.g., self-medication with nicotine, immune competence, and cardiovascular activity). An article was placed in the personality category if its focus was on individual differences (e.g., perfectionism, emotional expressiveness, psychological mindedness). Last, a study was placed in the social category if it looked at a variable or topic of interest tapping interactions with the environment, other people, or networks (e.g., self-comparison, social interaction in relation to social anxiety, attributions about others, and attitudes about surrounding people or events). The percentages by article foci were as follows: social and personality, 27%; clinical and personality, 12%; clinical, personality, and social, 9%; clinical only, 9%; clinical, health, and personality, 7%; personality, 7%; health only, 6%; clinical and social, 6%; health, personality, and social, 4%; social and health, 3%; personality and health, 3%; clinical, health, and social, 2%; clinical and health, 2%; social only, 2%; and all four, 1%.

A second survey item classified the type of research design, with 57% being correlational, 10% being manipulation, and 33% being both correlational and manipulation. Percentages of studies that used particular analyses were also examined, and they were as follows: regressions, 64%; analyses of variance, 60%; bivariate, 49%; chi square, 22%; path analysis, 21%; multivariate analysis of variance, 18%; factor analysis, 7%; discriminant function, 3%; cluster analysis, 2%; and odds ratio, 1%.

Next, we examined whether the studies focused on the weaknesses or strengths of people. Results showed that independent variables falling into each category were as follows: weakness, 60%; neutral, 87%; strength, 36%; and strengths and weaknesses, 21%. Dependent variables falling into each category were as follows: weakness, 65%; neutral, 62%; strength, 29%; and strengths and weaknesses, 22%. Percentages add up to more than 100% because many articles have multiple variables that differentially tap strengths and weaknesses.

The next tabulations pertained to variables that, taken together, were labeled as the *extensiveness* of the articles. Of the 100 articles, 77 were single studies, 12 involved two studies, 11 contained three studies, and 4 had four studies. The mean number of independent variables was 7.15 ($SD = 5.67$, range = 1–29); for the dependent variables, the mean number of variables per study was 11.75 ($SD = 13.2$, range = 1–69). Sixty-two percent were cross-sectional, and 38% were longitudinal. The nomothetic approach was used in 89%, whereas 11% used the idiographic and nomothetic approaches together for data collection.

Our subsequent interest pertained to the modes of inquiry reflected in the dependent variables used in the sampled studies. Tabulation yielded the following breakdown of dependent variables: self-report and behavioral, 33%; self-report, 30%; self-report and physiological, 11%; self-report, behavioral, and interview, 8%; observed and behavioral, 5%; self-report and interview, 5%; self-report, behavioral, and physiological, 3%; self-report, interview, and physiological, 3%; behavioral, physiological, and interview, 1%; all four, 1%; physiological, 0%; physiological and interview, 0%; interview, 0%; behavioral and physiological, 0%; and behavioral and interview, 0%.

Regarding the makeup of the sampled participants, we were specifically interested in where and with whom research is being done. One variable of interest was the location from which participants were recruited. Those percentages were: college students, 45%; community residents, 24%; outpatients, 13%; children and adolescents, 9%; hospital health patients, 8%; and psychiatric inpatients, 1%. Across all studies, there were 56.38% female participants and 43.12% male participants. For the 50% of the articles that reported racial composition, the race breakdown was White, 75.61%; African American, 18.93%; Hispanic, 4.55%; Asian, 2.83%; and other, 1.80%. For the 65% of the studies reporting the ages of participant, the mean age was 30.33 ($SD = 12.76$, range = 4.3–69.4); the average age of the youngest participants in a study was 20.51 ($SD = 12.80$), and the average age of the oldest participants in a study was 43.75 ($SD = 21.46$). The average number of research participants was 478.1 ($SD = 1510.75$, range = 12–14,555); when removing the one outlier study with 14,555 participants, the average number was 306.3 ($SD = 421.85$, range = 12–2,810).

Last, we explored the theoretical orientations of the research: Some studies examine small-scale theories that explain the relation of a few variables, and yet others use midscale theories implicating a moderate number of variables. Finally, some involve large-scale theories that address many facets of human behavior. More specifically, studies coded as small-scale theories were those addressing just the variables in that study and that do not make ties to any other variables (e.g., ambivalence, regret, and discomfort related just to psychological adjustment after abortion, or stress related specifically to upper respiratory infections). Medium-level theories included variables beyond the topic of the particular article and discussed how these variables affect one another; this midlevel included directionality as opposed to the "these variables are related" stance of small-scale theories, and extended beyond the variables of a given study but not to a degree that was very far reaching (e.g., theory of self-regulated decision making and symptom perception, and the theory of transactive memory systems and communication). Large-scale theories encompass most variables of human experience and offer some explanatory mechanism; for example, theories of dependent and self-critical personality styles or those regarding personality effects (Big Five Personality Factors, positive and negative affectivity) on social relationships. Using these three categories, plus a no-theory classification, 2% of the studies were atheoretical, 39% were small-scale theoretical, 42% were midscale theoretical, and 17% were large-scale theoretical.

Interpreting and Extrapolating From the Survey Results

Theory is alive and well. Prior to the survey, we were uncertain as to the degree and type of theory guiding interface research. Our sampled research clearly is theory driven. In regard to the type of theory, the small-scale and midscale theories together account for 81% of the studies. Or, looking at the mix somewhat differently, combining the mid- and large-scale research encapsulates 59% of the research. Thus, not only are the interface scholars building their work on theoretical foundations, but they evidence considerable variability in the size of their theories. The most prevalent theories that we found involved cognitive aspects of depression, attachment style, coping related to type of situation, positive and negative affectivity, and objectification and gender roles. One criticism that sometimes is heard about psychology more generally is that it involves too much raw empiricism, with very little theorization behind the work. For the sampled interface studies, however, virtually all were based on theory.

The pathology versus strength emphasis. Recently, with the influence of past American Psychological Association President Martin Seligman, as well as through the granting support of philanthropist Sir John Templeton, there have been calls for studies of human strengths rather than the previous traditional focus on pathologies (see McCullough & Snyder, in press; Snyder & McCullough, in press). It is difficult to interpret the results of this survey because it is not discernable whether these foci in recently published articles reflect a change relative to previous work. Taken as a one-time snapshot, however, it appears that the traditional pathology and weakness approach still holds sway. What is intriguing, also, is that 21% (independent variables) and 22% (dependent variables) of the sampled studies were examining both strengths and weaknesses. Obviously, these latter percentages reveal some openness to a range of variables. In future work, it also would be helpful to see if book contents are embracing a strength approach. Although there is more discussion given to strengths than previously, it will be important to track the contents of convention papers, published articles and books, as well as grant awards.

Health psychology often is practiced within medical settings where problems are the focus, but psychologists are exploring the psychological assets of people as they may relate to health matters. Historically, clinical psychology has been based on a pathology model, although there is some movement toward positive psychology (this change is happening at a time when women are forming the majority in the clinical psychology field; Snyder, McDermott, Leibowitz, & Cheavens, 2000). Social and personality psychologists have gravitated toward normal behaviors, and are positioned well to contribute to this strength approach.

Personality as a major tributary. The field of personality is represented individually as the focus of 7% of the studies, but has an additional interface of 63% with other areas. For social, the individual contribution was 2%, with an additional 54% for interface; similarly, clinical had an individual contribution of 9% and an additional 48% interface. Health by itself was 6%, and 22% in additional interface articles. Due to the fact that only one of the six journals focused on health per se, these lower percentages for health may reflect, in part, that sampling characteristic rather than a lack of interest in health issues more generally. As a counter to this latter argument, however, social has a very small individual contribution (2%) and a large interface contribution (54%). This suggests that there is much room for growth in terms of health interfacing with the other areas.

Another inference is that personality is a robust interface contributor (63%), whereas the social and clinical areas appear to be intermediate interface contributors (54% and 48%, respectively). Again, it is interesting that personality also exhibits the two highest two-way interfaces (27% with social and 12% with clinical). These percentages bear out the assertion that personality is, and probably always has been, a very important part of the interface movement along with social, clinical, and health psychology (Snyder, 1997).

Research participants. The survey data confirm a common perception that the typical psychology research participants are White college students. This is a sample of convenience for university researchers. We do not take the strident position that college students are totally unrepresentative of the population more generally, however, nor do we hold that they lack stressors compared to other samples of persons. On this latter point, researchers examining writings about traumatic events have been surprised at the very high number and strong intensity of college students' reported stressors (Smyth & Pennebaker, 1999). Thus, the view that college students do not have "real" problems is not accurate. Having argued for the use of college students, we nevertheless believe that the interface could profit by expanding to other samples. For health psychologists working in medical settings, of course, this is an easier task than for university-based researchers.

It should be noted from our sample that the percentage of female participants (57%) was higher than that for male participants (43%). This runs counter to the perception that psychological research overwhelmingly is conducted with male participants (e.g., the early Type A behavior pattern research). We encourage interface researchers to continue their recent apparent efforts to include men and women in their research. Given the data showing the feminization of clinical psychology (see Snyder et al., 2000), female investigators probably will make a point of ensuring that female research participants are included along with male participants. Also, because of the preponderance of college students serving as research participants, it naturally follows that the larger percentages of female as compared to male introductory psychology students contribute to the prevalence of female participants overall in interface research.

Our sampling suggests that race is not even reported in half of the studies. Given the increasingly multiracial composition of the U.S. population, we call on researchers to reach out to persons of color so as to have them participate in interface research, in addition to systematic efforts to recruit and train individuals of color to conduct research in this field. Also, editors should require that the breakdown of this variable at least be reported so that race can be taken into account when making interpretations of research findings.

Similar to the race variable, age of participants is not reported in 35% of the sampled studies. Interface researchers obviously should focus more on research with the elderly. There are two societal trends that contribute to the burgeoning numbers of older people: Baby boomers are aging, and life expectancies are increasing. Besides the many health research possibilities with this population, we need to investigate how to keep older adults psychologically and physically active. At the risk of stating the obvious, there is much to learn from the elderly, but it cannot be done unless some interface scholars begin to study them. The sampled interface studies also virtually ignored the children who are at the other extreme of the age continuum. For the benefit of our society in general, interface research and theory is needed on issues of a preventative and remediational nature with children (Snyder & Ingram, 2000).

Criteria variables. What is obvious in these survey data is that self-report dependent variables outnumber the other types. Although self-report alone is a feature of just 29% of the articles, when it is added to various combinations of behavioral, physiological, and interview, it accounts for 93% of the dependent variables of the articles in this sample. The next closest are observed and behavioral measures alone at 5%, and in combination with other methods, these account for 50%. Interviews and physiological measures each make up less than 20% of the dependent variables, but the relatively low percentages of physiological data may reflect the fact that only one of the six journals focused on health (indeed, an analysis showed that of the 19 references to physiological data, 8 of those came from *HP*).

We suggest that we need to place more emphasis on hard markers, including behaviors and physiological indexes. Even interviews would expand the usual paper-and-pencil approach. Although it is rarely discussed, there is a design artifact wherein self-report predictor variables will yield robust relations with self-report markers because of shared response modes. Thus, the enormous numbers of correlations between self-reports reported in our journals probably are increased in magnitude by this instrument effect.

Correlation-related approaches. The sampled studies overwhelmingly involved one study, with the cross-sectional approach being used in roughly a 2:1 ratio relative to the longitudinal approach. The numbers of independent ($M = 7.15$) and dependent variables ($M = 11.75$) strike us as being quite high. The prevalence of correlation-based analytic approaches in the survey is consistent with the impressions held by Tennen and Snyder as the editors of two of the journals used in this survey (*Journal of Social and Clinical Psychology* and *Journal of Personality*, respectively). Furthermore, note that the overwhelming number of personality variables (discussed later) are conducive to correlation-based analyses. The prevalence of the correlational approach in the interface also, in part, may be instrument driven in that there has recently been a proliferation of individual differences measures. Individual differences measures, of course, lend themselves to correlational procedures. Likewise, although controversial, given the preponderance of reported correlational designs, it is quite possible that some of the published correlation-based studies reflect "fishing," wherein the "catches of the day" (i.e., the variables with the highest correlations) are neatly packaged post hoc into theories fitting the given relations.

To help reduce the prevalence of correlation-based studies and potentially increase longitudinal research, we have three suggestions. First, teach students that the number of publications should be less important than in-depth, extensive, causal design, longitudinal studies. (In our advocating more longitudinal studies, however, we note that the attrition of both participants and experimenters is a problem in our increasingly mobile society.) Second, journal editors could give some priority to elaborated, multistudy, programmatic, causal, long-term research. Third, although it may be difficult to implement given the present organization of granting agencies, they could be especially receptive to submissions using long-term methodologies. (In fairness, many granting agencies already have moved in this direction.) In all three of these suggestions, we advocate more encouragement and infrastructure support for multistudy, programmatic, long-term research.

River of Dreams: Channels for Future Investigations and Method and Analytic Strategies

The first part of this article summarized the survey findings from literature published in six journals. This survey revealed a fair amount of interface between these four disciplines. Now that the interface in 1998 has been discussed, we speculate about where this endeavor is going. We convey our enthusiasm for what we anticipate to be an extraordinarily productive decade of interface investigation. In the following pages, four areas are described that are ripe for interface study (psychological predictors of medical outcomes, the phenomenon of stress-related growth, enhancement of psychotherapy outcomes, and social comparison processes in health and illness), and one methodological and statistical method that will aid this type of research (the multilevel daily process paradigm).

Psychological Predictors of Medical Outcomes

A growing body of evidence indicates that depressive symptoms predict important health related outcomes, including morbidity, mortality, and service utilization. These provocative findings point to extraordinary opportunities for psychological investigators at the interface of personality, social, clinical, and health psychology. Although the literature we highlight focuses on depressive symptoms, this line of inquiry is just one of the myriad ways in which person factors and the cognitive appraisals commonly studied by personality and social psychologists can influence health and illness.

Depressive symptoms, measured through depression questionnaires that are well-known to personality and social psychologists, anticipate increased health service utilization (Johnson, Weissman, & Klerman, 1992), days lost from work (Broadhead, Blazer, George, & Tse, 1990), physical disability (Bruce, Seeman, Merrill, & Blazer, 1994), and compromised recovery from illness and surgery (Dunham & Sager, 1994; Frasure-Smith, Lesperance, & Taljic, 1993). Although personality and social psychologists have been part of this emerging body of knowledge, their contributions have been modest. We view the area of depressive symptoms and health outcomes as a "growth industry" for personality and social psychology at the start of the new millennium, and an opportunity to bring fresh theoretical perspectives to this area of inquiry. We selected for brief discussion several studies that both capture the potential contributions of investigators at the personality–social–clinical–health interface, and that employ design features found lacking in the review of the interface literature. For the reasons cited earlier about the growing number of elderly people, we focus on interface opportunities in the study of older adults. Thus, we follow one of the earlier suggestions for improved interface research.

Depressive symptoms and declines in physical functioning. The heterogeneity of functional ability among older adults led Penninx et al. (1998) to investigate whether such changes can be predicted by depressive symptoms. They followed more than 1,200 men and women over the age of 65 years for 4 years. After adjusting for baseline physical performance, age, gender, education, and marital status, depressive symptoms predicted declines in performance 4 years later on objective indicators of standing balance, walking speed, and the ability to rise from a chair. The predictive value of depressive symptoms was far from trivial: Individuals who at baseline scored 20 or above on the Center for Epidemiological Studies–Depression Scale (Radloff, 1977) were 1.55 times more likely to decline substantially over the next 4 years. The relation between clinical and health psychology is clear in this instance. However, findings such as these beg for personality and social psychological theories to guide and expand further investigation.

One such model that elucidates the relation between personality and depressive symptoms is the hope theory (see Snyder, 1994; Snyder, Cheavens, & Michael, 1999), in which the sustaining of goal-directed thinking results in coping and health benefits. Elevated hope, whether achieved through dispositional measures (Snyder et al., 1991) or interventions with older persons (age 65 years old and higher; Klausner, Snyder, & Cheavens, in press), has resulted in psychological and physical benefits for the elderly (see Cheavens & Gum, 2000). In addition to this model, the effectiveness of brief interventions for individuals who do not meet criteria for major depression, but who report depressive symptoms (Miranda, Munoz, & Shumway, 1990) begins to hint at the fruitful collaborations that may develop among personality, social, clinical, and health psychologists as the population of older adults peaks at the start of the new millennium.

Depressive symptoms and health status following hospitalization. Because hospitalization of an older person for acute illness can begin a process of compromised daily functioning, Covinsky, Fortinsky, Palmer, Kresevic, and Landefeld (1997) examined whether depressive symptoms at the time of hospital admission predicted subsequent poorer health status. Controlling for potentially confounding factors such as severity of acute illness and admission health status, persons who endorsed more depression symptoms were more likely to be dependent in basic, daily living activities, to report less life satisfaction, and have worse global health at both 1 and 3 months after discharge. Although we applaud Covinsky et al.'s efforts, and view this medical context as an ideal arena for examining the prognostic role of depressive symptoms, we believe that social psychological theory and methods, and studies of how personality moderates the relation between depression and health outcomes, has enormous potential in an area that, for the most part, has been applied and descriptive.

Depressive symptoms, the development of coronary disease, and mortality. The Covinsky et al. (1997) study followed participants for 3 months, and the Penninx et al. (1998) study tracked people for 4 years. Thus, these studies are prime examples of the longitudinal research that we advocated earlier in this article. Even longer term prospective studies have begun to examine depressive symptoms in the pathogenesis of coronary artery disease. Barefoot and Schroll (1996), for example, described a 27-year prospective study in which over 600 individuals were tracked from 1964 (at age 50 years) to 1991 to determine if acute myocardial infarction could be predicted from baseline risk factors, disease status, and depressive symptoms. After 27 years, 40% of the participants had died, and causes of death were determined from death certificates, autopsies, and hospital records. As expected, the most common causes of death were ischemic heart disease, myocardial infarction, other cardiovascular diseases, and malignant neoplasms. Depressive symptoms nearly 3 decades earlier were associated with increased risk of acute myocardial infarction, ischemic heart disease mortality, and mortality from all other causes even after controlling for risk factors and earlier signs of disease.

Personality and social psychology has much to offer future investigations of this genre, including tests of theory-driven mediators and moderators. Also, these longitudinal and prospective designs should, as reasoned earlier, serve as methodological benchmarks for investigators planning to contribute to interface research in the 21st century. We hope that funding opportunities in this and other applied research venues related to older adults will entice personality and social psychologists to test their theories and apply their methods to the pressing practical challenges of a growing elderly population, and increasing rates of depression (Klerman & Weissman, 1989; Lewinsohn, Rohde, Seeley, & Fischer, 1993). Such long-term designs also must be reinforced by promotion committees within the academic and research communities.

Stress-Related Growth

A nascent but rapidly growing literature crossing clinical, personality, and social psychology indicates that many people who experience adversity report ensuing personal growth. One is reminded of the saying, "That which does not kill you makes you stronger." Of course, reports of positive change cannot be taken at face value (Park, Cohen, & Murch, 1996). Yet, converging evidence is beginning to point to the possibility that some individuals are changed in profoundly positive ways in the aftermath of a traumatic experience (Ickovics & Park, 1998; O'Leary, 1998; Tedeschi & Calhoun, 1996). Although this area of investigation calls for the contributions of interface

21

scholars, this is not the reason we include it in this special issue on new directions and interdisciplinary connections for social and personality research. Rather, its inclusion reflects our belief that this work mirrors broader trends on the horizon, that it will force personality and social psychologists to think "out of the box," and that the phenomenon of stress-related growth provides an opportunity for us to challenge how we conceptualize personality and human change processes.

The study of stress-related growth is in keeping with several recent requests for a sweeping change in the focus of behavioral and social sciences from its nearly exclusive reliance on dysfunction, negative affect, and distress, toward a focus on strength, virtue, and well-being. The most strident of these calls are Snyder and McCullough's (in press) description of a "positive psychology," and Seligman's (1998) appeal for a "positive social science." Such appeals have been echoed recently in the clinical assessment literature through calls for the assessment of psychological health (Exner, 1998; Handler & Potash, 1999; Lopez, Ciarlelli, Coffman, Stone, & Wyatt, 2000; Wright, 1991). Although theories of adaptive aspects of personality have been available for decades (Erikson, 1963; Maslow, 1954; Rogers, 1961), the voices are gathering for a positive social science that will necessitate changes in our approach to scientific inquiry.

In addition to its potential links to positive psychology, the phenomenon of stress-related growth holds the promise of extending current personality and social psychological models of personal consistency and change. Dramatic positive changes in the aftermath of adversity have been reported in the clinical literature (Herman, 1992), despite the contextual and interpersonal pressures against personal change that have been described in detail by social psychologists (e.g., Baumeister, 1994), and people's tendencies to select social environments that homeostatically interrupt exceptional personal changes (Watzlawick, Weakland, & Fisch, 1974).

There is great intuitive appeal to linking pre-event personality with postevent personal growth, and even with the nature of positive change. Although numerous personality factors have been nominated (e.g., Tedeschi & Calhoun, 1995), there have been relatively few published empirical studies relating dispositional influences to crisis-related personal growth. A notable exception, however, is the optimism model as first articulated by Scheier and Carver (1985). Optimism, according to their model, taps the person's perception that good things will happen to him or her. As an individual difference measure of optimism, Scheier and Carver (1985) initially developed a brief self-report instrument called the Life Orientations Test (LOT), and later revised this instru-

ment (LOT–Revised [LOT–R]; Scheier, Carver, & Bridges, 1994). Studies with the LOT and LOT–R have shown that more optimistic people (a) adjust better and are less depressed after childbirth (Carver & Gaines, 1987; Park, Moore, Turner, & Adler, 1997), (b) recover better in terms of greater life satisfaction after failed in vitro fertilization (Litt, Tennen, Affleck, & Klock, 1992), (c) are less distressed during and long after breast cancer treatment (Carver et al., 1993), (d) navigate infertility with less distress (Stanton & Dunkel-Schetter, 1991), and (e) have better adjustment after an abortion (Cozzarelli, 1993). In summary, optimism does appear to moderate coping with major life stressors (Carver & Scheier, 1999), and serves as an example of successful linking of personality, social, health, and clinical factors.

With regard to how personality is viewed, McAdams (1993) speculated that identity is continuously being shaped to fit personal experiences into a coherent account. Instead of viewing adversity as an invitation to the dark side that cannot be refused, perhaps adversity provides an opportunity to fit one's experience into her or his life narrative and to reshape personal identity. With regard to new conceptions of personality change, preliminary yet highly provocative evidence suggests that by facing prolonged misfortune and dramatic or quantum changes (Miller & C'deBaca, 1994), one's personality may change in ways that cannot be incorporated easily into current conceptions of trait stability. Moreover, such change clearly challenges the current conceptions of adaptation to trauma (Greenberg, 1995). The opportunity afforded by the study of stress-related growth will demand sophisticated prospective designs that were not evidenced in the interface literature we reviewed. This line of inquiry during the first decade of the 21st century also may distinguish between characteristics that successfully guide our daily lives and those that benefit us in crisis (Gould, 1993; Lifton, 1993). This is not an undertaking for the timid, those who are comfortable with the status quo, or investigators whose work environment or personal inclinations demand that they publish a great deal in a short period of time.

Enhancing Psychotherapeutic Outcomes

In contrast to the unequivocally bright future we anticipate for interface psychologists who immerse themselves in studying how depressive symptoms influence health outcomes, and the major contributions awaited from those who endure prospective studies of posttraumatic growth, we are more cautious, yet intrigued, by the possibility that personality and social psychologists may make invaluable contributions to how psychotherapy is practiced in the 21st century. Specifically, as "empirically supported interventions" (Chambless, 1996) inevitably become the treatments for psychological disorders, we envisage a unique and important role for personality and social psychological theories and methods in evaluating whether and how individual differences predict the outcome of these interventions and in advancing efforts to match these treatments to client characteristics. Currently, we have no more than a rudimentary understanding of how pretreatment characteristics affect an individual's response to psychotherapy.

The recent emergence of empirically supported interventions for specific psychological disorders, and the leading role of clinical psychology in developing and evaluating these interventions, ushers a new era in the study and delivery of psychological treatments. It stands to reason that personality psychologists' accumulated knowledge of individual differences, and social psychologists' long history of studying interpersonal influence processes would position them for making fundamental contributions to these developing treatments (see Forsyth & Corazzini, 2000). Yet, studies examining personality as a treatment moderator have been disappointing (Lambert & Supplee, 1997), and few social psychologists have become involved in the development of effective therapeutic interventions.

Recently, however, persuasive arguments have been offered for the potential of individual difference approaches and social psychological theories in the development of empirically supported treatments. The central role of personality in effective treatment planning has been advocated by Harkness and Lilienfeld (1997) and others, who have drawn on Costa and McCrae's (1994) distinction between *basic tendencies*, which are resistant to change, and *characteristic adaptations*, which make more effective targets of therapeutic influence. Similarly, McAdams's (1994) distinctions among *dispositional traits*, *personal concerns*, and *life narratives* opens new opportunities for personologists to examine how people change through psychotherapy or through other life experiences (according to McAdams, the answer depends on which level of personality is considered). Although we need to learn more about personal concerns and life narratives before applying these constructs to interventions, it is intuitively appealing to speculate that some clients may more readily incorporate therapist suggestions into their personal narratives, and others may find that different aspects of the therapeutic interaction modify their life narratives.

Because characteristic adaptations, personal concerns, and life narratives have not been studied exten-

sively, the rather large literature that has examined how treatments interact with client characteristics has yet to address the possibility that these constructs may help us understand who is most likely to respond to a particular treatment. Personality at the level of dispositional traits, however, has neither provided an effective basis for treatment selection, nor reliable evidence that individual differences among clients interact with treatment type to differentially influence therapeutic outcomes (Cronbach & Snow, 1977; Petry, Tennen, & Affleck, 2000).

The inconsistent findings for the role of client traits present a formidable challenge to personality psychologists who may consider contributing to what will surely be a surge of research over the next decade into the development of empirically validated treatments. At the very least, attention to levels of personality would highlight the limitations of current outcome indicators. The most widely used indicators of treatment outcome measure depressive symptoms, anxiety, and global symptoms (Lambert & Supplee, 1997). However, therapeutically generated changes in personal concerns or shifts in life narratives do not necessarily leave people less distressed. Global symptom measures, although informative, seem inadequate to capture positive changes in personal concerns or life narratives. A shift to multidimensional outcomes would by no means be a trivial consequence of personality psychologists' involvement in the search for effective psychological treatments. Yet, recent work blending social psychological theory and individual difference methods suggests that this partnership may help to unravel this thorny clinical problem.

Shoham and associates' (Shoham, Bootzin, Rohrbaugh & Urry, 1996; Shoham & Rohrbaugh, 1995) study of psychotherapy outcomes anticipates the contributions that personality and social psychologists can make to the formulation of effective treatments and to matching treatments to individual differences. Their study was based on the social psychological theory of reactance (Brehm & Brehm, 1981). Shoham et al. (1996) hypothesized that individual differences in psychological reactance measured before and during therapy would moderate differential treatment effects for insomnia, with more highly reactant individuals benefitting more from paradoxical interventions (PI), which involved prescribing the very symptom the client sought to change, and those low in reactance showing more favorable outcomes from progressive muscle relaxation (PMR). Clients who met criteria for primary sleep onset insomnia were randomly assigned to PI, PMR, or an attention-measurement control group. Client reactance moderated treatment effects as hypothesized: Paradoxical interventions were more effective for high- than for low-reactance clients, whereas PMR was more effective for clients with low reactance.

Findings such as these should stimulate further research into how individual differences may be used effectively to match treatments to client characteristics. Furthermore, the case for examining therapist characteristics as they interact with client characteristics may provide some clarity (Teyber & McClure, 2000). Obviously, the future of individual differences (in client and therapist) and treatment matching in the development of empirically supported interventions is going to be a complicated enterprise. Nevertheless, the possibility of interactions between personality, social, and clinical psychologists to guide theoretically driven client variables (Shoham-Salomon & Hannah, 1991; Smith & Sechrest, 1991) and therapist variables (Teyber & McClure, 2000), as well as to select individual difference and outcome indicators, is foreseen. Although a high-risk endeavor, there is tremendous potential in such collaborative efforts.

Social Comparison

Social comparison processes have been incorporated into psychological theories of how people interpret health threats (Suls, Marco, & Tobin, 1991), how they understand their own health risks (Gibbons & Gerrard, 1997), how and when they decide to seek care for physical symptoms (Leventhal, Hudson, & Robitaille, 1997), and how they adapt to serious illness (Taylor, Aspinwall, Giuliano, Dakof, & Reardon, 1993), including rheumatoid arthritis, impaired fertility, the birth of a medically fragile infant, cancer, multiple sclerosis, sickle cell disease, and chronic pain. Unlike the three emergent areas of interdisciplinary research described thus far, social comparison already has connected social and health psychology for nearly 2 decades. Although scores of studies have been published on the significance of comparison processes in health and illness, the most important conceptual and methodological advances are yet to come and, during the next decade, this blend of social and health psychology has the potential to influence the practice of medicine and public health. The enthusiasm for this area of research is fueled not only by its implications for health care but also by how it has tested well-formulated social psychological principles in real-world settings, and its elegant blend of experimental and field studies.

There is now evidence that individuals facing medical threats engage in both upward and downward social comparison. Research has supported Wills's (1981) contention that downward comparisons are often made by persons facing medical threats so as to increase subjective well-being. Additionally, findings have supported Taylor and Lobel's (1989) position that although persons facing threatening events often prefer downward evaluations, certain types of comparisons, specifically those involving information seeking and affiliation, typically will be upward, so as to provide the person making the comparison with problem-solving information, hope, and inspiration.

Whereas social comparison studies among the seriously ill have implications for how health care providers respond to patients' spontaneous comparisons, and when they decide to offer such comparisons, investigations of comparison processes among healthy people holds great promise for increasing our understanding of perceived risk and risk reduction efforts. As the health care system shifts (slowly) from its current focus on treating illness to a dual focus of preventing and treating illness, investigators engaged in social comparison research during the early decades of the 21st century almost surely will play a pivotal role in guiding public health efforts.

Croyle's (1992; Sun & Croyle, 1995) work in this area offers an example of how elegantly designed laboratory studies of social comparison hold the potential to inform large scale prevention campaigns. In his studies, participants were tested for a fictitious enzyme deficiency, which ostensibly placed one at risk for the development of pancreatic problems. Studies employing this paradigm show that when people are told that they are one of four members of a group of five who test positive for the deficiency (i.e., high consensus), they rate the disorder as a less serious health threat, and they are less likely to request information or a follow-up exam than those who are told they are the only member of a group of five who tested positive (i.e., low consensus). Interestingly, earlier research revealed a similar sequence of cognitions and behaviors for people who did not have the target problem (Snyder & Ingram, 1983). In this latter study, however, they also included persons who had the problem (debilitating anxiety), and when these persons were given high consensus information about the prevalence of the problem, they rated it as more serious and they were more likely to seek help. This study implies that if actuarial information about the high prevalence of a given problem via public service announcements is presented, it will be those persons who actually have the problem who will take it seriously and seek treatment. This is precisely the impact wanted for such public health announcements.

Field and experimental studies of social comparison in relation to "unrealistic optimism" (Weinstein, 1980) also hold potential for guiding the 21st-century's health care system toward prevention. Klein and Weinstein's (1997) review revealed that people across all age groups are unrealistically optimistic regarding many potential health and safety problems, and they hold self-serving biases about specific health behaviors associated with problems (e.g., believe they eat less salt than others, sunbathe less often, etc.). Across studies, unrealistic optimism is reduced when the person making the comparison does not have an image of the stereotypical victim (e.g., the typical accident victim as careless; see also Gibbons & Gerrard, 1997), when the target is a specific person rather than the average person, when the target is perceived as similar to the person making the comparison, and when the person making the comparison has personal contact with the target. These findings suggest that using similar, specific, and physically present others as comparison targets in health promotion campaigns may improve the effectiveness of such interventions.

We see the very real possibility that social comparison research may have an impact on society. In an enlightened health care delivery system, findings from comparison research will affect how care is provided. In a forward-looking public health system, this social comparison work will guide prevention efforts in areas ranging from health screening, to safety precautions, risky sex, and alcohol and drug use among adolescents. Before social comparison theory and research is taken to the streets, however, a number of conceptual and methodological issues will need to be faced directly. One such issue is when comparisons are best conceived as efforts to regulate emotions, and when they actually change commitment patterns (Lazarus, 1991). Most studies have limited their focus to the relation between comparisons and emotional well-being and subjective distress. Theory also suggests that social comparisons should appear more frequently and intensely during early phases of a medical threat to produce maximal impact, and that impact may vary as a function of what an individual expects to happen in the future (Aspinwall, 1997; Festinger, 1954). These predictions will require the regular use of longitudinal investigations in concert with laboratory studies. We expect these challenging issues to draw researchers into this line of research, to bring closer collaborations between social and health psychologists, and to increase further the growing number of investigators who identify themselves as social and health psychologists. Likewise, with the increasing presence of health psychology specialties within clinical psychology programs, there will be growing numbers of clinical health psychologists.

The Multilevel Daily Process Paradigm

The multilevel daily process paradigm is providing investigators with new methodological and statistical tools for interface research. This approach features time-intensive prospective measurement of dependent variables that are thought to change in meaningful ways from day to day or within a day. In the parlance of multilevel modeling, the repeated observations are called Level 1 (or lower level) variables, which are nested within Level 2 units, or persons providing the observations. This design and the statistical approaches now available to analyze such multilevel data sets enable researchers to answer idiographic and nomothetic research questions simultaneously. (By itself, this is a methodological improvement of major importance.) These questions take the following general form: "Are there relations between variables within individuals over time that generalize across individuals or that relate to differences between individuals?" (Larsen & Kasimatis, 1991; Tennen & Affleck, 1996).

The methodological and statistical options available for multilevel daily process studies have been elaborated in reviews and commentaries appearing in this decade's literature in personality psychology (e.g., Stone, Kessler, & Haythornthwaite, 1991; West & Hepworth, 1991), health psychology and behavioral medicine (e.g., Berry, 1997; Brown & Moskowitz, 1998; Schwartz & Stone, 1998), clinical psychology (e.g., Affleck, Zautra, Tennen, & Armeli, 1999), and social psychology (e.g., Kenny, Kashy, & Bolger, 1997).

Perhaps an example will help to elucidate this new paradigm. Consider a study by Steiger, Gauvin, Jabalpurwila, Seguin, and Stotland (1999) of women who were actively or formerly bulimic or who never had an eating disorder (this interface is between clinical and social psychology). They used an experience sampling procedure to obtain within-day Level 1 ratings of social interactions, self-concepts, moods, and eating behaviors, and used a hierarchical linear modeling procedure to analyze the Level 2 effects of eating disorder status on the relations between the Level 1 ratings. Individuals meeting criteria for a current eating disorder experienced more negative encounters and self-criticism than those with a previous history of eating disorders and those with no eating disorder history. The two eating disorder groups remained alike, however, in their inclination to exhibit self-criticism following a negative social interaction, and both of these groups differed from the group with no history of eating disorder. This uncovers a subtle vulnerability associated with having had an eating disorder history that could not have been readily detected in more conventional research designs.

Interface research in the next millennium also will use multilevel daily process designs to assess the outcomes of behavioral interventions in clinical and health psychology. In a study in progress, two of us

(Affleck and Tennen) are using these methods to evaluate the effects of brief interventions with problem drinkers. Participants are using electronic interviewers to describe their fleeting emotions, social pressure to drink, and interpersonal conflict. After 3 baseline weeks of daily self-monitoring, they are randomly assigned to one of three treatment conditions: (a) coping skills training, which identifies new ways of responding to emotions, social pressure to drink, and interpersonal conflict; (b) brief motivational intervention, which explores readiness to change problem drinking; or (c) a waiting list control group. A second 3-week self-monitoring period follows the intervention. Although both coping skills training and the motivational intervention should result in reduced drinking, a greater change in the within-person association between drinking and interpersonal conflict, positive and negative emotions, and social pressures to drink is anticipated for participants treated with the coping skills approach.

A second illustration of the marriage between multilevel daily process methods and intervention research comes from a series of studies in progress by F. Keefe (personal communication, July 14, 1998) and colleagues on the effects of several intervention strategies (e.g., exercise, cognitive–behavioral intervention, and couples-oriented intervention) on chronic pain patients' within-person relations among daily pain, mood, and coping. Such studies invite application of three-level hierarchical models: nesting daily observations, within multiple occasions of daily data collection, and within persons receiving different treatments (Schwartz & Stone, 1998). An illustrative hypothesis is that individuals receiving Treatment A will differ from those receiving Treatment B not only in the amount of pain reported daily before and after treatment but also in the extent to which certain coping strategies are used more frequently on days that are relatively more painful.

Closing Exhortations

We will not close with the usual repetition of what we have said—that can be obtained in short form by visiting the abstract, and in long form by revisiting the article itself. Instead, we make two exhortations.

Our first point relates to the integration and cooperation of interface scholars. Any combination of social, clinical, personality, and health psychologists can work together fruitfully. Sometimes, the interface may involve persons from any two areas or there may be triads; yet at other times, all four may unite to research a shared research focus. Although breakthroughs in the history of science occasionally have been accomplished by a single investigator, more often it is the case that such advances result from the sustained, co-

operative efforts of many persons sharing viewpoints and productively disagreeing. Thus, we should acknowledge the power of shared efforts. To be true to the spirit of what we have advocated in this article, we also believe that we could profit even more by "inviting others to the party." As just two possible examples, counseling psychologists could be added to the mix; so too could we move our thinking forward by collaborating with epidemiologists. The net scientific yield of interface cooperation transcends that knowledge obtained by merely summing individual contributions. Instead, it is the synergistic, catalytic, combined process and results of many minds focused on a common problem that produce the discoveries that advance our field, and our society more generally. Because of this, we would ask that you teach your students how to cooperate with others and show them how to do it.

Second, we sincerely believe in the potential power of interface scholars not only to shape the field of psychology but also to send positive ripples throughout our society more generally. Poised at the edge of the next millennium in psychology, the new psychology will be crafted by those with the innovative and integrative ideas, along with the motivation to do the hard work that goes with those ideas. We invite interface scholars to seize this opportunity, to caste away on this merging scholarly "river of dreams."

References

Affleck, G., Zautra, A., Tennen, H., & Armeli, S. (1999). Multilevel daily process designs for consulting and clinical psychology: A preface for the perplexed. *Journal of Consulting and Clinical Psychology, 67,* 746–754.

American Psychiatric Association. (1994). *Diagnostic and statistical manual of mental disorders* (4th ed.). Washington, DC: Author.

Aspinwall, L. G. (1997). Future-oriented aspects of social comparisons: A framework for studying health-related comparison activity. In B. P. Buunk & F. X. Gibbons (Eds.), *Health, coping, and well-being: Perspectives from social comparison theory* (pp. 125–166). Mahwah, NJ: Lawrence Erlbaum Associates, Inc.

Barefoot, J., & Schroll, M. (1996). Symptoms of depression, acute myocardial infarction, and total mortality in a community sample. *Circulation, 93,* 1976–1980.

Baumeister, R. F. (1994). The crystallization of discontent in the process of major life change. In T. F. Heatherton & J. L. Weinberger (Eds.), *Can personality change?* (pp. 281–297). Washington, DC: American Psychological Association.

Berry, C. (1997). Multilevel statistical models for psychosomatic research. *Psychosomatic Medicine, 59,* 350–351.

Brehm, S. S., & Brehm, J. W. (1981). *Psychological reactance: A theory of freedom and control.* New York: Academic.

Broadhead, W., Blazer, D., George, L., & Tse, C. (1990). Depression, disability days, and days lost from work in a prospective epidemiologic survey. *JAMA: Journal of the American Medical Association, 264,* 2524–2528.

Brown, K., & Moskowitz, D. (1998). It's a function of time: A review of the process approach to behavioral medicine research. *Psychosomatic Medicine, 20,* 109–117.

Bruce, M., Seeman, T., Merrill, S., & Blazer, D. (1994). The impact of depressive symptomatology on physical disability: MacArthur studies of successful aging. *American Journal of Public Health, 84,* 1796–1799.

Carver, C. S., & Gaines, J. G. (1987). Optimism, pessimism, and post-partum depression. *Cognitive Therapy and Research, 11,* 449–462.

Carver, C. S., Poza, C., Harris, S. D., Noriega, V., Scheier, M. F., Robinson, D. S., Ketchum, A. S., Moffat, F. L., & Clark, K. C. (1993). How coping mediates the effect of optimism on distress: A study of women with early stage breast cancer. *Journal of Personality and Social Psychology, 65,* 375–390.

Carver, C. S., & Scheier, M. F. (1999). Optimism. In C. R. Snyder (Ed.), *Coping: The psychology of what works* (pp. 182–204). New York: Oxford University Press.

Chambless, D. L. (1996). In defense of dissemination of empirically supported psychological interventions. *Clinical Psychology: Science and Practice, 3,* 230–235.

Cheavens, J., & Gum, A. (2000). Hope and older persons. In C. R. Snyder (Ed.), *Handbook of hope* (pp. 201–222). New York: Academic.

Costa, P. T., Jr., & McCrae, R. R. (1994). Set like plaster? Evidence for the stability of adult personality. In T. F. Heatherton & J. L. Weinberger (Eds.), *Can personality change?* (pp. 21–40). Washington, DC: American Psychological Association.

Covinsky, K., Fortinsky, R., Palmer, R., Kresevic, D., & Landefeld, C. (1997). Relation between symptoms of depression and health status outcomes in acutely ill hospitalized older persons. *Annals of Internal Medicine, 126,* 417–425.

Cozzarelli, C. (1993). Personality and self-efficacy as predictors of coping with abortion. *Journal of Personality and Social Psychology, 65,* 1224–1236.

Cronbach, L. J., & Snow, R. E. (1977). *Aptitudes and instructional methods.* New York: Irvington.

Croyle, R. T. (1992). Appraisal of health threats: Cognition, motivation, and social comparison. *Cognitive Therapy and Research, 16,* 165–182.

Dunham, N., & Sager, M. (1994). Functional status, symptoms of depression, and the outcomes of hospitalization in community-dwelling elderly patients. *Archives of Family Medicine, 3,* 676–681.

Erikson, E. (1963). *Childhood and society.* New York: Wiley.

Exner, J. E., Jr. (1998, February). *The future of the Rorschach.* Master lecture presented at annual meeting of the Society for Personality Assessment, Boston, MA.

Festinger, L. A. (1954). A theory of social comparison processes. *Human Relations, 7,* 117–140.

Forsyth, D. R., & Corazzini, J. G. (2000). Groups as change agents. In C. R. Snyder & R. E. Ingram (Eds.), *Handbook of psychological change: Psychotherapy processes and practices for the 21st century* (pp. 309–336). New York: Wiley.

Frasure-Smith, N., Lesperance, F., & Taljic, M. (1993). Depression following myocardial infarction. Impact on 6-month survival. *JAMA: Journal of the American Medical Association, 270,* 1819–1825.

Gibbons, F. X., & Gerrard, M. (1997). Health images and their effects on health behavior. In B. P. Buunk & F. X. Gibbons (Eds.), *Health, coping, and well-being: Perspectives from social comparison theory* (pp. 63–94). Mahwah, NJ: Lawrence Erlbaum Associates, Inc.

Gould, S. J. (1993). *Eight little piggies: Reflections on natural history.* New York: Norton.

Greenberg, M. A. (1995). Cognitive processing of traumas: The role of intrusive thoughts and reappraisals. *Journal of Applied Social Psychology, 25,* 1262–1296.

Handler, L., & Potash, H. M. (1999). Assessment of psychological health. *Journal of Personality Assessment, 72,* 181–184.

Harkness, A. R., & Lilienfeld, S. O. (1997). Individual differences science for treatment planning: Personality traits. *Psychological Assessment, 9,* 349–360.

Herman, J. L. (1992). *Trauma and recovery: The aftermath of violence from domestic abuse to political terror.* New York: Basic Books.

Ickovics, J. R., & Park, C. L. (1998). Paradigm shift: Why a focus on health is important. *Journal of Social Issues, 54,* 237–244.

Johnson, J., Weissman, M., & Klerman, G. (1992). Service utilization and social morbidity associated with depressive symptoms in the community. *JAMA: Journal of the American Medical Association, 267,* 1478–1483.

Kenny, D., Kashy, D., & Bolger, N. (1997). Data analysis in social psychology. In D. Gilbert, S. Fiske, & G. Lindzey (Eds.), *Handbook of social psychology* (4th ed., pp. 233–265). New York: McGraw-Hill.

Klausner, E., Snyder, C. R., & Cheavens, J. (in press). A hope-based group intervention for depressed older adult outpatients. In G. M. Williamson, P. A. Parmelee, & D. R. Shaffer (Eds.), *Physical illness and depression in older adults: A handbook of theory, research, and practice.* New York: Plenum.

Klein, W. M., & Weinstein, N. D. (1997). Social comparison and unrealistic optimism about personal risk. In B. P. Buunk & F. X. Gibbons (Eds.), *Health, coping, and well-being: Perspectives from social comparison theory* (pp. 25–64). Mahwah, NJ: Lawrence Erlbaum Associates, Inc.

Klerman, G. L., & Weissman, M. M. (1989). Increasing rates of depression. *Journal of the American Medical Association, 261,* 2229–2235.

Lambert, M. J., & Supplee, E. C. (1997). Trends and practices in psychotherapy outcome assessment and their implications for psychotherapy and applied personality. In S. Briggs (Ed.), *Handbook of personality psychology* (pp. 947–967). New York: Academic.

Larsen R., & Kasimatis, M. (1991). Day-to-day physical symptoms: Individual differences in the occurrence, duration, and emotional concomitants of minor daily illnesses. *Journal of Personality, 59,* 387–424.

Lazarus, R. S. (1991). *Emotion and adaptation.* New York: Oxford University Press.

Leventhal, H., Hudson, S., & Robitaille, C. (1997). Social comparison and health: A process model. In B. P. Buunk & F. X. Gibbons (Eds.), *Health, coping, and well-being: Perspectives from social comparison theory* (pp. 411–432). Mahwah, NJ: Lawrence Erlbaum Associates, Inc.

Lewinsohn, P. M., Rohde, P., Seeley, J. R., & Fischer, S. A. (1993). Age-cohort changes in the lifetime occurrence of depression and other mental disorders. *Journal of Abnormal Psychology, 102,* 110–120.

Lifton, R. J. (1993). *The protean self: Human resilience in an age of fragmentation.* New York: Basic Books.

Litt, M. D., Tennen, H., Affleck, G., & Klock, S. (1992). Coping and cognitive factors in adaptation to in vitro fertilization failure. *Journal of Behavioral Medicine, 15,* 171–187.

Lopez, S., Ciarlelli, R., Coffman, L., Stone, M., & Wyatt, L. (2000). Diagnosing for hope. In C. R. Snyder (Ed.), *Handbook of hope* (pp. 57–85). New York: Academic.

Maslow, A. H. (1954). *Motivation and personality.* New York: Harper & Row.

McAdams, D. P. (1993). *The stories we live by: Personal myths and the making of the self.* New York: Morrow.

McAdams, D. P. (1994). Can personality change? Levels of stability and growth in personality across the life span. In T. F. Heatherton & J. L. Weinberger (Eds.), *Can personality change?* (pp. 299–313). Washington, DC: American Psychological Association.

McCullough, M., & Snyder, C. R. (in press). Classical sources of human strength: Revisiting an old home and building a new one. *Journal of Social and Clinical Psychology.*

Miller, W. R., & C'deBaca, J. (1994). Quantum change: Toward a psychology of transformation. In T. F. Heatherton & J. L. Weinberger (Eds.), *Can personality change?* (pp. 253–280). Washington, DC: American Psychological Association.

Miranda, J., Munoz, R., & Shumway, M. (1990). Depression prevention research: The need for screening scales that truly predict. In C. Attkisson & J. Zich (Eds.), *Depression in primary care: Screening and detection* (pp. 232–250). New York: Routledge.

O'Leary, V. E. (1998). Strength in the face of adversity: Individual and social thriving. *Journal of Social Issues, 54,* 425–446.

Park, C., Cohen, L., & Murch, R. (1996). Assessment and prediction of stress-related growth. *Journal of Personality, 64,* 71–105.

Park, C. L., Moore, P. J., Turner, R. A., & Adler, N. E. (1997). The roles of constructive thinking and optimism in psychological and behavioral adjustment during pregnancy. *Journal of Personality and Social Psychology, 73,* 584–592.

Penninx, B., Guralnik, J., Ferrucci, L., Simonsick, E., Deeg, D., & Wallace, R. (1998). Depressive symptoms and physical decline in community-dwelling older persons. *JAMA: Journal of the American Medical Association, 279,* 1720–1726.

Petry, N. M., Tennen, H., & Affleck, G. (2000). Stalking the elusive client variable in psychotherapy research. In C. R. Snyder & R. E. Ingram (Eds.), *Handbook of psychological change: Psychotherapy processes and practices for the 21st century* (pp. 88–108). New York: Wiley.

Radloff, L. S. (1977). The CES–D scale: A self-report depression scale for research in the general population. *Applied Psychological Measurement, 1,* 385–401.

Rogers, C. (1961). *On becoming a person: A therapist's view of psychotherapy.* Boston: Houghton Mifflin.

Scheier, M. F., & Carver, C. S. (1985). Optimism, coping and health: Assessment and implications of generalized outcome expectancies. *Health Psychology, 4,* 219–247.

Scheier, M. F., Carver, C. S., & Bridges, M. W. (1994). Distinguishing optimism from neuroticism (and trait anxiety, self-mastery, and self-esteem): A reevaluation of the Life Orientation Test. *Journal of Personality and Social Psychology, 67,* 1063–1078.

Schwartz, J., & Stone, A. (1998). Strategies for analyzing ecological momentary assessment data. *Health Psychology, 17,* 6–16.

Seligman, M. E. P. (1998). Positive social science. *American Psychological Association Monitor, 29*(4), 2,5.

Shoham, V., Bootzin, R. R., Rohrbaugh, M., & Urry, H. (1996). Paradoxical versus relaxation treatment for insomnia: The moderating role of reactance. *Sleep Research, 24,* 365.

Shoham, V., & Rohrbaugh, M. J. (1995). Aptitude X treatment interaction (ATI) research: Sharpening the focus, widening the lens. In M. Aveline & D. Shapiro (Eds.), *Research foundations for psychotherapy practice* (pp. 73–95). Sussex, England: Wiley.

Shoham-Salomon, V., & Hannah, M. T. (1991). Client–treatment interaction in the study of differential change processes. *Journal of Consulting and Clinical Psychology, 59,* 217–225.

Smith, B., & Sechrest, L. (1991). Treatment of Aptitude × Treatment interactions. *Journal of Consulting and Clinical Psychology, 59,* 233–244.

Smyth, J. M., & Pennebaker, J. W. (1999). Sharing one's story: Translating emotional experiences into words as a coping tool. In C. R. Snyder (Ed.), *Coping: The psychology of what works* (pp. 70–89). New York: Oxford University Press.

Snyder, C. R. (1994). *The psychology of hope: You can get there from here.* New York: Free Press.

Snyder, C. R. (1997). The state of the interface. *Journal of Social and Clinical Psychology, 16,* 231–242.

Snyder, C. R., Cheavens, J., & Michael, S. T. (1999). Hoping. In C. R. Snyder (Ed.), *Coping: The psychology of what works* (pp. 205–231). New York: Oxford University Press.

Snyder, C. R., Harris, C., Anderson, J. R., Holleran, S. A., Irving, L. M., Sigmon, Y. L., Gibb, J., Langelle, C., & Harney, P. (1991). The will and the ways: Development and validation of an individual-differences measure of hope. *Journal of Personality and Social Psychology, 60,* 570–585.

Snyder, C. R., & Ingram, R. E. (1983). "Company motivates the miserable": The impact of consensus information on help seeking for psychological problems. *Journal of Personality and Social Psychology, 45,* 1118–1126.

Snyder, C. R., & Ingram, R. E. (2000). Psychotherapy: Questions for an evolving field. In C. R. Snyder & R. E. Ingram (Eds.), *Handbook of psychological change: Psychotherapy processes and practices for the 21st century* (pp. 707–726). New York: Wiley.

Snyder, C. R., & McCullough, M. E. (in press). A positive psychology field of dreams: "If you build it, they will come ..." *Journal of Social and Clinical Psychology.*

Snyder, C. R., McDermott, D. S., Leibowitz, R. Q., & Cheavens, J. (2000). The roles of female clinical psychologists in changing the field of psychotherapy. In C. R. Snyder & R. E. Ingram (Eds.), *Handbook of psychological change: Psychotherapy processes and practices for the 21st century* (pp. 640–659). New York: Wiley.

Stanton, A. L., & Dunkel-Schetter, C. (Eds.). (1991). *Infertility: Perspectives from stress and coping research.* New York: Plenum.

Steiger, H., Gauvin, L., Jabalpurwila, S., Seguin, J., & Stotland, S. (1999). Hypersensitivity to social interactions in bulimic syndromes: Relationship to binge eating. *Journal of Consulting and Clinical Psychology, 67,* 765–775.

Stone, A., Kessler, R., & Haythornthwaite, J. (1991). Measuring daily events and experiences: Decisions for the researcher. *Journal of Personality, 59,* 575–608.

Suls, J., Marco, C. A., & Tobin, S. (1991). The role of temporal comparison, social comparison, and direct appraisal in the elderly's self-evaluations of health. *Journal of Applied Social Psychology, 21,* 1125–1144.

Sun, Y., & Croyle, R. T. (1995). Level of health threat as a moderator of social comparison preferences. *Journal of Applied Social Psychology, 25,* 1937–1952.

Taylor, S. E., Aspinwall, L. G., Giuliano, T. A., Dakof, G. A., & Reardon, K. K. (1993). Storytelling and coping with stressful events. *Journal of Applied Social Psychology, 23,* 703–733.

Taylor, S. E., & Lobel, M. (1989). Social comparison activity under threat: Downward evaluation and upward contacts. *Psychological Review, 96,* 569–575.

Tedeschi, R. G., & Calhoun, L. G. (1995). *Trauma and transformation: growing in the aftermath of suffering.* Thousand Oaks, CA: Sage.

Tedeschi, R. G., & Calhoun, L. G. (1996). The post-traumatic growth inventory: Measuring the positive legacy of trauma. *Journal of Traumatic Stress, 9,* 455–471.

Tennen, H., & Affleck, G. (1996). Daily processes in coping with chronic pain: Methods and analytic strategies. In M. Zeidner & N. Endler (Eds.), *Handbook of coping* (pp. 151–180). New York: Wiley.

Teyber, E., & McClure, F. (2000). Therapist variables. In C. R. Snyder & R. E. Ingram (Eds.), *Handbook of psychological change: Psychotherapy processes and practices for the 21st century* (pp. 62–87). New York: Wiley.

Watzlawick, P., Weakland, J. H., & Fisch, R. (1974). *Change: Principles of problem formation and problem resolution.* New York: Norton.

Weinstein, N. D. (1980). Unrealistic optimism about future life events. *Journal of Personality and Social Psychology, 39,* 806–820.

West, S., & Hepworth, J. (1991). Statistical issues in the study of temporal data: Daily experiences. *Journal of Personality, 59,* 609–662.

Wills, T. A. (1981). Downward comparison principles in social psychology. *Psychological Bulletin, 90,* 245–271.

Wright, B. A. (1991). Labeling: The need for greater person–environment individuation. In C. R. Snyder & D. R. Forsyth (Eds.), *Handbook of social and clinical psychology: The health perspective* (pp. 469–487). New York: Pergamon.

Personality and Social Psychology Review
2000, Vol. 4, No. 1, 30–44

Interpersonal Flourishing: A Positive Health Agenda for the New Millennium

Carol D. Ryff
Department of Psychology
University of Wisconsin–Madison

Burton Singer
Office of Population Research
Princeton University

Quality ties to others are universally endorsed as central to optimal living. Social scientists have extensively studied the relational world, but in somewhat separate literatures (e.g., attachment, close relationships, marital and family ties, social support). Studies of intimacy and close connection are infrequently connected to health, whereas studies of health and social support rarely intersect with literatures on relational flourishing. Efforts to probe underlying physiological processes have been disproportionately concerned with the negative (e.g., adverse effects of relational conflict). A worthy goal for the new millennium is promoting greater cross talk between these realms via a focus on the positive health implications of interpersonal flourishing. Vital venues for the future include mapping the emotional configurations of quality social relationships and elaborating their physiological substrates.

Defining *health* as the absence of illness or disease does not get to the heart of what it means to be well and thriving (Ickovics & Park, 1998; Ryff & Singer, 1998). Construed positively, health encompasses diverse aspects of flourishing, such as leading a meaningful and purposeful life as well as having quality ties to others and how these core features of the well-lived life affect biology. That is, positive health requires probing the physiological substrates of flourishing—mapping how positive psychological or relational experience is instantiated in neural circuitry, downstream endocrinological and immunological systems, and ultimately culminates in vitality and longevity. The discipline of psychology has much to contribute to this story via its expertise in studies of social interaction, interpersonal relationships, emotion, and psychophysiology. In broadening its purview to other realms of empirical inquiry, psychology also has much to gain from joining the new millennial pursuit of health as wellness.

Our first objective in this article is to make the case, on philosophical as well as psychological grounds, that interpersonal flourishing is a core feature of quality living across cultures and across time. We then shift to the empirical realm, highlighting what is known about relational flourishing and interpersonal well-being. Many realms of inquiry bear on this question, but few have been explicitly concerned with health. When social life has been linked to health (e.g., morbidity and mortality), the conceptualization and measurement of the interpersonal realm has often lacked the depth and scope of social relationships as studied by developmental, personality, and social psychologists. There has also been, as we illustrate, a pervasive tendency to focus on the negative—thwarted attachments, relational difficulties, belongingness deficits, and marital conflict—particularly when reaching for physiological substrates, or mental or physical health outcomes.

Our objective, broadly speaking, is to promote a future vision and agenda that integrates these diverse realms of study, underscoring that each of them tells part, but only part, of the story about relational flourishing and health. To bring the future into clear focus, we call for multiple initiatives built on neglected territories and unmapped intersections in the aforementioned areas of research as well as promising, innovative, and even outlandish (i.e., out of the ordinary) new directions, substantive and methodological. The goal is to challenge psychologists to think in cre-

This research was supported by the John D. and Catherine T. MacArthur Foundation Research Networks on Successful Midlife Development and Socioeconomic Status and Health as well as National Institute on Aging Grant R01–AG13613 and National Institute of Mental Health Grant P50–MH61083.

Requests for reprints should be sent to Carol D. Ryff, Department of Psychology, Brogden Hall, University of Wisconsin, Madison, WI 53706. E-mail: cryff@facstaff.wisc.edu.

ative new ways about how relational well-being keeps people healthy and well.

Quality Ties to Others: The Ultimate Criterial Good

Those of diverse ideological persuasions are quicker to agree about the meaning of sickness (physical and mental) than they are about what comprises core facets of quality living and well-being. Articulating the contours of positive health unavoidably requires stepping into the realm of human values and socially constructed ideals, and then considering the implications of such ideals for biology. There are, of course, multiple views of what constitutes quality living, flourishing, and the good life, in both philosophical (Becker, 1992; Griffin, 1986; Norton, 1976; Nozick, 1989) and social scientific accounts (Coan, 1977; Jahoda, 1958; Keyes, 1998; Ryff, 1985, 1989a). Despite the variety, important points of convergence can be found, and they provide useful starting points for advancing the science of positive human health (Ryff, 1989b; Ryff & Singer, 1998).

Central among the core criterial goods comprising optimal living is having quality ties to others. Across time and settings, people everywhere have subscribed to the view that close, meaningful ties to others is an essential feature of what it means to be fully human. Moreover, in philosophical accounts of the good life, notable prominence is given to mutual love, affection, and empathy (Becker, 1992), deep personal relationships (Griffin, 1986), and love's bond, intimacy, and parent–child connection (Nozick, 1989). Zest in life, according to Russell (1930/1958), comes, more than anything, from feeling loved and from giving love and affection.

Such consensus is likely rooted in evolutionary history (Trivers, 1971, 1985) as well as the first and most immediate human relationships (Bowlby, 1969). Across the broad span of time, nurturing and caring for others has been fundamental to survival, and thereby, the transmission of genes to the next generation. In the current era, a greater appreciation of differential priorities accorded across cultures to agentic and individualist versus collectivitist and communal modes of being is afforded (Markus & Kitayama, 1991, 1994; Triandis, 1989), but these varieties rest on bedrock recognition of abiding needs for close connection to others that transcend cultural nuance and variety.

Within the discipline of psychology, efforts to delineate core features of what it means to be psychologically well repeatedly invoke the interpersonal realm. Maslow (1955, 1968) described self-actualizers as having strong feelings of empathy and affection for all human beings and having the capacity for greater love, deeper friendship, and more complete identification with others than those who are not self-actualized. Allport (1961) formulated maturity as the capacity for great intimacy in love, whether with family members or friends, and also the showing of compassion, respect, and appreciation for others. Erikson's (1959) adult developmental tasks were highly interpersonal, including the establishment of close unions with others (intimacy) and the showing of concern for guiding and directing others (generativity). Jahoda (1958) defined the ability to love as a key criterion of positive mental health. Baumeister and Leary (1995) described the need to form and maintain strong, stable interpersonal relationships as a fundamental human motive. Drawing on sociological theory, Keyes (1998) described multiple dimensions of social well-being, such as being integrated into one's community and able to contribute to society and the social good.

In sum, from diverse philosophical and scholarly vantage points there is ringing endorsement that interpersonal connection is essential to human thriving. In the following section, scientific agendas pertinent to relational flourishing are briefly examined (e.g., studies of attachment—in childhood and adulthood; research on personal relationships and related topics of love, intimacy, and attraction; and studies of marital quality and family ties). For the most part, these literatures have not been connected to questions of human health. Where their consequences for health have been explored, the focus has been predominantly on the side of adverse effects following from dysfunctional, conflictual, or inadequate relational ties.

Empirical Coordinates of the Relational World

Studies of Attachment

A vast literature has been built on Bowlby's (1969) initial formulation of attachment theory, which gave fundamental importance to early ties between infant and caregiver. The rich proliferation of agendas that followed, exemplified by the recent 36-chapter handbook of attachment (Cassidy & Shaver, 1999), addresses core features of the theory (e.g., nature of the child's ties, normative development of attachment, individual differences in caregiver attachment), the cross-species evidence of attachment and separation responses (including psychophysiology), the relational sequelae of early attachments through childhood and adolescence into adulthood, and clinical applications. Emergent topics carry the attachment perspective to realms of caregiving, loss and bereavement, and religious experience.

Hazan and Shaver (1994) suggested that attachment theory provides a useful framework to organize and extend the large literature on close relationships in general. The theory encompasses a behavioral system designed to maintain proximity and close contact with the caregiver, which is subsequently linked to feelings of security, love, confidence, and interpersonal effectiveness. Disruption or dissolution of attachments contribute to reactions of anxiety, protest, and even detachment. Repeated interactions with the caregiver lead to expectations (i.e., internal working models that forecast caregiver availability and responsiveness). Individual differences in such processes and their stability over time are central questions of empirical study.

Extrapolating beyond infancy and childhood, Hazan and Shaver (1994) proposed that attachment theory provides a framework for understanding how adult relationships are formed, what makes partners appealing or unappealing, and why relationships endure or dissolve. Their claims prompted extensive reaction and exchange among contemporary relationship and attachment researchers (see 13 commentaries to Hazan & Shaver's 1994 *Psychological Inquiry* article).

Despite its broad scope, attachment research has not been strongly linked to health. When implications for overall functioning (e.g., adjustment, health) have been addressed, the focus has been almost exclusively negative; that is, how avoidant or anxious attachments, disruption, or loss of significant relationships create vulnerability to behavioral and psychiatric problems as well as compromised cardiovascular, immune, or neuroendocrine function, and even death (e.g., Bloom, Asher, & White, 1978; Coe & Lubach, in press; Feeney & Kirkpatrick, 1996; Goodwin, Hurt, Key, & Sarret, 1987; Kiecolt-Glaser et al., 1984). How stable and secure attachments that promote feelings of being loved and confident influence various physiological systems, and ultimate health outcomes, has rarely received scientific attention.

Close and Personal Relationships: The Emergent Field of "Relationship Science"

Related to, and sometimes intersecting with, the attachment field (e.g., Hazan & Shaver, 1987; Reis & Patrick, 1996) are studies of intimacy, love, attraction, and close relationships. Berscheid and Reis (1998) provided a comprehensive overview of the field of relationship science and showed its distant historical roots in social psychology. Acknowledging the conceptual and methodological challenges inherent in studying social interaction, they summarized extensive findings on how relationships begin (i.e., antecedents and consequents of attraction in first encounters), how they develop (i.e., progression of relationships over time), what makes them satisfying and stable (i.e., factors determining whether relationships will endure or dissolve), and what social relationships contribute to well-being.

With regard to the latter, relationships have been studied for their contributions to happiness (Argyle, 1987; Myers & Diener, 1995) as well as health outcomes (e.g., morbidity and mortality). However, as Berscheid and Reis's (1998) review revealed, it has been primarily epidemiologists, not social psychologists, who have built bridges between the social world and health. In the main, the expansive literature on close and personal relationships, exemplified by their review as well as recent handbooks (Duck, 1997) and future formulations of relationship science (e.g., Berscheid, 1999; Sarason, Sarason, & Pierce, 1995) has been surprisingly distant from questions of human health. Emphasis, rather, has been on understanding relational development and interpersonal communication, broadly defined, with future visions emphasizing the need for unifying theory (Berscheid, 1995; Hazan & Shaver, 1994; Rook, 1995), methodological innovation (Kenny, 1995), and attending to cultural and demographic factors (Sarason et al., 1995). The net effect, paradoxically, is that those with the most comprehensive, in-depth knowledge of the relational realm are frequently absent in the building of scientific agendas that link the social world to health.

As with the attachment literature, when implications for overall functioning have been considered, the downside has priority—the adverse consequences of deficits in belongingness (Baumeister & Leary, 1995), the dispositional and cognitive factors contributing to loneliness (Marangoni & Ickes, 1989; Rook, 1988), and the nature of toxic relationships such as those involving violence, jealousy, or conflict (see Berscheid & Reis, 1998; Bradbury, 1998). There are, of course, counterpoint studies of love, intimacy, and satisfactions in close relationships (Barnes & Sternberg, 1997; Hatfield & Rapson, 1993; Hendrick & Hendrick, 1997; Reis & Patrick, 1996; Sternberg, 1986; Sternberg & Barnes, 1988; Sternberg & Hojjat, 1997), but these salubrious aspects of social connection are rarely explored for their health consequences.

Marital Quality and Family Ties

The primary social relationships in most individuals' lives are those within the family—ties between parents and children, husbands and wives. Empirical study of these relationships intersects with the realms of child and adult attachment, close and personal relationships, but goes beyond them. For example, extensive work pertains exclusively to the development of survey instruments to assess marital quality and adjustment (Fincham & Bradbury, 1987; Glenn, 1990; Sabatelli, 1988). These instruments have differentiated various dimensions of marital intimacy (e.g., emotional, sexual, social, intellectual; Schaefer & Olson, 1981) as well as specific aspects of spousal interaction (e.g., problem-solving communication, time spent together, conflict over children or finances; Snyder, 1983). When concern extends beyond the theoretical basis or psychometric properties of such measures, emphasis is typically on questions of why marriages succeed or fail. Karney and Bradbury's (1995) recent review of 115 longitudinal studies, representing over 45,000 marriages, included a stress-vulnerability/ stress-adaptation model to account for variations in marital quality and stability over time. Gottman and Levenson (1992) also proposed a cascade model of marital dissolution to identify precursors of separation or divorce.

Looking to the future, Karney and Bradbury (1995) called for numerous priorities, including more studies of marital quality over time (noting that prior work has targeted the independent variables predicting change in marital stability, rather than the course of marital quality itself); more homogeneous marital samples (to reduce interpretive difficulties in studies that combine marriages at different stages, of diverse sociodemographic backgrounds, and varying initial levels of satisfaction, etc.); and more comprehensive longitudinal designs allowing for assessment of reciprocal effects (e.g., between stress, adaptive processes, and marital quality). Pertinent to this article, they also advocated more longitudinal research that examines nonmarital outcomes, including physical health problems (Burman & Margolin, 1992), depression (Beach, Sandeen, & O'Leary, 1990), and children's adjustment (Markman & Jones-Leonard, 1985). Marital contributions to the positive health and well-being of spouses or children was not part of the future vision.

Marital dysfunction and conflict comprises a large and somewhat distinctive realm of inquiry (see Bradbury, 1998; Leonard & Roberts, 1998; Noller & Feeney, 1998; O'Leary & Cascardi, 1998). This work is pertinent to health because numerous studies have linked marital conflict to physiological consequences, such as cardiovascular, neuroendocrine, and immunological parameters. For example, Kiecolt-Glaser et al. (1997) showed that, among older adults in long-term marriages, 30 min of conflict discussion was associated with changes in cortisol, adrenocorticotropic hormone, and norepinephrine in women, but not men. Both husbands and wives showed poorer immunological response during conflict. Among newlyweds, Kiecolt-Glaser, Newton, et al. (1996) found higher cortisol and epinephrine levels among wives whose husbands had higher probabilities of withdrawal in response to their negative communication. More frequent positive behaviors were also associated with lower epinephrine and higher prolactin levels among wives. No significant associations were found between the behavioral and endocrine data of newly married husbands.

Other studies have linked marital conflict with high blood pressure (Ewart, Taylor, Kraemer, & Agras, 1991), pituitary and adrenal hormones (Malarkey, Kiecolt-Glaser, Pearl, & Glaser, 1994), and physiological arousal (Levenson, Carstensen, & Gottman, 1994). During discussion of marital problems, Miller, Dopp, Myers, Stevens, and Fahey (1999) showed that displays of anger in husbands high in cynical hostility were associated with greater elevations in systolic and diastolic blood pressure, cortisol, and increases in natural killer (NK) cell numbers and cytotoxicity, whereas for men low in cynical hostility, anger was associated with smaller increases in heart rate and NK cell cytotoxicity. None of women's affect scores were related to cardiovascular, neuroendocrine, or immunologic outcomes, leading the authors to suggest that other emotions (e.g., sadness) may be more relevant for wives' physiological responses.

Apart from marital conflict, other aspects of family relationships have also been linked to biology. A growing literature on caregiving shows that the chronic stress of caring for a relative with dementia has been linked with immune consequences, such as poorer proliferative responses of peripheral blood leukocytes (Kiecolt-Glaser, Dura, Speicher, Trask, & Glaser, 1991), lowering of NK cell response (Esterling, Kiecolt-Glaser, Bodnar, & Glaser, 1994), and impaired antibody response to influenza virus vaccine (Kiecolt-Glaser, Glaser, Gravenstein, Malarkey, & Sheridan, 1996).

Reflecting more general perspectives on families and health, Burg and Seeman (1994) elaborated the ways in which family life contributes to stress and dysfunctional coping as well as detrimental health behaviors (e.g., smoking, sedentary lifestyles, poor eating habits, Type A behavior patterns). This formulation was presented as a counterpoint to the mainstream literature on social support (see later), which has emphasized primarily the positive effects derived from social ties. Taylor, Repetti, and Seeman (1997) also explored the nature of "unhealthy environments" and how they get under the skin. Their review points to three characteristics of the family social environment that undermine the health of children and adolescents: (a) a social climate that is conflictual and angry, or even violent and abusive; (b) parent–child relationships that are unresponsive and lacking in cohesiveness, warmth, and emotional support; and (c) a parenting style that is either overly controlling and dominating, or uninvolved with little imposition of rules and structure. Such characteristics were linked to depression and maladaptive ways of coping in children as well as health-threatening behaviors in adolescents. A relevant counterpoint, focusing on life course perspectives, are studies of parent–child solidarity and exchange and affection between the generations (Rossi & Rossi, 1990).

Summary

Taken as a whole, the aforementioned literature reveals the remarkable scope of research on significant social relationships. Collectively, the work represents major empirical strides in understanding how key relationships are formed, how they evolve and change over time, what makes them satisfying and fulfilling, and why they frequently become conflictual, dysfunctional, or both. Viewed from the standpoint of interpersonal flourishing and positive health, two key points emerge. First, studies of the beneficial and positive features of social relationships, be they secure attachments in childhood and adulthood, or loving and intimate relationships in adulthood, are rarely connected to health. Second, when health or biology has entered the picture, it is overwhelmingly on the side of negative social interaction and adverse health consequences, including an expansive array of physiological systems (cardiovascular, neuroendocrine, immunological). The counterpart agenda (i.e., mapping the physiological substrates of relational flourishing and their role in promoting health, well-being, and longevity) has received dramatically less empirical attention.

Missing from this overview thus far has been the vast literature on social support and health. The following section briefly examines this realm, which extends well beyond the field of psychology into epidemiology, sociology, and demography. Of particular interest in summarizing this domain is the degree of cross talk (or lack thereof) between social support researchers and those working in realms of study previously described.

The Social World and Health

Over the last 2 decades epidemiologists have repeatedly put forth evidence that social isolation is consequential for health. Berkman and Syme (1979), in a community-based prospective investigation (the Alameda County Study), showed that those who lacked ties to others were two to three times more likely to have died 9 years later than those who were socially connected. Subsequent inquiries extended the documentation of social isolation, or lack of social support, to include increased risk of various diseases as well as reduced length of life (Berkman & Breslow, 1983; House, Landis, & Umberson, 1988; Seeman, 1996; Seeman et al., 1993). Review of eight major epidemiological studies (Berkman, 1995) indicated that, in each case, mortality was significantly lower among persons who were more socially integrated.

Relative to the psychologically oriented studies previously described, these epidemiological inquiries are unique for their focus on specific health outcomes (i.e., rates of cancer, coronary heart disease, stroke, etc.) and mortality, as well as their large, population-based samples that overcome the nonrandom selection bias, and thereby, the limited generalizability of the preceding literature. Nonetheless, psychologists note the limited capacity of epidemiological studies to address questions of causality between social relationships and health (Berscheid & Reis, 1998), given the large number of factors (sociodemographic, geographic, occupational, personality) that covary with measures of social integration. Some of these are dealt with as statistical controls, but many are frequently not assessed, given limitations on the scope of data collection in large, population-based samples.

The social support literature follows from and extends these epidemiological findings. Initial assessments of social isolation (or integration) tended to emphasize objective features of social support such as the size or density of one's social network and frequency of contact with relatives and friends. Subsequent studies elaborated the more subjective and functional aspects, such as the perception that one is emotionally and instrumentally supported and assisted by others (Cohen, 1988; Cohen & Wills, 1985; Vaux, 1988). Along the way, research on social support became increasingly differentiated into specific substantive areas, such as the role of social support in stress and coping (Thoits, 1995), social support in family relationships (Pierce, Sarason, & Sarason, 1996), social support and personality (Pierce, Lakey, Sarason, & Sarason, 1997), and social support and differential survival from various health challenges, such as myocardial infarction (e.g., Ruberman, Weinblatt, Goldberg, & Chaudhary, 1984) or cancer (Spiegel, Bloom, & Yalom, 1981).

With regard to how various aspects of support influence health outcomes, there have been numerous formulations. Cohen (1988) distinguished between a main effects model, which suggests that social support is beneficial whether or not one is under stress, and a buffering model (see also Cohen & Willis, 1985), which states that social support is beneficial for health only when one is confronted with stress or adversity. Buffering is said to occur when the quality of support matches one's needs for support, thereby underscoring the importance of measuring "perceived" support. These distinctions between buffering and direct effects models continue to guide empirical studies (e.g., Gerin, Milner, Chawla, & Pickering, 1995).

In addition to such analytic distinctions, the mechanisms through which social support impacts health have implicated behavioral routes, such as how significant others promote and encourage positive health practices (Berkman, 1995; Spiegel & Kimerling, in press; Taylor et al., 1997). The most extensive proliferation of research on mechanism, however, pertains to the underlying physiological routes through which social ties influence health. For example, Uchino et al.'s (1996) recent review of 81 studies revealed that social support has been reliably related to beneficial effects in cardiovascular, endocrine, and immune systems. Seeman has been particularly influential in elaborating the links between social ties and neuroendocrine function (e.g., Seeman, 1996, in press; Seeman, Berkman, Blazer, & Rowe, 1994; Seeman & McEwen, 1996), whereas Coe, Cohen, and Kiecolt-Glaser, among others (e.g., Coe & Lubach, in press; Cohen & Herbert, 1996; Kang, Coe, Karaszewski, & McCarthy, 1998; Kiecolt-Glaser, Malarkey, Cacioppo, & Glaser, 1994), have elaborated connections between the social realm and immune function . Reflecting the vitality and scope of current inquiry, such studies span a wide array of human and animal models.

Looking to the future, Uchino et al. (1996) called for more studies of social support as a multidimensional, rather than a unidimensional, construct, noting Seeman et al.'s (1994) finding that emotional support was a more consistent predictor of neuroendocrine function than informational support. They also emphasized the importance of assessing both positive and negative aspects of social relationships in future research as well as further analytical refinement (e.g., specific tests for mediating and moderating effects). Reflecting the need to integrate what is known about cardiovascular, endocrine, and immune systems, they noted that only 5 of the 81 studies reviewed obtained simultaneous measurements from even two of the different systems, and none measured all three. Thoits (1995) also called for greater attention to the negative effects of social support as well as the importance of giving (not just getting) social support, and optimal matches between individuals' needs and the support received. Berkman (1995) emphasized that for social support to be health promoting, it must provide a sense of belonging and intimacy, and help individuals to be more competent and efficacious.

When juxtaposing the aforementioned studies of social support with preceding literatures on attachment and close personal relationships, what is notable is the missing interchange between these realms. Those in the social support arena have been explicitly concerned with health outcomes, and as such, have contributed outstanding advances with regard to social influences on morbidity and mortality, and more recently, the physiological mechanisms that may underlie such effects. Although the focus has been primarily on the side of positive effects (there is increasing interest given to the dark side of social support, however), extant instruments do not probe the depths of relational flourishing—what it means to have loving, intimate, fulfilling, and enjoyable ties to significant others (spouse, parent, children, coworkers, friends). This is undoubtedly because studies of social integration and social support never had as their objective the conceptualization and measurement of optimal relational experience and how it affects multiple physiological systems, and ultimately, health.

Alternatively, social relationship researchers who probe early and later life attachments, and close personal relationships, including marital and family ties, have elaborated some of the features of deep, meaningful, loving human connection, but their agendas have rarely entered the health arena. Moreover, their literatures rarely intersect with formulations of optimal human functioning (see Becker, 1992; Ryff, 1985; Ryff & Singer, 1998) as they reach to articulate key elements of relational well-being. When social relationship researchers have probed the health significance of key social ties, inquiries have been heavily weighted on the side of relational conflict and dysfunction as risk factors for behavioral, mental, and physical health problems.

Building on these observations, in the remainder of this article we propose new venues for the study of relational flourishing and positive health. Many follow from observations about unmapped territories, missing connections, or both, in the aforementioned realms of inquiry. Together, they herald a new era of multidisciplinary inquiry seeking to understand the relational side of optimal human health.

Promising Venues for the Future

What Are the Emotions of Interpersonal Flourishing?

Alongside the proliferation of relational research in recent years has been dramatic growth in the study of emotion (Ekman & Davidson, 1994; Izard, 1991; Lewis & Haviland, 1993). This work has addressed taxonomic issues (i.e., what are the basic emotions); the biological and neurophysiological underpinnings of emotion; their developmental course; how they are linked to temperament, personality, memory, and cognition; and how they are controlled and regulated. Although social processes have been part of this unfolding enterprise, core interpersonal emotions (e.g., love, desire, hate, jealousy, shame) occupy a relatively small space within the larger field of "affective science."

There are, of course, major programs of study and clinical intervention that deal explicitly with emotion in social relationships. Numerous investigations have probed the nature of affect in intimate relationships, its developmental course over time, and related expressions of emotion during marital interaction, particularly when dealing with conflict (Carstensen, Graff, Levenson, & Gottman, 1996; Carstensen, Levenson, & Gottman, 1995; Gottman, 1993, 1994; Gottman & Levenson, 1992; Levenson, Carstensen, & Gottman, 1994; Levenson & Gottman, 1985). Evidence suggests a general trend toward declining marital satisfaction following the birth of a child, which persists until children leave home, although the manner in which couples resolve emotionally charged conflicts predicts marital satisfaction throughout adulthood. Happily, with time, older couples appear to derive more pleasure than distress from their marriages and also show more displays of affection during conflict than do younger couples.

Dealing with more general social functions of emotion, Keltner and Kring (1998) discussed the ways in which emotion coordinates social interaction by conveying information (about the sender, objects, or events, or all of these, in the social environment), by serving evocative functions (e.g., to elicit helping, soothing, sympathy, forgiveness), and by providing incentives that reinforce another's social behavior (e.g., laughter serving as a reward for desirable social behaviors). Although the role of these social functions in understanding social interaction disturbances in psychopathology has been explored, their contributions to maintaining positive, healthy social relationships comprise open territory for future inquiry.

Interest in positive emotions is also on the rise (Fredrickson, 1998), despite the prevailing problem focus in psychological research and the fact that positive emotions have been faulted for being less differentiated and lacking in direct action tendencies than negative emotions. Seeking to liberate the positive side, Fredrickson argued that feelings such as joy and interest can prompt individuals to pursue novel and creative paths of thought and action, whereas feelings of contentment can prompt the savoring and integration of events and experiences. Love is construed as varied (e.g., romantic, companionate, attachment, caregiving) and involving a fusion of many positive emotions, the combination of which broadens the scope of thought and action as well as building personal, social, and physical resources. Empirical illus-

trations are offered, along with a final section emphasizing the role of positive emotions as antidotes to negative feelings—that is, how they can undo the hold that negative emotions have on mind and body.

Folkman's (1997) research on coping with the stress of providing care to a partner who is dying elaborates the importance of attending to positive experience. Longitudinal assessments of caregiving partners of men with AIDS revealed experiences of intense negative and positive psychological states over the course of this profoundly difficult experience. Noting that coping theory has traditionally focused on the management of stress, Folkman called for greater attention to the role of positive psychological states in effective coping processes.

Collectively, these promising lines of new inquiry clarify that future studies of interpersonal flourishing must give greater attention to the emotional upside of significant social relationships—that is, elaborate the nature of the joyful, nurturing, meaningful, loving interactions that characterize enduring ties to those most central in one's life. It is important to note that they also clarify that optimal relational well-being is probably not well characterized by simple models, which promote an abundance of positive and a dearth of negative emotions. The deeper challenge is to understand that the positive and negative are blended together in ways that are nourishing and health promoting.

The delicate dance between positive and negative emotion thus constitutes a vitally important venue for future studies linking social relationships to health (see Ryff & Singer, in press). Three lines of current work highlight the potential of this direction. First, Gottman's (in press; Gottman, Katz, & Hooven, 1996) innovative work on emotion coaching clarifies the emotional styles, or meta-emotions, that parents bring to the task of rearing children. A bedrock assumption is that negative emotions are fundamental to healthy social relationships. The decisive question is how such feelings are handled. Emotion-coaching parents see children's expressions of anger, fear, or sadness as frequently legitimate and even valuable, in providing opportunities for intimacy, teaching, or both. Expression of these negative states are, in fact, deemed "magical moments" in parent–child interaction when the parent can play a vital role in helping the child explore, label, and respond to difficult feelings. Doing so strengthens the bond between parent and child, and gives the child a greater sense of control and optimism in managing personal feelings. Emotion-dismissing parents, in contrast, equate negative emotions with loss of control, passivity, cowardice, or selfishness. It is important to note that this work reveals that children with emotion-coaching rather than emotion-dismissing parents, have a greater capacity for self-calming after emotional upset, thereby clarifying possible routes to emotion self-regulation, and even better health (measured by fewer infectious illnesses). Speaking to underlying mechanisms, Gottman (in press) suggested that emotion coaching may contribute to higher vagal tone among these children (for further perspectives on parental socialization of emotion, see Eisenberg, Cumberland, & Spinrad, 1998).

Shifting to adult social interaction, Reis (in press) used daily experience methods to probe the kinds of relational interactions that promote (or hinder) secure attachments, adult intimacy, and a sense of emotional well-being. He argued that intimacy interactions are those in which self-disclosure occurs and there is partner responsiveness to such disclosure. This kind of exchange can be, and frequently is, in the context of difficult, negative, painful topics, including relational conflict. The strongest predictor of "affirmative social interactions" (i.e., those satisfying needs for autonomy, competence, and relatedness) were ones in which the individual felt understood and appreciated by the other. Conflict, per se, was not found to diminish feeling close and connected in daily interaction.

Intimacy formulated as self-disclosure calls for connection to research showing that disclosure of stressful events is related to decreased physiological activity and better self-reported health (Pennebaker, 1989, 1993; Pennebaker & Susman, 1988). This work launched numerous inquiries, such as research linking emotional disclosure to improved affect and better physical functioning among rheumatoid arthritis patients (Kelley, Lumley, & Leisen, 1997). The key point for understanding relational flourishing and positive health is the need to connect studies of intimacy defined as self-disclosure with agendas probing the health consequences of such disclosure. If there are beneficial health consequences of disclosing emotion, it is important to recognize that the forum in which this most likely occurs, naturalistically, is in exchanges between significant others.

Finally, Spiegel's (Spiegel, 1990, 1998; Spiegel, Bloom, Yalom, 1981; Spiegel & Kimerling, in press) group psychotherapy for women with breast cancer also gives explicit emphasis to the benign, indeed beneficial, effects of expressing negative emotion. Particular emphasis in these interventions is given to the need to access, express, and work through difficult emotions related to the stress of cancer. Suppression of such emotion is seen to reduce intimacy in families and social networks, and limit opportunities for expressions of affection, concern, and support. Naturally, much of this expression is about negative feelings, indeed the prospect of dying. However, what their qualitative data eloquently reveal are the rich interminglings of laughter and tears as family members deal with the trauma of cancer. Families that adopt an atmosphere of open and shared problem solving are found to help reduce anxiety and depression among cancer patients. Positive effects associated with the psychotherapy also include increased survival time and lower rates of recurrence. More important, the emotional expression at the core of the intervention is facilitated, as Spiegel and colleagues emphasized, by close relationships.

Taken as a whole, these observations call for a new era of inquiry that addresses the emotional configurations of quality social relationships—not only their capacities to revel in and nurture varieties of good feelings but also their honed abilities to deal constructively with the negative experiences that inevitably enter all lives, albeit to differing degrees. Mapping the emotional terrain of relational flourishing stands to extend what can be learned about physiological substrates of quality ties to others (see the later topic), but may also provide vital insight to why close relationships sometimes fail to provide the needed emotional support during times of stress (e.g., Bolger, Vinokur, Foster, & Ng, 1996), and what can be done to constructively intervene in such situations.

Finally, regarding the empirical payoff of studying positive versus negative emotions, it is noted that negative emotions have frequently shown stronger effects than positive, particularly when building bridges to biology (e.g., being nasty matters more than being nice when it comes to high blood pressure; Ewart et al., 1991). These findings should be viewed as preliminary. They may even be misleading. The main message conveyed by such findings may be that positive emotions are not less consequential, but that efforts to properly identify and measure relevant, powerful positive emotions lag woefully behind scientific advances on the negative side.

What Are the Physiological Substrates of Relational Flourishing?

Advancing the science of positive human health requires linking criterial goods in life, such as quality social relationships, to biology (Ryff & Singer, 1998). This necessitates new and innovative directions regarding the complex physiological systems that underlie quality human connection. Preceding sections have illustrated the impressive scope of scientific agendas linking relational problems (marital conflict, caregiving stress) to cardiovascular, neuroendocrine, and immunological functioning. Studies of social integration and support, in both human and animal models, and in naturalistic as well as laboratory contexts, are also advancing understanding of neurophysiological underpinnings. One critical avenue for future inquiry, as emphasized by Uchino et al. (1996), is the need to link multiple, interacting physiological systems to social ties, and to examine their cumulative impact through time.

Allostatic load, introduced by McEwen and Stellar (1993) is a construct referring to the cumulative physiological toll exacted on the body in repeated attempts to adapt to life's demands. Seeman, Singer, Rowe, Horwitz, & McEwen (1997) developed an operational definition of allostatic load that included assessments of multiple physiological systems (hypothalamic–pituitary–adrenal [HPA] axis, sympathetic nervous system, cardiovascular system, and metabolic processes) and showed in a longitudinal aging sample that, over a 2½-year period, high allostatic load predicted incident cardiovascular disease, decline in physical function, and decline in cognitive function. Recent findings covering a 7½-year follow-up showed that high allostatic load was also a significant predictor of mortality (Seeman, Singer, Wilkinson, & McEwen, 1999).

A relevant question is what predicts high allostatic load? Might social relational experiences, for example, particularly when viewed cumulatively over the long term, provide insight as to who has high versus low allostatic load? Utilizing another longitudinal study of midlife adults, these questions were recently examined (Ryff, Singer, Wing, & Love, in press). Using multiple assessments of early life relationships with the mother and father as well as various ratings of intimacy with an adult spouse, we created positive and negative relationship pathways. As predicted, those on the positive relationship pathway had significantly lower allostatic load than those on the negative pathway. The findings were significant for both men and women, although the effects were notably stronger for men. This work augments a related longitudinal study (Russek & Schwartz, 1997) showing that adults who perceived greater feelings of warmth and closeness with parents during childhood had, 35 years later, fewer diagnosed diseases (coronary artery disease, hypertension, duodenal ulcer, alcoholism) than those not perceiving warmth or closeness with parents.

To fully track the physiological substrates of relational flourishing entails going beyond such investigations to map new routes of behavioral and physiological assessment. It is animal models, particularly studies of positive affiliation (Carter, 1998; Panksepp, 1998a) that may lead the way with regard to the neurobiology of relational flourishing. Carter (1998) provided a neuroendocrine perspective on social attachment and love, noting that in animals attachment can be operationalized as selective social or emotional bonds, and thus facilitate observation and experimentation connecting the phenomenon to physiological substrates. A review of caregiver–infant and adult-heterosexual pair bonds revealed recurrent associations between high levels of activity in the HPA axis and subsequent expression of social behaviors and attachments. In turn, positive social behaviors (e.g., social bonds) may reduce HPA axis activity, whereas negative interactions sometimes have the opposite effects. Central neuropeptides, especially oxytocin and vasopressin, are implicated in social bonding and central control of the HPA axis. In prairie voles, which show clear evidence of pair bonds, oxytocin has been shown to increase social behavior, and both oxytocin and social interaction reduce activity in the HPA axis. These processes, Carter suggested, may be relevant for understanding the health benefits that underlie loving relationships.

Uvnäs-Moberg (1997, 1998; Petersson, Alster, Lundeberg, & Uvnäs-Moberg, 1996) further elaborated how oxytocin may mediate the benefits of positive social interaction and emotions. Oxytocin levels are raised by somatosensory stimulation (e.g., breast feeding or suckling) as well as touch and warm temperatures. In both male and female rats, oxytocin exerts potent antistress effects, such as decreases in blood pressure, heart rate, and cortisol levels, with effects lasting from 1 week to several weeks. Rates of wound healing and weight gain are also promoted by oxytocin treatments. Thus, oxytocin appears strongly implicated in future efforts to track the neuroendocrine substrates of positive social experiences. Viewed over the long term, social bonds lead to repeated exposure to positive social stimuli, and thereby repeated release of oxytocin. More important, in humans such positive social experiences can be stored in memories, which in themselves may reactivate these physiological processes.

What are the implications of these findings for new millennial studies of interpersonal flourishing and positive health? Primarily, they point to new directions, both in terms of relevant neuropeptides as well as the physiological cascades associated with them, that may be consequences of (as well as contributors to) positive social interaction. Related venues on the human side include work on the beneficial effects of massage therapy (Field, 1998), which include facilitating growth, reducing pain, increasing alertness, diminishing depression, and enhancing immune function. This work intersects with the innovative animal studies described previously, but a key point from the relational angle is the importance of touch in quality human relationships. Few formulations of quality attachments or fulfilling marriages include assessments about the nature or scope of touch in key relationships (e.g., frequency of hugs or back rubs from parents to children; extent of physical affection between spouses). Research on adult sexuality, an obvious forum for studying the beneficial effects of quality human contact, has, like many other realms, tended toward the negative (i.e., studies of sexually transmitted diseases), or has asked only rudimentary questions about number of sexual partners or frequency of sexual intercourse. Questions relevant for advancing knowledge of "sexually transmitted health" (Ryff & Singer, 1998) may pertain to the duration of periods of lovemaking between partners and the extent to which such experience heightens feelings of intimacy, love, and connection.

Further innovative avenues for linking positive human experience, particularly of the relational variety, to health pertain to interest in nerve growth factors (see Panksepp, 1998b) and the anabolic growth promoting hormones that embody thriving (Epel, McEwen, & Ickovics, 1998) and help maintain and repair the body. A major task for future inquiry is to identify the naturally occurring interactions and activities (e.g., zestful group play in children; optimistic life outlooks in adulthood, loving and supportive relationships) that activate these growth promoting processes.

Finally, at the behavioral level, an aspect of social relationships, which likely has importance not only for monitoring their quality but also their health-promoting substrates, is research on humor and laughter. How often do parents and children, spouses, coworkers, and other combinations of significant others have a good laugh together? Keltner and Kring (1998) emphasized the rewarding, and thereby, sustaining nature of humor in social relationships, but others, most notably Cousins (1979; see also Hafen, Karren, Frandsen, & Smith, 1996), have pointed to the potentially healing power of laughter and humor. Explicating how such effects occur is an important venue for the future, but the key point for present purposes is that laughing, having fun, and enjoying the time spent with significant others may be vital ingredients of relational flourishing.

Gender Differences in Emotion, Social Relationships, and Health

Pervasive throughout much of the aforementioned literature are findings that men and women differ in their relational experiences and related physiological substrates. There are also notable gender differences in emotion, particularly in expressions of anger and affection in marriage (e.g., Gottman & Levenson, 1992) as well as in intimacy and related behaviors (Reis, 1998). Men, for example, rely on women for intimacy, but women report confiding in both genders (Reis, in press). The links between relational experience, particularly marital conflict, and biology also underscore prominent gender differences, as illustrated with prior findings by Kiecolt-Glaser and colleagues (Kiecolt-Glaser et al., 1997; Kiecolt-Glaser, Newton, et al., 1996). In the social support realm, there are further results documenting differences between men and women in the links between social ties and neuroendocrine function (Seeman, in press; Seeman et al., 1994).

Some of the prior work suggests that women may be more physiologically reactive to negative aspects of social relationships than men. Women's more traditional roles as caretakers within the family may also subject them to greater relational demands and stress. Alternatively, across multiple samples (varying in age, socioeconomic standing, and cultural background), women rate themselves as having higher quality social relationships than do men (Ryff, Singer, Wing, & Love, in press). Men, in fact, rate their interpersonal well-being as the lowest of six different aspects of positive psychological functioning. Thus, an important avenue for future studies is better understanding of gender differences in social relational strengths and vulnerabilities, and of course, how these feed into biology.

The fundamental links between the social realm and mortality implicate gender differences (House et al., 1988), showing that social ties are more strongly associated with lower risk of mortality for men compared to women. Nonetheless, women, on average, tend to live 6 to 7 years longer than men, adding further complexity to the larger puzzle combining social relationships, neurobiology, and health. In short, questions of gender must be kept center stage in new millennial studies of social relationships and health.

Relational Flourishing and Resilience

Resilience, or the capacity to maintain or recover high well-being in the face of life adversity (Ryff, Singer, Love, & Essex, 1998) is another promising realm for delineating the significance of quality social relationships. At the biographical level, stories such as Mark Mathabane's account of surviving the horrors of poverty and apartheid in South Africa (see Singer & Ryff, 1997) speak eloquently to the sustaining power of a committed and tenacious mother and a nurturing grandmother in saving him from a violent street life destined for early mortality. Studies of resilient children also underscore the importance of family cohesion and warmth, having a close bond with a nurturing, emotionally stable adult, and external social supports (Garmezy, 1993; Rutter, 1987; Werner, 1995) vis-à-vis the difficulties of poverty, troubled environments, or parental psychopathology. Life histories of women regaining high well-being following depression (Singer, Ryff, Carr, & Magee,

1998) also feature significant others in prominent roles, both as possible contributors to the depression (e.g., growing up with an alcoholic parent, living with an alcoholic spouse, experiencing death of parent or spouse) as well as sources of strength in recovering well-being (e.g., close, supportive spouse; community ties and involvement). In short, a major category of protective factors enabling individuals to overcome the life challenges, from childhood through old age, derive from social relational ties.

How these protective benefits have their effects are vital avenues for future inquiry. Although the stress buffering effects of social relationships are well recognized, there is need for richer formulation, conceptually and empirically, of the emotional routes through which these effects occur. As described previously, more differentiated assessment of discrete emotions (positive, negative, and their blends) that comprise socially derived protection are critically needed. Another social psychological venue ripe for new inquiry builds on the interpersonal self (Markus & Cross, 1990), that is, the fundamentally social nature of self-conception. Traditions of symbolic interactionism, reflected appraisals, and the looking glass self elaborate these ideas, but such literatures have been missing in formulations of quality social relationships (viz., how significant others come to shape each others' core views of self as competent, worthy, fun, or lovable). The power of these reflected appraisals may be particularly significant in the face of life adversity.

Quality relationships may also contribute to biological resilience in the face of life challenges. Singer and Ryff (1999) explored this possibility in the context of social inequalities (i.e., the socioeconomic disparities that have increasingly been linked to differences in health; Adler et al., 1994). Those with life histories of economic hardship were more likely to have high allostatic load, described previously as a risk factor for various health problems and earlier mortality. However, the important finding from the standpoint of relational flourishing was that those with low socioeconomic status profiles who were also on the positive social relationship pathway had lower incidence of high allostatic load (i.e., good, enduring social ties appeared to afford protection at the biological level). Other avenues for probing protective effects follow from new interest in anabolic growth hormones and their actions in maintaining and repairing the body's resources (Epel et al., 1998). These ideas merge with the growing interest in the capacity to thrive and do well despite adversity (Carver, 1998; Ickovics & Park, 1998; Park, 1998). What we draw attention to are the relational features of thriving.

The Need for Methodological Innovation

The scientific agenda advocated earlier requires novelty in the methodological realm as well. In connecting relational flourishing to health, including underlying physiological mechanisms, there is a concerted need for long-term studies that track cumulative processes. It is not single, isolated incidents of positive interaction, but the repeated, enduring nature of salubrious encounters that likely impact health. Accompanying the call to study relational experience longitudinally is the need to utilize person-centered strategies (Singer et al., 1998) that allow for charting life history pathways that link relational experience (across time and across life domains) with related physiological systems, and ultimately health outcomes. Such methods swim against the variable-centered tide extant in social scientific research, but multidisciplinary inquiry of the sort advocated herein creates new levels of complexity in integrating expansive biobehavioral phenomena. Keeping the person in focus, not as a case study, but a route to finding group patterns, is exceedingly valuable in managing such complexity.

Finally, those who would advance knowledge of relational flourishing would do well to embark on new empirical pursuits that combine qualitative and quantitative methods. How do we get to the heart, literally, of what it means to have deep connection to one's child, parent, spouse, or lover? What are the powerful, memorable moments of human connection? How do we probe the relevant depths of significant relational experiences? Although structured surveys provide exceedingly valuable tools to empirically grasp the social world, there is far more to be learned about the phenomenology of relational flourishing via the use of narrative techniques. The diaries of Leo and Sonya Tolstoy, the letters of Elizabeth Barrett Browing and Robert Browning, and even the artistic expressions of Frida Kahlo illustrate the powerful gains derived in understanding significant social relationships via the use of qualitative accounts (Ryff, Singer, Wing, & Love, in press). Others who study social relationships or emotion have also advocated the use of such procedures (see Berscheid & Reis, 1998, p. 252–253; Pennebaker, 1989; Sternberg, 1995). As science becomes ever more precise in probing the physiological substrates of social relationships, it is equally imperative to ever refine our abilities to capture the subjective essence of relational flourishing.

Conclusions

The opportunity to push forward understanding of positive human health—how we take care of ourselves, each other, and the planet—may be a distinguishing feature of the new millennium. No longer running from predators, pestilence, and natural disasters, the contemporary challenge is to mobilize our remarkable talent as a species to make the most of our lives and our world. Advancing the science of interpersonal flourishing is one vital route to promoting positive human health; so doing will require concerted focus on upside of relational experience and the biology that accompanies it. The time for such inquiry is at hand.

References

Adler, N. E., Boyce, T., Chesney, M. A., Cohen, S., Folkman, S., Kahn, R. L., & Syme, S. L. (1994). Socioeconomic status and health: The challenge of the gradient. *American Psychologist, 49,* 15–24.

Allport, G. W. (1961). *Pattern and growth in personality.* New York: Holt, Rinehart & Winston.

Argyle, M. (1987). *The psychology of happiness.* London: Methuen.

Barnes, M. L., & Sternberg, R. J. (1997). A hierarchical model of love and its prediction of satisfaction in close relationships. In R. L. Sternberg & M. Hojjat (Eds.), *Satisfaction in close relationships* (pp. 79–101). New York: Guilford.

Baumeister, R. F., & Leary, M. R. (1995). The need to belong: Desire for interpersonal attachments as a fundamental human motivation. *Psychological Bulletin, 117,* 497–529.

Beach, S. R. H., Sandeen, E. E., & O'Leary, K. D. (1990). *Depression in marriage.* New York: Guilford.

Becker, L. C. (1992). Good lives: Prolegomena. *Social Philosophy and Policy, 9,* 15–37.

Berkman, L. F. (1995). The role of social relations in health promotion. *Psychosomatic Medicine, 57,* 245–254.

Berkman, L. F., & Breslow, L. (1983). *Health and ways of living.* New York: Oxford University Press.

Berkman, L. F., & Syme, S. L. (1979). Social networks, host resistance, and mortality: A nine year follow-up study of Alameda County residents. *American Journal of Epidemiology, 100,* 186–204.

Berscheid, E. (1995). Help wanted: A grand theorist of interpersonal relationships, sociologists or anthropologist preferred. *Journal of Social and Personal Relationships, 12,* 529–533.

Berscheid, E. (1999). The greening of relationship science. *American Psychologist, 54,* 260–266.

Berscheid, E., & Reis, H. T. (1998). Attraction and close relationships. In D. T. Gilbert, S. T. Fiske, & G. Lindzey (Eds.), *Handbook of social psychology* (Vol. 2, 4th ed., pp. 193–281). Boston: McGraw-Hill.

Bloom, B. L., Asher, S. J., & White, S. W. (1978). Marital disruption as a stressor: A review and analysis. *Psychological Bulletin, 85,* 867–894.

Bolger, N., Vinokur, A. D., Foster, M., & Ng, R. (1996). Close relationships at adjustment to a life crisis: The case of breast cancer. *Journal of Personality and Social Psychology, 70,* 283–294.

Bowlby, J. (1969). *Attachment and loss.* New York: Basic Books.

Bradbury, T. N. (Ed.) (1998). *The developmental course of marital dysfunction.* Cambridge, England: Cambridge University Press.

Burg, M. M., & Seeman, T. E. (1994). Families and health: The negative side of social ties. *Annals of Behavioral Medicine, 16,* 109–115.

Burman, B., & Margolin, G. (1992). Analysis of the association between marital relationships and health problems: An interactional perspective. *Psychological Bulletin, 112,* 39–63.

Carstensen, L. L., Graff, J., Levenson, R. W., & Gottman, J. M. (1996). Affect in intimate relationships: The developmental course of marriage. In C. Magai & S. H. McFadden (Eds.), *Handbook of emotion, adult development, and aging* (pp. 227–247). San Diego, CA: Academic.

Carstensen, L. L., Levenson, R. W., & Gottman, J. M. (1995). Emotional behavior in long-term marraige. *Psychology and Aging, 10,* 140–149.

Carter, C. S. (1998). Neuroendocrine perspectives on social attachment and love. *Psychoneuroendocrinology, 23,* 779–818.

Carver, C. S. (1998). Resilience and thriving: Issues, models, and linkages. *Journal of Social Issues, 54,* 245–266.

Cassidy, J., & Shaver, P. R. (1999). *Handbook of attachment: Theory, research, and clinical applications.* New York: Guilford.

Coan, R. W. (1977). *Hero, artist, sage, or saint? A survey of views on what is variously called mental health, normality, maturity, self-actualization, and human fulfillment.* New York: Columbia University Press.

Coe, C. L., & Lubach, G. R. (in press). Social context and other psychological influences on the development of immunity. In C. D. Ryff & B. Singer (Eds.), *Emotion, social relationships, and health.* New York: Oxford University Press.

Cohen, S. (1988). Psychosocial models of the role of social support in the etiology of physical disease. *Health Psychology, 7,* 269–297.

Cohen, S., & Herbert, T. B. (1996). Health psychology: Psychological factors and physical disease from the perspective of human psychoneuroimmunology. *Annual Review of Psychology, 47,* 113–142.

Cohen, S., & Wills, T. A. (1985). Stress, social support, and the buffering hypothesis. *Psychological Bulletin, 98,* 310–357.

Cousins, N. (1979). *Anatomy of an illness as perceived by the patient: Reflections on healing and regeneration.* New York: Norton.

Duck, S. (1997). *Handbook of personal relationships: Theory, research, and interventions* (2nd ed.). New York: Wiley.

Eisenberg, N., Cumberland, A., & Spinrad, T. L. (1998). Parental socialization of emotion. *Psychological Inquiry, 9,* 241–273.

Ekman, P., & Davidson, R. J. (1994). *The nature of emotion: Fundamental questions.* New York: Oxford University Press.

Epel, E. S., McEwen, B. S., & Ickovics, J. R. (1998). Embodying psychological thriving: Physical thriving in response to stress. *Journal of Social Issues, 54,* 301–322.

Erikson, E. (1959). Identity and the life cycle. *Psychological Issues, 1,* 18–164.

Esterling, B., Kiecolt-Glaser, J. K., Bodnar, J., & Glaser, R. (1994). Chronic stress, social support, and persistent alterations in the natural killer cell response to cytokines in older adults. *Health Psychology, 13,* 291–299.

Ewart, C. K., Taylor, C. B., Kraemer, H. C., & Agras, W. S. (1991). High blood pressure and marital discord: Not being nasty matters more than being nice. *Health Psychology, 10,* 155–163.

Feeney, B. C., & Kirkpatrick, L. A. (1996). Effects of adult attachment and presence of romantic partners on physiological responses to stress. *Journal of Personality and Social Psychology, 70,* 255–270.

Field, T. M. (1998). Message therapy effects. *American Psychologist, 53,* 1270–1281.

Fincham, F. D., & Bradbury, T. N. (1987). The assessment of marital quality: A reevaluation. *Journal of Marriage and the Family, 49,* 797–809.

Folkman, S. (1997). Positive psychological states and coping with severe stress. *Social Science and Medicine, 45,* 1207–1221.

Fredrickson, B. L. (1998). What good are positive emotions. *Review of General Psychology, 2,* 271–299.

Garmezy, N. (1993). Vulnerability and resistance: In D. C. Funder, R. D. Parke, C. Tomlinson-Keasey, & K. Widaman (Eds.), *Studying lives through time: Personality and development* (pp. 377–398). Washington, DC: American Psychological Association.

Gerin, W., Milner, D., Chawla, S., & Pickering, T. G. (1995). Social support as a moderator of cardiovascular reactivity in women: A test of the direct effects and buffering hypotheses. *Psychosomatic Medicine, 57,* 16–22.

Glenn, N. D. (1990). Quantitative research on marital quality in the 1980s: A critical review. *Journal of Marriage and the Family, 52,* 818–831.

Goodwin, J. S., Hurt, W. C., Key, C. R., & Sarret, J. M. (1987). The effect of marital status on stage, treatment and survival of cancer patients. *Journal of the American Medical Association, 258,* 3125–3130.

Gottman, J. M. (1993). The roles of conflict engagement, escalation, and avoidance in marital interaction: A longitudinal view of five types of couples. *Journal of Consulting and Clinical Psychology, 61,* 6–15.

Gottman, J. M. (1994). *What predicts divorce? The relationship between marital processes and marital outcomes.* Hillsdale, NJ: Lawrence Erlbaum Associates, Inc.

Gottman, J. M. (in press). Meta-emotion, children's emotional intelligence, and buffering children from marital conflict. In C. D. Ryff & B. Singer (Eds.), *Emotion, social relationships, and health.* New York: Oxford University Press.

Gottman, J. M., Katz, L. F., & Hooven, C. (1996). Parental meta-emotion philosophy and the emotional life of families: Theoretical models and preliminary data. *Journal of Family Psychology, 10,* 243–268.

Gottman, J. M., & Levenson, R. W. (1992). Marital processes predictive of later dissolution: Behavior, physiology, and health. *Journal of Personality and Social Psychology, 63,* 221–233.

Griffin, J. (1986). *Well-being.* Oxford, England: Clarendon.

Hafen, B. Q., Karren, K. J., Frandsen, K. J., & Smith, N. L. (1996). The healing power of humor and laughter. In *Mind/body health* (pp. 541–561). Boston: Allyn & Bacon.

Hatfield, E., & Rapson, R. L. (1993). *Love, sex, and intimacy.* New York: HarperCollins.

Hazan, C., & Shaver, P. R. (1987). Romantic love conceptualized as an attachment process. *Journal of Personality and Social Psychology, 52,* 522–524.

Hazan, C., & Shaver, P. R. (1994). Attachment as an organization framework for research on close relationships. *Psychological Inquiry, 5,* 1–22.

Hendrick, S. S., & Hendrick, C. (1997). Love and satisfaction. In R. L. Sternberg & M. Hojjat (Eds.), *Satisfaction in close relationships* (pp. 56–78). New York: Guilford.

House, J. S., Landis, K. R., & Umberson, D. (1988). Social relationships and health. *Science, 241,* 540–545.

Ickovics, J. R., & Park, C. L. (1998). Paradigm shift: Why a focus on health is important. *Journal of Social Issues, 54,* 237–244.

Izard, C. E. (1991). *The psychology of emotions.* New York: Plenum.

Jahoda, M. (1958). *Current concepts of positive mental health.* New York: Basic Books.

Kang, D. H., Coe, C. L., Karaszewski, J., & McCarthy, D. O. (1998). Relationship of social support to stress responses and immune function in healthy and asthmatic adolescents. *Research in Nursing and Health, 21,* 117–128.

Karney, B., & Bradbury, T. N. (1995). The longitudinal course of marital quality and stability: A review of theory, method, and research. *Psychological Bulletin, 118,* 3–34.

Kelley, J. E., Lumley, M. A., & Leisen, J. C. C. (1997). Health effects of emotional disclosure in rheumatoid arthritis patients. *Health Psychology, 16,* 331–340.

Keltner, D., & Kring, A. M. (1998). Emotion, social function, and psychopathology. *Review of General Psychology, 2,* 320–342.

Kenny, D. A. (1995). Relationship science in the 21st century. *Journal of Social and Personal Relationships, 12,* 597–600.

Keyes, C. L. M. (1998). Social well-being. *Social Psychology Quarterly, 61,* 121–140.

Kiecolt-Glaser, J. K., Dura, J. R., Speicher, C. E., Trask, O. J., & Glaser, R. (1991). Spousal caregivers of dementia victims: Longitudinal changes in immunity and health. *Psychosomatic Medicine, 53,* 345–362.

Kiecolt-Glaser, J. K., Glaser, R., Cacioppo, J. T., MacCallum, R. C., Snydersmith, M., Cheongtag, K., & Malarkey, W. B. (1997). Marital conflict in older adults: Endocrinological and immunological correlates. *Psychosomatic Medicine, 59,* 339–349.

Kiecolt-Glaser, J. K., Glaser, R., Gravenstein, S., Malarkey, W. B., & Sheridan, J. (1996). Chronic stress alters the immune response to influenza virus vaccine in older adults. *Proceedings of the National Academy of Sciences, 93,* 3043–3047.

Kiecolt-Glaser, J. K., Malarkey, W. B., Cacioppo, J. T., & Glaser, R. (1994). Stressful personal relationships: Immune and endocrine function. In R. Glaser & J. K. Kiecolt-Glaser (Eds.), *Handbook of human stress and immunity* (pp. 321–340). San Diego, CA: Academic.

Kiecolt-Glaser, J. K., Newton, T., Cacioppo, J. T., MacCallum, R. C., Glaser, R., & Malarkey, W. B. (1996). Marital conflict and endocrine function: Are men really more physiologically affected than women? *Journal of Consulting and Clinical Psychology, 64,* 324–332.

Kiecolt-Glaser, J. K., Ricker, D., George, J., Messick, G., Speicher, G. E., Garner, W., & Glaser, R. (1984). Urinary cortisol levels, cellular immunocompetence, and loneliness in psychiatric inpatients. *Psychosomatic Medicine, 46,* 15–23.

Leonard, K. E., & Roberts, L. J. (1998). Marital aggression, quality, and stability in the first year of marriage: Findings from the Buffalo Newlywed Study. In T. N. Bradbury (Ed.), *The developmental course of marital dysfunction* (pp. 44–73). Cambridge, England: Cambridge University Press.

Levenson, R. W., Carstensen, L. L., & Gottman, J. M. (1994). The influence of age and gender on affect, physiology, and their interrelations: A study of long-term marriage. *Journal of Personality and Social Psychology, 67,* 56–68.

Levenson, R. W., & Gottman, J. M. (1985). Physiological and affective predictors of change in relationship satisfaction. *Journal of Personality and Social Psychology, 49,* 85–94.

Lewis, M., & Haviland, J. M. (1993). *Handbook of emotions.* New York: Guilford.

Malarkey, W., Kiecolt-Glaser, J. K., Pearl, D., & Glaser, R. (1994). Hostile behavior during marital conflict alters pituitary and adrenal hormones. *Psychosomatic Medicine, 56,* 41–51.

Marangoni, C., & Ickes, W. (1989). Loneliness: A theoretical review with implications for measurement. *Journal of Social and Personal Relationships, 6,* 93–128.

Markman, H. J., & Jones-Leonard, D. (1985). Marital discord and children at risk: Implications for research and prevention. In W. Frankenberg & R. Emde (Eds.), *Early identification of children at risk* (pp. 59–77). New York: Plenum.

Markus, H. R., & Cross, S. (1990). The interpersonal self. In L. Pervin (Ed.), *Handbook of personality theory and research* (pp. 576–608). New York: Guilford.

Markus, H. R., & Kitayama, S. (1991). Culture and the self: Implications for cognition, emotion, and motivation. *Psychological Review, 98,* 224–253.

Markus, H. R., & Kitayama, S. (1994). A collective fear of the collective: Implications for selves and theories of selves. *Personality and Social Psychology Bulletin, 20,* 568–579.

Maslow, A. (1955). Deficiency motivation and growth motivation. In M. R. Jones (Ed.), *Nebraska symposium on motivation* (pp. 1–30). Lincoln: University of Nebraska Press.

Maslow, A. (1968). *Toward a psychology of being* (2nd ed.). New York: Van Nostrand.

McEwen, B. S., & Stellar, E. (1993). Stress and the individual: Mechanisms leading to disease. *Archives of Internal Medicine, 153*, 2093–2101.

Miller, G. E., Dopp, J. M., Myers, H. F., Stevens, S. Y., & Fahey, J. L. (1999). Psychosocial predictors of natural killer cell mobilization during marital conflict. *Health Psychology, 18*, 262–271.

Myers, D. G., & Diener, E. (1995). Who is happy? *Psychological Science, 6*, 10–19.

Noller, P., & Feeney, J. A. (1998). Communication in early marriage: Responses to conflict, nonverbal accuracy, and conversational patterns. In T. N. Bradbury (Ed.), *The developmental course of marital dysfunction* (pp. 11–43). Cambridge, England: Cambridge University Press.

Norton, D. (1976). *Personal destinies*. Princeton, NJ: Princeton University Press.

Nozick, R. (1989). *The examined life*. New York: Simon & Schuster.

O'Leary, K. D., & Cascardi, M. (1998). Physical aggression in marriage: A developmental analysis. In T. N. Bradbury (Ed.), *The developmental course of marital dysfunction* (pp. 343–376). Cambridge, England: Cambridge University Press.

Panksepp, J. (1998a). *Affective neuroscience: The foundations of human and animal emotions*. New York: Oxford University Press.

Panksepp, J. (1998b). The quest for long-term health and happiness: To play or not to play, that is the question. *Psychological Inquiry, 9*, 56–65.

Park, C. L. (1998). Stress-related growth and thriving through coping: The roles of personality and cognitive processes. *Journal of Social Issues, 54*, 267–278.

Pennebaker, J. W. (1989). Confession, inhibition and disease. *Advances in Experimental Social Psychology, 22*, 211–244.

Pennebaker, J. W. (1993). Putting stress into words: Health, linguistic, and therapeutic implications. *Behavior Research and Therapy, 31*, 539–548.

Pennebaker, J. W., & Susman, J. R. (1988). Disclosure of traumas and psychosomatic processes. *Social Science and Medicine, 26*, 327–332.

Petersson, M., Alster, P., Lundeberg, T., & Uvnäs-Moberg, K. (1996). Oxytocin causes long-term decrease of blood pressure in female and male rats. *Physiology and Behavior, 60*, 1311–1315.

Pierce, G. R., Lakey, B., Sarason, I. G., & Sarason, B. R. (1997). *Sourcebook of social support and personality*. New York: Plenum.

Pierce, G. R., Sarason, B. R., & Sarason, I. G. (1996). *Handbook of social support and the family*. New York: Plenum.

Reis, H. T. (1998). Gender differences in intimacy and related behaviors: Context and process. In D. C. Canary & K. Dindia (Eds.), *Sex differences and similarities in communication* (pp. 203–231). Mahwah, NJ: Lawrence Erlbaum Associates, Inc.

Reis, H. T. (in press). Relationships experiences and emotional well-being. In C. D. Ryff & B. Singer (Eds.), *Emotion, social relationships, and health*. New York: Oxford University Press.

Reis, H. T., & Patrick, B. C. (1996). Attachment and intimacy: Component processes. In E. T. Higgins & A. Kruglanski (Eds.), *Social psychology: Handbook of basic principles* (pp. 367–389). Chichester, England: Wiley.

Rook, K. S. (1988). Towards a more differentiated view of loneliness. In S. Duck (Ed.), *Handbook of personal relationships: Theory, research and interventions* (pp. 571–590). Chichester, England: Wiley.

Rook, K. S. (1995). Relationship research at the crossroads: Commentary on the special section. *Journal of Social and Personal Relationships, 12*, 601–606.

Rossi, A. S., & Rossi, P. H. (1990). *Of human bonding: Parent–child relations across the life course*. New York: deGruyter.

Ruberman, W., Weinblatt, E., Goldberg, J. D., & Chaudhary, B. S. (1984). Psychosocial influences on mortality after myocardial infarction. *New England Journal of Medicine, 311*, 552–559.

Russek, L. G., & Schwartz, G. E. (1997). Feelings of parental caring predict health status in midlife: A 35-year follow-up of the Harvard Mastery Study of Stress. *Journal of Behavioral Medicine, 30*, 1–13.

Russell, B. (1958). *The conquest of happiness*. New York: Liveright. (Original work published 1938)

Rutter, M. (1987). Psychosocial resilience and protective mechanisms. *American Journal of Orthopsychiatry, 22*, 323–356.

Ryff, C. D. (1985). Adult personality development and the motivation for personal growth. In D. Kleiber & M. Maehr (Eds.), *Advances in motivation and achievement: Motivation in adulthood* (Vol. 4, pp. 55–92). Greenwich, CT: JAI.

Ryff, C. D. (1989a). Beyond Ponce de Leon and life satisfaction: New directions in quest of successful aging. *International Journal of Behavioral Development, 12*, 35–55.

Ryff, C. D. (1989b). Happiness is everything, or is it?: Explorations on the meaning of psychological well-being. *Journal of Personality and Social Psychology, 57*, 1069–1081.

Ryff, C. D., & Singer, B. (1998). The contours of positive human health. *Psychological Inquiry, 9*, 1–28.

Ryff, C. D., & Singer, B. (in press). Integrating emotion into the study of social relationships and health. In C. D. Ryff & B. Singer (Eds.), *Emotion, social relationships, and health*. New York: Oxford University Press.

Ryff, C. D., Singer, B., Love, G. D., & Essex, M. J. (1998). Resilience in adulthood and later life: Defining features and dynamic processes. In J. Lomranz (Ed.), *Handbook of aging and mental health: An integrative approach* (pp. 69–96). New York: Plenum.

Ryff, C. D., Singer, B., Wing, E. H., & Love, G. D. (in press). Elective affinities and uninvited agonies: Mapping emotion with significant others onto health. In C.D. Ryff & B. Singer (Eds.), *Emotion, social relationships, and health*. New York: Oxford University Press.

Sabatelli, R. M. (1988). Measurement issues in marital research: A review and critique of contemporary survey instruments. *Journal of Marriage and the Family, 50*, 891–915.

Sarason, I. G., Sarason, B. R., & Pierce, G. R. (1995). Social and personal relationships: Current issues, future directions. *Journal of Social and Personal Relationships, 12*, 613–619.

Schaefer, M. T., & Olson, D. (1981). Assessing intimacy: The PAIR Inventory. *Journal of Marriage and Family Therapy, 7*, 47–60.

Seeman, T. E. (1996). Social ties and health: The benefits of social integration. *Annals of Epidemiology, 6*, 442–451.

Seeman, T. E. (in press). How do others get under our skin: Social relationships and health. In C. D. Ryff & B. Singer (Eds.), *Emotion, social relationships, and health*. New York: Oxford University Press.

Seeman, T. E., Berkman, L. F., Blazer, D., & Rowe, J. (1994). Social ties and support and neuroendocrine function: The MacArthur Studies of Successful Aging. *Annals of Behavioral Medicine, 16*, 95–106.

Seeman, T. E., Berkman, L. F., Kohout, F., LaCroix, A., Glynn, R., & Blazer, D. (1993). Intercommunity variation in the association between social ties and mortality in the elderly: A comparative analysis of three communities. *Annals of Epidemiology, 3*, 325–335.

Seeman, T. E., & McEwen, B. S. (1996). Impact of social environment characteristics on neuroendocrine regulation. *Psychosomatic Medicine, 58,* 459–471.

Seeman, T. E., Singer, B., Rowe, J. W., Horwitz, R., & McEwen, B. S. (1997). The price of adaptation: Allostatic load and its health consequences, MacArthur Studies of Successful Aging. *Archives of Internal Medicine, 157,* 2259–2268.

Seeman, T. E., Singer, B., Wilkinson, C., & McEwen, B. S. (1999). *Exploring a new concept of cumulative biological risk—Allostatic load and its health consequences: MacArthur studies of successful aging.* Unpublished manuscript.

Singer, B., & Ryff, C. D. (1997). Racial and ethnic inequalities in health: Environmental, psychosocial, and physiological pathways. In B. Devlin, S. E. Feinberg, D. Resnick, & K. Roeder (Eds.), *Intelligence, genes, and success: Scientists respond to the Bell Curve* (pp. 89–122). New York: Springer-Verlag.

Singer, B., & Ryff, C. D. (1999). Hierarchies of life histories and health risk. *Annals of the New York Academy of Sciences, 896,* 96–115.

Singer, B., Ryff, C. D., Carr, D., & Magee, W. J. (1998). Life histories and mental health: A person-centered strategy. In A. Raftery (Ed.), *Sociological methodology, 1998* (pp. 1–51). Washington, DC: American Sociological Association.

Snyder, D. K. (1983). Clinical and research applications of the marital satisfaction inventory. In E. E. Filsinger (Ed.), *Marriage and family assessment: A sourcebook for family therapy* (pp. 169–189). Beverly Hills, CA: Sage.

Spiegel, D. (1990). Facilitating emotional coping during treatment. *Cancer, 66,* 1422–1426.

Spiegel, D. (1998). Effects of psychosocial treatment in prolonging cancer survival may be mediated by neuroimmune pathways. *Annals of the New York Academy of Sciences, 840,* 674–683.

Spiegel, D., Bloom, J. R., & Yalom, I. (1981). Group support for patients with metastatic cancer: A randomized outcome study. *Archives of General Psychiatry, 38,* 527–533.

Spiegel, D., & Kimerling, R. (in press). Group psychotherapy for women with breast cancer: Relationships among social support, emotional expression, and survival. In C. D. Ryff & B. Singer (Eds.), *Emotion, social relationships, and health.* New York: Oxford University Press.

Sternberg, R. (1986). A triangular theory of love. *Psychological Review, 93,* 119–135.

Sternberg, R. (1995). Love as a story. *Journal of Social and Personal Relationships, 12,* 541–546.

Sternberg, R. J., & Barnes, M. I. (1988). *The psychology of love.* New Haven, CT: Yale University Press.

Sternberg, R., & Hojjat, M. (Eds.). (1997). *Satisfaction in close relationships.* New York: Guilford.

Taylor, S. E., Repetti, R. L., & Seeman, T. (1997). Health psychology: What is an unhealthy environment and how does it get under the skin? *Annual Review of Psychology, 48,* 411–447.

Thoits, P. A. (1995). Stress, coping, and social support processes: Where are we? What next? [Special extra issue]. *Journal of Health and Social Behavior,* 53–79.

Triandis, H. C. (1989). The self and social behavior in differing cultural contexts. *Psychological Review, 96,* 506–520.

Trivers, R. (1971). The evolution of reciprocal altruism. *Quarterly Review of Biology, 46,* 35–56.

Trivers, R. (1985). *Social evolution.* Menlo Park, CA: Benjamin/Cummings.

Uchino, B. N., Cacioppo, J. T., & Kiecolt-Glaser, J. K. (1996). The relationship between social support and physiological processes: A review with emphasis on underlying mechanisms and implications for health. *Psychological Bulletin, 119,* 488–531.

Uvnäs-Moberg, K. (1997). Physiological and endocrine effects of social contact. *Annals of the New York Academy of Science, 807,* 146–163.

Uvnas-Moberg, K. (1998). Oxytocin may mediate the benefits of positive social interaction and emotions. *Psychoneuroendocrinology, 23,* 819–835.

Vaux, A. (1988). *Social support: Theory, research, and intervention.* New York: Praeger.

Werner, E. (1995). Resilience in development. *Current Directions in Psychological Science, 4,* 81–85.

Personality and Social Psychology Review
2000, Vol. 4, No. 1, 45–56

Personal Memory Telling and Personality Development

Avril Thorne

Department of Psychology
University of California, Santa Cruz

Although personal memories have been appreciated by psychologists for nearly a century, their significance for personality development has tended to be relegated to internalized representations of early childhood experiences. Recent research, however, suggests that adolescence and early adulthood are the most memorable parts of the life span and perhaps the broadest period of memory telling. This article integrates recent work in cognitive and developmental psychology into a framework for studying how and why tellers proffer and make sense of momentous emotional events, and how families and friends collude in self-making. Promising areas for future research include individual differences in readiness for memory telling, gendered ecologies of memory telling, the developmental significance of parents' stories, and reconciling personal memories and personality traits. Personal memory telling is not just for fun and entertainment, but, more important, drives social and emotional development in concrete moments of social life.

When I was 5, I lived down the road from an old man who didn't like my dog. He would say horrible things about her and I would become enraged. So I propped nails against his tires but he came out and discovered me. He chased me away and I got into a lot of trouble for standing up for my dog. I told my friend in high school about this event and she flipped out and said I was a "nasty little kid." I thought this was wrong and argued about it with her. I told her that it was only in protection of my family and she said, "Well, what kind of a family is a dog?"—19-year-old man

What do personal memories do for personality? In this article, I argue that the telling of personal memories is not merely for fun or entertainment, but, more important, drives personality development in concrete

A preliminary version of this article was presented at the 50th Anniversary Colloquium Series of the Institute of Personality and Social Research, University of California, Berkeley, April 1999.

I am grateful to Erin Davis, Deborah Reichle, Raina Nishino, Michael Maciel, Marie Sarte, Gretchen Dix, Kim Howerton, and Antoinette Dasbach for helping to collect data about parent and adolescent memory tellings. Discussions with Joe Christy, Kenneth H. Craik, Gerald A. Mendelsohn, and Gary Gregg contributed to my thinking about the framework presented in this article.

Requests for reprints should be sent to Avril Thorne, Department of Psychology, 277 Social Sciences 2, University of California at Santa Cruz, Santa Cruz, CA 95064. E-mail: avril@cats.ucsc.edu.

moments of social life. I begin by identifying three unique features of personal memories that have emerged in recent research on autobiographical memory. Extending the work of McAdams (1995), I contrast these features of personal memories with those of personality traits. I then advance an agenda for exploring the unique role of personal memories in personality development. This agenda focuses on coparticipation in memory telling during a highly formative period of personality and personal memory development: adolescence and early adulthood.

I will use the terms *personal memory* and *personal story* somewhat interchangeably. *Personal memory* has been defined as the subset of autobiographical memory that involves the recollection of specific emotional events from one's past, events that are enduring aspects of the self-concept (Nelson, 1993). A *personal story* is the narrative representation of a personal memory. Narratives usually describe location, action, people, and thoughts, and often take the form of stories. The telling of personal stories is often associated with a high degree of vividness so that the teller, and sometimes the audience, relives the past experience (Brewer, 1988). I distinguish between the memory and the story because memory carries more freight of being internalized; memories may be ruminated on or otherwise kept to oneself. In this article, I draw heavily from personal memory research but emphasize the telling of personal memories, which tend to emerge as stories.

Personality Traits, Motives, and Personal Memories

McAdams (1995) attracted considerable attention by proposing that the most frequently studied level of personality, *the trait,* is insufficiently personal, conditional, and developmental. Traits such as extraversion are readily assessed in people and chimpanzees because they are summary terms for act trends that are publicly observable and pervasive across situations. In addition, some traits are substantially heritable or present at birth, and show considerable stability across the life span (McCrae & Costa, 1990). Citing such genetic and biological evidence, Cantor (1990) referred to personality traits as things that people "have."

However, knowing that someone is an extravert does not reveal much about a person. There are millions of extraverts in the world, and no two extraverts share exactly the same motives or life experiences. Although extraverts can routinely be found associating with groups of people, their relational motives vary. Some extraverts desire close and intimate contacts with others, whereas other extraverts prefer to control or compete with others (Winter, John, Stewart, Klohnen, & Duncan, 1998). Compared to traits, *motives* offer more specific information about what people desire or want to do.

A third level of personality is much more personal than traits and motives, and more cognitively complex, for it requires the capacity to make sense of lived experience both at one point in time and across the life span. This level, *the life story,* reveals how people construct meaningful accounts of their lives, selecting from a myriad of experiences those events that are the most important, and linking the events into a coherent and personally meaningful life story. Recognizing that the process of making sense of one's life is an interpretive feat (Bruner, 1987), McAdams (1995) referred to life stories as things that people "make."

Although life stories have long been recognized as crucial windows into personality (Adler, 1937; Murray, 1938), systematic studies of life stories have only begun to emerge in the last decade with the turn toward narrative in the social sciences. McAdams's (1988) work is widely recognized for appreciating the identity-making functions of life stories, and for elaborating their components. With regard to components, McAdams viewed very important, specific personal memories as the smallest units and basic data of the extended and developing life story. The story form that often structures personal memories facilitates their serving as basic data for the life story because stories are an efficient and memorable way of organizing events (Mandler & Johnson, 1977).

Although the term *story* suggests an arbitrary construction of events, longitudinal studies have shown that the basic story lines of memorable events tend to be stable across time. Stability in basic story lines has been found in longitudinal studies of "flashbulb memories," or memories of vivid, culturally significant events such as where one was when John F. Kennedy was shot (e.g., Brown & Kulik, 1977; Christianson & Safer, 1996; Pillemer, 1984). More recently, stability in basic story lines was found in a longitudinal study of personal memories. Thorne, Cutting, and Skaw (1998) solicited 16 important or problematic personal memories from each of 46 young adults during open-ended interviews. Six months later, informants were recontacted and reinterviewed. A different interviewer was used for the second session, and informants were told that it did not matter whether or not they repeated any memories from the prior interview. Of the events that were selected for telling both times, 71% showed the same basic story line from one telling to the next in terms of what was wanted from whom and what happened at the end. This stability in a basic story line, although not perfect, was remarkable because an identical story line required a precise matching among seven categories of significant others, seven motives, and three outcomes—a very low probability of chance concordance.

It is important to note that *stability* in basic story lines refers to what basically happened during the original event—not implications or larger meanings. For example, the basic story line of the childhood event that introduced this article can be summarized as "I tried to stand up for my dog, who was abused by an old man, and I got into a lot of trouble." This basic story line can be expected to be quite stable across tellings, but what it means to the teller may change with the telling. For example, the young woman's reaction to the dog story seemed to take the young man by surprise, for she interpreted the story as meaning he was a nasty little kid, a meaning that he did not intend and that must now be reckoned with as he ponders the meaning of the story. For now, suffice it to say that findings of story line stability suggest that the basic facts of personal memories—what happened—tend to anchor in memory and can potentially serve as foundations for the extended, developing life story. In this sense, personal stories are not only things that people make but also things that people have, perhaps somewhat like people have traits.

Nonetheless, personal stories are more contextual and personal than traits. In the next section, I identify some recently documented features of personal memories that suggest their unique role in human development. Most of these features have been identified by cognitive psychologists. Although much of this research has not yet filtered into personality and social psychology, I have imported these findings because I think they are enormously useful for understanding the developmental affordances of personal memories.

Three Felicitous Features of Personal Memories

Studying traits is a relative breeze for researchers because traits tend to be reliably and widely exhibited across time and place. Not so with personal memories. Personal memories are not about typical events, but about atypical, rare events. Furthermore, personal memories are not evenly distributed across the life course; the landscape of personal memory has got a bump. Even worse, memorable events are not visible unless one chooses to tell them, and what gets told is hard to predict. In an effort to make lemonade out of these lemons, I discuss each of these features in turn.

Personal Memories Are About Atypical, Emotionally Disruptive Events

Traits, by virtue of being summary terms of one's typical conduct to date, signify the kinds of routines that are counterpoints to the disruptions that characterize personal memories. A recent set of diary studies nicely demonstrates the atypicality of memorable events. Thompson, Skowronski, Larsen, and Betz (1996; see also Thorne, 1998), asked six college students to keep a written diary of two events per day for periods ranging from 18 to 30 months. Students were periodically tested for the memorability of these events. Event memorability was found to decline dramatically over the first 300 days, and then to bottom out. Only about 3% of the events were rated highly memorable after 300 days, an average of about one event every 3 weeks. Clearly, personal memories that endure for at least 1 year to achieve some kind of "permastore" are rare events.

Why do we remember atypical events? To answer this question, it is instructive to examine the kinds of events that get remembered. Specific events that get remembered are about equally distributed among positive and negative outcomes (e.g., Thorne, 1995), ranging from memories of abuse, illness, and death of loved ones, to falling in love, the birth of one's first child, and one's first drug experience (e.g., Robinson & Taylor, 1997). All of these events disrupt everyday routines and are highly emotional, features that are widely recognized as crucial for event memorability (e.g., Brewer, 1988; Linton, 1978). Furthermore, many memorable events depict first-time experiences, which are presumably more emotional, unusual, and surpris-

ing than are subsequent similar experiences, such as one's third kiss.

Rehearsal also enhances event memorability. The more emotionally disruptive the event, the more likely it is to be rehearsed covertly, and overtly shared with others. In a recent study of six European samples, Rimé, Mesquita, Philippot, and Boca (1991) found that the more emotionally disruptive the original event, the more likely it was to be rehearsed privately as well as shared with others. Furthermore, the majority of highly disruptive events were likely to be shared with others initially within a day of the event occurring. The authors speculated that sharing highly emotional events helps to disambiguate their meanings by assessing others' reactions to the events (Festinger, 1954). Meanings are not automatically attached to emotional events, but develop over time through reflection, sharing, and comparing with other experiences.

The high probability of sharing disruptive events with others soon after the event occurs suggests that *personal memories* is a misnomer, because most memories are not kept to oneself. However, neither are most memories told widely; instead, the telling audience is likely to be close friends and family (Rimé et al., 1991). Perhaps a better term is *intimate memories*, because this term targets the telling audience more accurately than does *personal memories,* which suggests that memories are kept to oneself. In any event, findings that personal memories tend to be shared primarily with close friends and family suggests that the developmental context for personal memories is much more focused than that of traits, and thereby lessens the terrain that researchers must tread to locate and observe a representative sampling of the phenomenon.

In sum, the highly emotional nature of memorable events has some unique advantages for understanding personality and self-development. Due to the fact that personal memory tellings are usually restricted to close friends and family, the phenomenon traverses a more circumscribed territory for researchers than traits do. In addition, personal memory tellings provide crucial windows for understanding how people mutually participate in interpreting and narratively regulating important emotional experiences.

Personal Memories Cluster in Adolescence and Early Adulthood, Not Pervasively Across the Life Course

Whereas the atypicality of personally memorable events has been recognized for the last 20 years, the age-related "bump" in their life-span distribution is a relatively more recent recognition. Personal memories are not randomly distributed across the life course; rather, the landscape of personal memory has got a bump between 10 and 30 years of age (e.g., Rubin, Rahhal, & Poon, 1998). The comparatively high density of personal memories for events that occurred between 10 and 30 years of age is a very robust phenomenon in later life; it has been found with adults ranging in age from 45 to 80 years, and with methods ranging from memory priming using single words, requests for vivid autobiographical memories (reviewed in Rubin et al., 1998) and studies of event–age clustering in autobiographies (Mackavey, Malley, & Stewart, 1991).

Rubin et al. (1998) advanced several complementary explanations for the greater density of events between ages 10 and 30 years. One explanation concerned age-developmental peaks in some aspects of cognitive functioning. A second explanation derived from life-span studies of socioemotional networks (Carstensen, 1995). Highly emotional events, as previously discussed, are particularly likely to be told to others, and adolescence is an intensely emotional period of development. Freeman, Csikszentmihalyi, and Larson (1986) found more dramatic hour-to-hour mood fluctuations in a late adolescent sample than in a sample of adults. Recognizing the high emotionality of the adolescent period, clinical psychologists have now developed a special adolescent version of the Minnesota Multiphasic Personality Inventory (MMPI) to take into account the "tendency for normal adolescents in a temporary state of turmoil to score like adult psychopaths on the original MMPI" (Aiken, 1997, p. 317). The disproportionate clustering of vivid emotional memories during adolescence and early adulthood may not only reflect a higher base rate of highly emotional experiences during this age period but also a higher frequency of emotional event telling. This possibility is suggested by recent work by Carstensen (1995), who found that socioemotional contacts are broader for adolescents and young adults than for other age groups. Although family members and friends appear to be the primary audience for personal memory telling across the life span, a wider array of family and friends is likely to participate in memory telling during adolescence and young adulthood than during other age periods.

A third explanation for the disproportionate clustering of personal memories between 10 and 30 years of age concerns the developmental tasks of this age period, which center on the formation of identity and intimacy (Erikson, 1968; Fitzgerald, 1996). Identity is partly achieved by sorting through the events of one's life to understand who one is and where one is going, and intimacy is partly achieved by sharing one's personal past with significant other people. Many memo-rable events occurring between ages 10 and 30 concern first time experiences, first jobs, and first loves, which reflect the kinds of explorations that seem foundational for the formation of identity and intimacy (Robinson & Taylor, 1997).

The high density of memories between ages 10 and 30 has important implications for personality psychology because it directs attention to self-making in adolescence and young adulthood. Research on personality and personal memory has tended to focus on early childhood memories, often working from an Adlerian perspective (Adler, 1937). Some time ago, Kihlstrom and Harackiewicz (1982) questioned the assumption that early memories have a privileged status in personality development. More recently, Josselson (1997) voiced somewhat similar concerns in her longitudinal study of early memories of women interviewed between college and midlife. Josselson observed that her participants regarded their early childhood memories as emotionally distanced and disconnected from later life experiences. In addition to being more numerous and more representative of the life course, bump memories have also been found to be more elaborated and motivationally diverse than early childhood memories, and much more narratively enriched (Thorne, 1995).

Personal Stories Show a High Turnover From One Telling to the Next in Young Adulthood

In our previously discussed cross-time study of personal memory telling in a young adult sample (Thorne et al., 1998), we expected to find a considerable number of twice-told tales across 6-months time. Instead, we discovered an exceedingly high turnover rate. Only 12% of the events at Time 1 were also chosen for telling at Time 2. Furthermore, this high turnover rate held for different kinds of memories, including earliest memories, high points, and low points. At least in the identity and intimacy era, we do not have an earliest memory or a core set of later memories that we choose to tell when we are asked to describe meaningful events in our lives. Rather, we choose from a relatively large repertoire of memorable events, and are unlikely to choose the same events for telling each time.

It is important to note that the high turnover in the repertoire of events that were told each time produced quite different aggregated themes from one telling to the next. We found no significant correlations for significant others in the events; that is, a person may tell mostly events involving parents at Time 1 and mostly events involving friends at Time 2 (Thorne et al., 1998). Other elements of the basic story line, motive and outcome, showed somewhat more stability across time. The most stable aggregated motives involved themes of wanting to avoid other people, and of wanting to help other people. Positive and negative aggregated outcomes were also somewhat stable from one telling to the next. For example, people who primarily told memories about positive outcomes at Time 1 continued to do so at Time 2, albeit by offering an almost entirely different set of events at each time. However, the significant cross-time stabilities were very modest in magnitude (averaging $r = .30$), suggesting that aggregated themes will also shift so that each audience gets a quite different display of overall trends in motives and outcomes. Although systematic, large sample, long-term longitudinal studies of personal memory are still rare, Josselson's (1997) findings suggest the possibility of less turnover in midlife, or more consolidation of a core set of stories.

My focus is on the most densely formative period of personal memory telling, adolescence and early adulthood. Although the role of personal memories in personality development is a nascent field of inquiry (Pillemer, 1998), the peak period of personal memory making and telling seems a good place to embark. In the next section, I advocate a proximal, situated focus on what develops during memory telling.

Personal Memory Telling and Proximal Personality Development

Proximal development refers to teachable moments in which some kind of learning takes place through social activity (e.g., Rogoff & Mistry, 1990). Self and personality, in the sociocultural approach to human development, are derivative of social transactions during joint activities. When the social transactions involve personal memory telling, what develops is a joint product of personal, interpersonal, and cultural values, which jointly contour what is reportable and toward what ends.

In terms of familiar frameworks in personality psychology, perhaps the closest companion to the concept of proximal development is that of *reciprocal interactionism,* the view that persons, situations, and behaviors fluidly and reciprocally influence each other (Endler, 1981). However, models of reciprocal interactionism have tended to neglect the larger cultural systems that constrain what happens during immediate interactions. Proximal studies of self-telling have shown that parents teach their children early on which events are reportable and how to report them, and that these lessons are contoured by culture and gender. Cultures differ in the degree to which children are encouraged to tell adults about their own ex-

periences. For example, whereas U.S. mothers often encourage their children to report personal experiences, Japanese and Mayan children are not encouraged to do so (Minami & McCabe, 1991; Rogoff & Mistry, 1990). In addition, White, middle-class U. S. mothers tend to emphasize independence and the development of the child's full potential in the stories they tell to their children; Chinese mothers, on the other hand, tend to tell stories for the purpose of imparting a moral lesson (Miller, Wiley, Fung, & Liang, 1997).

With regard to gender, a number of studies, primarily with White, middle-class U.S. samples, have found that talk about emotional events is a sex-typed activity. Gender differences in emotion talk are promoted early on by parents, who have been found to elicit more elaborated emotional memories from preschool-age daughters than sons. Mothers have been found to talk more about emotions and about more emotions to daughters than sons, differences that were later reflected in the daughters' and sons' own emotion talk by the end of their preschool years (Fivush & Kuebli, 1997). Perhaps partly reflecting these early childhood practices, adult women tend to report more memories from early childhood, earlier memories, and more detailed and vivid memories than their male counterparts (Cowan & Davidson, 1984; Friedman & Pines, 1991; Mullen, 1994), and reportedly share their emotional past experiences with a wider array of significant others than do men (Rimé et al., 1991).

Finally, functions of memory telling tend to vary with age. Older adults more often share memories for the purpose of teaching by example, whereas adolescents more often tell memories for the purpose of identity making (Webster, 1995). These findings suggest that conversations between parents and teenagers about past events may sometimes be at cross purposes because the parent wants to constrain the teens' experience by channeling the teen toward or away from the parents' own past experiences, whereas the teen seeks to find himself or herself through telling his or her own experiences.

I have touched on a number of ways in which the larger forces of culture, gender, and age help to contour preferences and functions of personal memory telling. I now consider how to parse memory telling into components to facilitate proximal studies of what develops during memory telling. Recent work by Davies and Harré (1990) and Bamberg (1997) provides a useful framework for addressing where to look to capture developments through story telling. This framework demarcates three sites of development: (a) within the story itself, (b) within the self, and (c) between the teller and the listener. In discussing each of these sites of development, I identify new arenas for research on personal memory telling and personality development.

Personal Development Within the Story Itself

One site of development concerns the characters within the story and the nature of their relationship. As the story unfolds, a certain posture develops between self and others in the story. The main character positions himself or herself vis-à-vis the other and portrays a certain intention (Bamberg, 1997; Davies & Harré, 1990). From observing developments between the story characters, we may get an impression of the kind of person that the teller is. Stories themselves are fertile ground for personality development not just because we use them internally to guide our future, as Adler (1937) emphasized, but because we proffer these stories to others as vivid examples of what we have been through. We try them on for size and gauge other's reactions to them. The dog story that introduced this article is a perfect example. The teller's story conveyed the impression that he was a "nasty little boy," an impression that he apparently did not intend. He intended the story to demonstrate his loyalty, but the story missed the mark.

Intentions or motives in stories can obviously be identified from several perspectives. My own research has usually focused on outside coders' viewpoints of the protagonist's intentions, as have most studies of motives in the Thematic Apperception Test (TAT; Murray, 1943) stories. Although restricting attributions of intent to the viewpoint of outside coders has its drawbacks, interest in consensual views is unlikely to wane in empirical research. Still, we could make more demands on coders than we often do. Instead of restricting coders to inferring motives in memories, we could also ask them to infer character or traits from the stories that people choose to tell.

To date, systematic research on the personological impressions that particular stories make on others has been surprisingly rare. One study is relevant because the personal memory interviewer provided a Q-sort (Block, 1961/1978) description of the informant after the interview (Thorne & Klohnen, 1993). Linkages between the interviewer's Q-sort description and particular kinds of story lines were notably sparse. However, a few observed attributes, independence in young women and depression in young men, were significantly related to story lines. Specifically, young women who impressed the interviewer as independent produced repeated story lines about adults failing to come to their rescue. This theme was vividly illustrated by a 23-year-old informant. Six of her 14 stories showed the same basic story line. The ear-

liest story involved her father's refusing to retrieve her teddy bear after it had fallen out of her crib: "I was really mad at him, that he wouldn't come." Her most recent story described an episode with her high school principal, in which she unsuccessfully tried to get him to suspend some athletes who had assaulted her. The theme of negligent authorities is apparent, but why the link with independence? A proximate possibility is that the interviewer was impressed by the informant's repeated insistence, story after story, that she could not depend on elders for help and had to rely on her own devices. Male depression was the other observed attribute that was found to be correlated with a repeated story line. Male participants who appeared depressed to interviewers told repeated stories about failed romantic relationships. The message of these stories seemed to come through loud and clear to the interviewer: "I am depressed by my repeated failures at romance."

I speculate that story lines that most impress observers as characterological are those that portray a relatively high density of counternormative themes: in this case, a young woman's repeated claims that elders do not help her, and a young man's repeated stories about failures at love. These themes seem to run counter to sex-role stereotypes, in which women, supposedly the weaker gender, should be helped, and in which men, supposedly sturdy oaks, should not whine and seek sympathy. It is important to note that this interpretation directs attention to the role of cultural norms in attributing meanings to stories.

The aforementioned study (Thorne & Klohnen, 1993) is not ideal because it aggregated across memories to identify shared story lines. Although such aggregation is possible, it blurs the exquisite detail of personal memories and the ways in which tellers spontaneously form connections between episodes. Although focusing on specific personal stories would seem to restrict research to single occurrences, it is important to recognize that personal memories are not usually one-time events because most personal memories get told multiple times (Rimé et al., 1991). Furthermore, because vivid memories tend to be relived in the telling (Brewer, 1988), one-time events can be experienced again and again with successive tellings.

Development Within Selves: Differentiating "Then" and "Now"

Whereas developments within the story are circumscribed by what happened "back then," tellers often add codas to their stories or in other ways comment on the current meaning of the event. When tellers comment on the meaning of the story, we can often get a feeling for developments within the self. Take, for example, the following narrative from one college-age informant. This reportedly self-defining event occurred at age 13:

> I was sitting on the living room couch watching TV with my mother. The movie was one of those really boring ones, so we had an excuse to chat. All of a sudden, I felt as though the woman next to me was just another woman, not my mother. It felt scary to hear her voice because I did not see at the time who this woman really was. We talked about love and life, and how people come and go in our lives. I remember feeling for the first time a different type of connection between my mother and me from that conversation on. She was reminiscing to when she was my age, and I could relate so much to what she was saying. It was the first time that I saw my mother as more than just my parent, and my relationship with my mother has really changed. I feel that I have grown up.

This young woman's story displays growth in her relationship with her mother, a broadening of bonds from the daughter position to the peer position. If studied in the traditional way by coding motives, the meaning may be need for intimacy or communion. Viewed in terms of self-development, the story is one of a developmental transition in the teller's relationship with her mother. The transition to a more differentiated view of self and other is one of the hallmarks of maturing stories (McAdams, 1993). Other features of mature stories may also begin to emerge in adolescence, including coherence, openness, credibility, conflict resolution, and integration (McAdams, 1993).

Commentaries on how one has changed for the better are not uncommon in adolescent self-telling. The self-defining memories that we have been collecting are sometimes tagged with spontaneous reflections about how one has changed for the better as a result of an experience (e.g., "I became a whole different person after acting in that play;" "I found a new self-confidence in high-school sports;" "When the light shone through the window at my bar mitzvah, I felt that I finally became a man").

McCabe, Capron, and Peterson (1991) also observed that adolescent memory narratives sometimes include commentary about how one's perspective on the event has changed. For example, one informant described having fallen in a pond in childhood, and having believed for some time that his brother had tried to drown him, an interpretation that he now no longer believes. Other commentaries implicitly referred to personality changes, such as "I was insecure, back then." McCabe et al. found that nearly half of their informants spontaneously turned their memorable adolescent experiences into lessons learned (e.g., about whom to trust, the value of hard work, accepting death, and being more kind to girlfriends).

Noting that Erikson (1968) viewed the transition to adulthood as a time of self-exploration and personality growth, Pals, Hendin, and Beer (1998) examined written self-defining memories for statements of transformation or personal growth. One fourth of the college sample memories were identified by coders as transforming on the basis of explicit statements that the event had changed some aspect of oneself. Compared to nontransformative events, tranformative events were more negative at the time they occurred, suggesting a profiting from adversity (Affleck & Tennen, 1996). Furthermore, follow-ups 1 year later found that students who reported transformative memories viewed themselves as having increased during the subsequent year in openness to experience, independence, and self-esteem. Pals et al. concluded that negative life events can promote emotional and self-definitional development across time, a conclusion supported by stress and coping research (e.g., Park, Cohen, & Murch, 1996).

If researchers are not clear about the time frame that they wish respondents to tell, or about distinguishing between informants' past and current meanings, memory findings can be a muddle. We are especially impressed with two kinds of muddles. One concerns affect. The distinction between what happened then and what it means now is particularly important in coding affect because negative events can take on positive meanings. In one of our pilot studies (Nishino & Reichle, 1996) with college age samples, we asked for two vivid memories, one positive and one negative. Although most of the negative events looked negative to us because they were often traumatic, many of the positive events also looked negative, so much so that we suspected that our participants were not reading the instructions. In examining the content of many of these suspiciously positive memories, we found that their contents concerned lessons learned as a result of long-term reminiscing and coping with an initially traumatic event.

A second related peril with regard to studying memories is that if instructions are not clear about what time slice one is seeking for an account of a past event—then, now, or then and now—respondents will be left to their own devices in deciding how much of the event to report. Although researchers often tend to view differences in the degree of resolution or coherence of a story as reflecting preexisting personality differences, such findings are also contoured by different assumptions on the part of participants about what is wanted, either a concrete past event circumscribed by time and place, or an update on its current meanings. People seem to differ in the degree to which they tend to make larger meanings of events, but to date, researchers have not examined what happens when informants are uniformly pressed to go beyond the circumscribed content of past events to infer larger meanings.

Developments Between
Teller and Listener

The third and final site of self-development in story telling lies at the heart of proximal development because it concerns what people learn about themselves in the process of telling emotional past events to others. These lessons sometimes endure beyond the event telling to become memorable moments in themselves. Self-learning through self-telling can be captured using retrospective as well as in situ methods. Some results of retrospective research are first described, and then I consider the more difficult and enriched terrain of ongoing studies of self-telling.

We have recently been focusing on vivid and important personal event memories that are at least 1 year old, which Singer and Salovey (1993) termed *self-defining memories* (Thorne & McLean, 2000). Working from the assumption that adolescents and young adults frequently share personal memories with others, we ask informants not only to describe three self-defining memories but also, for each memory, to describe a vivid memory of telling that memory to someone else. We found that most of the self-defining memories have reportedly been told to others, and that about half of the self-defining memories are accompanied by a vivid account of telling the memory to someone else. As expected, accounts of memorable tellings reveal that the original event can take on new meanings because of the reactions of the telling audience.

A dramatic example comes from an 18-year-old named Mac. One of Mac's self-defining memories described an event in which he experienced a 5-day ordeal from ingesting amphetamines. He recounted in vivid detail being awake for 5 days, being manic, tense, and completely miserable. "The comedown was horrible, I was nauseated but I couldn't vomit. I was weak and tired but equally restless." When asked for an account of a memorable telling, Mac responded:

About two days later, I told my friend and former speed buddy how I felt. He told me, "Oh, you'll get used to that," and that was when I totally realized that I didn't want to be a drug user. I didn't want to "get used to" such a miserable existence. I got kind of weirded out because I couldn't understand how you could let yourself become used to pain like that. That was when I finally decided to stop using drugs.

Telling his drug buddy about his ordeal completed a trend that had begun with the ordeal itself. The buddy's reaction, "You'll get used to it," confirmed to Mac that he wanted to quit drugs altogether.

Telling emotional events can be risky because tellers may not be able to anticipate what kind of reaction they will get. Due to the fact that self-telling in late adolescence is presumably in high gear, with important events being told numerous times, tellers can accumulate a range of audience reactions to the same event. An exquisite example comes from a 19-year-old woman who told about the consequences of serially telling various friends about being raped at age 15. The guys (nonboyfriends) whom she told would get frustrated because they did not know how to console her. The successive boyfriends she told blamed her reluctance to have sex with them on the man who had earlier raped her. Subsequently, she told some close girlfriends about the rape and they cried with her and helped her to realize that what happened was not her fault.

In testing out audience reactions to emotional event telling, adolescents may increasingly develop layers of experiences that are differentially revealed to particular people. The work of Mead (1934) helps to describe the psychological process by which different selves develop, become accepted or revised, and synthesized. Mead viewed the social self as developing through playing at social roles and increasingly taking the perspective of other players on one's own performances. By adulthood, as roles become more complex and significant others more extensive, Mead believed that these various "me's" became consolidated into an encompassing social self evaluated from the perspective of the generalized other, who challenges the appropriateness and genuineness of the me's. Self-defining memories are very useful instantiations of particular me's, and the perceived meanings of other's reactions to particular tellings are useful instantiations of the generalized other. Whether one generalized other develops, or whether adults retain multiple generalized others in evaluating the personal and social meanings of their stories is a question that awaits future research.

Instances in which one chooses *not* to elaborate a self-defining memory can also reveal formative moments for developing generalized others. Another participant in our retrospective study (Thorne & McLean, 2000) of self-defining memory tellings told the story of his bar mitzvah. At one moment during the ceremony, he said that a light shone through the windows and it was at that moment that he felt he became a man. The memorable telling of this moment occurred right after the ceremony, when his buddies commented that he "looked funny" at one point during the ceremony. Sensing that he would be teased for disclosing a spiritual moment, he clammed up because he suddenly understood that spiritual experiences were not to be told to the guys. Another male participant learned that his father did not want him to crow about a compliment he had received. His father seemed uninterested so he did not pursue the story and reportedly had not told anyone until he was asked for a self-defining memory. Surveys of emotional event sharing have found that shame memories are least likely to be told to others (Rimé et al., 1991). The aforementioned nontold stories suggest that shame may be defined more by other's curtailments of attempted tellings than by the content of the original event. For example, a spiritually uplifting experience is not shameful in itself, but the guys defined it as shameful by their reactions. Similarly, a personal triumph is not shameful in itself, but may be regarded as such by parents who value modesty in their children. Shame memories thus may be useful in revealing the kinds of emotions that valued communities do not deem reportable.

From the accounts of telling that we have collected thus far, it appears that memorable moments of telling span the gamut from positive to negative audience reactions, but are more likely to be positive than negative. Although it is tempting to attribute the greater likelihood of positive telling outcomes to a self-enhancing bias, the original self-defining events in this ongoing study showed a bias in the opposite direction. Research has found that telling about traumas can be particularly salutary (Pennebaker & Beall, 1986).

Avenues for Future Research

Although personality development through self-telling appears to be in high gear during adolescence and early adulthood, ongoing studies of past event telling are currently more prominent with parent–child dyads than older samples. Due to the fact that personality and social psychologists more often study adolescents and young adults than do developmental psychologists, and because self-telling reflects both individual and social forces, we are nicely positioned to fill this gap. In this concluding section, I suggest some promising avenues for future research.

Individual Differences in Readiness for Story Telling

Each time one tells a personal story about one's past, one transfers one's past onto people in the present, creating one's past anew in the present (Thorne, 1989). These self-constructions may or may not be de-

liberate, but they can take on a life of their own (Van Langenhove & Harré, 1993). People vary in the degree to which they tend to share their past with others. Some of this difference seems captured by individual differences in need for intimacy, a concept that is measured by the content of TAT stories and centers on preferences for mutual self-disclosure (McAdams, 1980). In casting about for a term that conveys the readiness to tell self stories to others, my students and I have come to call this tendency "proferring personal information about the past" ("PPIPing").

In talking with students about whether they like to PPIP, it is clear that some do and some do not, and that most have a decided opinion about whether such tellings are appropriate, seemly, and wise. Reluctance to PPIP can stem from fear of creating a certain reputation, and clearly, reputations can be made in such tellings (Craik, 1985; Gergen, 1994). The stories that we choose to tell about ourselves can create lasting impressions that can take on a life of their own. The more broadly we share our stories, the more control we exert over our reputations but also the more fodder we provide for alternative interpretations. Sharing the self can be perilous because one can never be certain how the story will be interpreted by others. Presumably, the more experience one has in self-telling, the more confident one will feel about others' reactions.

Whether confidence and breadth of self-telling can be captured by customary measures of individual differences is unknown. For example, *need for intimacy* refers to preference to disclose to close friends, but how broadly does this extend to other friends and family members? *Extraversion* refers to preference to associate with a broad array of others, but not necessarily to telling personal stories to a wide array of others. *Secure attachment,* as identified by the Adult Attachment Interview (AAI; Main & Goldwyn, 1996), which centers on the coherence of discourse about early relationships with caregivers, may identify comfort and skill in telling emotional events to a wide array of people because the interview is administered by strangers. However, secure attachment in the AAI is based on an overall discourse style and does not center on personal memories per se.

Readiness for story telling may be shown in measures of latency, frequency, and breadth of story telling. Sharing personal memories soon after the emotional event, and on many successive occasions, and to different people, affords more opportunities for feedback vis-à-vis the emotional experiences of others. People who choose to keep events to themselves may be less likely to grow from the experience because they do not get the kinds of reciprocal feedback that bring alternative interpretations to the experience.

Gendered Ecologies of Self-Telling

Parent–child discourse is the most frequent site of self-telling in childhood, increasingly moving to same-sex peers from midchildhood to adolescence, and to spouses in adulthood (Burhmester & Prager, 1995). However, disclosure audiences tend to narrow earlier for boys in adolescence, and continue to be more narrow in adulthood. Boys begin restricting disclosure to same-sex friends earlier in adolescence than do girls, and although parents continue to be targeted for disclosure, this is more true of female than male adolescents (Burhmester & Prager, 1995). In adulthood, spouses are the primary audience for men's self-telling, whereas for women, self-telling continues to include friends and other family members (Rimé et al., 1991). The narrower ecology of self-telling for men would seem to have important consequences for emotional development.

The Developmental Significance of Parents' Stories

Parents' story telling is often done for the purposes of teaching the younger generation (Webster, 1995). This phenomenon can be likened to that of genetics: Whereas genes constrain biological development, parents' stories can constrain children's social and emotional development. Parents can accentuate trends in their children's personality by emphasizing particular stories. For example, one informant said that her mother often tells her about a trip to the mall when the daughter was 3 years old:

> There was a piano store and a man was playing an organ out front. As soon as I heard the music, I ran to it and started dancing. Soon there was a large crowd around me, but I didn't mind, I just kept going.

This story about herself was appropriated from an elder who told her about it. Memories of what one did in early life typically are appropriated from elders because the capacity to verbalize personal event memories does not usually emerge until language skills are established (Nelson, 1993). This finding suggests that adults who report many early memories may have experienced more extensive past event discussions with their parents during childhood.

Parents also use stories of their own personal past to try to teach by example. The process by which parents decide what to tell their children about their own personal past, and what not to tell, is fascinating and almost entirely unexplored. Presumably, when a child has an experience that the parent has also experi-enced in the past, the parent is tempted to comfort, warn, or inform the child by relaying his or her own experience, or at least the part that is deemed appropriate for telling. Whether the PPIPing has the intended effect is another question. In our interviews with teenagers about their parents' PPIPing, we have found a wide array of opinions about whether it is useful. Parent PPIPing can sometimes be oppressive, and can sometimes be salutary, as when a mother in an aforementioned episode relayed stories of her own teenage years to her teenage daughter.

Because temperament tends to differ among siblings, siblings are likely to find different kinds of events surprising and therefore to engage different domains of their parents' own childhood experiences. This phenomenon, too, remains to be explored. In addition, there are few studies of how teens and parents co-coordinate their own past experiences through discourse, although there is plentiful advice about how parents should try to talk with their kids about their own experiences, especially with regard to illicit drugs. Due to the fact that sons, relative to daughters, begin to exclude parents as a disclosure audience relatively early in adolescence, parental stories may be less meaningful for teenage sons than daughters, a difference that may continue into adulthood.

Reconciling Personal Memories and Personality Traits

Despite important epistemological differences raised earlier, traits and personal memories are both important aspects of self-presentation (Harré & Van Langenhove, 1991). Recent work by Woike (1995) suggests that the settings and routines that are conveyed in personal memories provide a useful bridge to traits, whereas the emotional themes of memories provide a useful bridge to motives. It is also possible that momentous events can trigger changes in formerly stable personality traits. Imagine a typically reserved person experiencing an atypical event in which he or she suddenly feels the excitement that comes from entertaining others. This event is a self-defining memory because it defies his or her routines; it needs the routines to seem out of the ordinary. Personal memories may derive their personal and interpersonal distinctiveness, in part, from the backdrop of personality traits.

There is another sense in which traits and personal stories interweave in that they are both important aspects of self-presentation and therefore subject to feedback from others. Whenever we claim that we have certain tendencies, such as extraversion or introversion, we may encounter acceptance or resistance just as when we tell particular stories. We cannot be anything in the eyes of others without their implicit or explicit consent, and our communities support and constrain self-development in important but presently mysterious ways. Trait-like presentations may be as prone to community collusion, approval, and censure as are richly elaborated personal stories.

Because the relation of traits and life stories is not well charted, researchers will profit from including participants' accounts of why they chose to tell particular stories about themselves and what they learn from telling them (e.g., Thorne, 1987). In addition, researchers need to be alert to natural settings in which emotional event telling is in high gear. Developmental psychologists have been especially innovative in capturing memory telling on the hoof. Events that press for immediate sharing with friends and family are those that disrupt our routines, such as bar mitzvahs, menstruation, and other rites of passage; first dates; romantic breakups; and physical injuries.

Summary and Conclusions

Although personal memories have been appreciated by psychologists for nearly a century, their significance for personality development has tended to be relegated to internalized representations of early childhood memories. However, recent studies of autobiographical memories reveal that ages 10 to 30 are the most memorable period of the life span, and that events that are most likely to be remembered are highly emotional and disruptive of everyday routines and likely to be told to others soon after the event occurs. Studies of how tellers proffer and make sense of momentous events, and how families and friends collude in sense making can importantly extend our understanding of a phenomenon that was formerly relegated to psychoanalysts. Personality and social psychologists can make important contributions to the burgeoning interest in self-telling because self-telling seems to be particularly dense during the age periods that we are most inclined to study—adolescence and early adulthood. Furthermore, the gap that has customarily divided studies of persons (personality) and situations (social psychology) is necessarily bridged in studies of self-telling. Although we have tended to neglect the ways in which personality is constructed and maintained through self-telling, developmental psychologists have prepared fertile ground for personality research.

References

Adler, A. (1937). The significance of early recollections. *International Journal of Individual Psychology, 3,* 283–287.

Affleck, G., & Tennen, H. (1996). Construing benefits from adversity: Adaptational significance and dispositional underpinnings. *Journal of Personality, 64,* 899–922.

Aiken, L. R. (1997). *Psychological testing and assessment.* Boston, MA: Allyn & Bacon.

Bamberg, M. G. W. (1997). Positioning between structure and performance. *Journal of Narrative and Life History, 7,* 335–342.

Block, J. (1978). *The Q-sort method in personality assessment and psychiatric research.* Palo Alto, CA: Consulting Psychologists Press. (Original work published 1961)

Brewer, W. F. (1988). Memory for randomly sampled autobiographical events. In U. Neisser & E. Winograd (Eds.), *Remembering reconsidered: Ecological and traditional approaches to the study of memory* (pp. 21–90). Cambridge, England: Cambridge University Press.

Brown, R., & Kulik, J. (1977). Flashbulb memories. *Cognition, 5,* 73–99.

Bruner, J. S. (1987). Life as narrative. *Social Research, 54,* 11–32.

Burhmester, D., & Prager, K. (1995). Patterns and functions of self-disclosure during childhood and adolescence. In K. J. Rotenberg (Eds.), *Disclosure processes in childhood and adolescence* (pp. 10–56). New York: Cambridge University Press.

Cantor, N. (1990). From thought to behavior: "Having" and "doing" in the study of personality and cognition. *American Psychologist, 45,* 735–750.

Carstensen, L. L. (1995) Evidence of a life-span theory of socioemotional selectivity. *Current Directions in Psychological Science, 4,* 151–156.

Christianson, S.-Å., & Safer, M. A. (1996). Emotions in autobiographical memories. In D. C. Rubin (Ed.), *Remembering our past: Studies in autobiographical memory* (pp. 218–243). New York: Cambridge University Press.

Cowan, N., & Davidson, G. (1984). Salient childhood memories. *Journal of Genetic Psychology, 145,* 101–107.

Craik, K. H. (1985). Multiple perceived personalities: A neglected consistency issue. In E. E. Roskam (Ed.), *Measurement and personality assessment* (pp. 333–338). New York: Elsevier.

Davies, B., & Harré, R. (1990). Positioning: The discursive production of selves. *Journal for the Theory of Social Behaviour, 20,* 43–63.

Endler, N. S. (1981). Persons, situations, and their interactions. In A. I. Rabin, J. Aronoff, A. M. Barclay, & R. A. Zucker (Eds.), *Further explorations in personality* (pp. 114–151). New York: Wiley.

Erikson, E. H. (1968). *Identity: Youth and crisis.* New York: Norton.

Festinger, L. (1954). A theory of social comparison processes. *Human Relations, 7,* 117–140.

Fitzgerald, J. M. (1996). Intersecting meanings of reminiscence in adult development and aging. In E. Winograd & E. Neisser (Eds.), *Affect and accuracy in recall: Studies of "flashbulb" memories. Emory Symposia in Cognition* (Vol. 4, pp. 360–383). New York: Cambridge University Press.

Fivush, R., & Kuebli, J. (1997). Making everyday events emotional: The construal of emotion in parent–child conversations about the past. In N. L. Stein, P. A. Ornstein, B. Tversky, & C. Brainerd (Eds.), *Memory for everyday and emotional events* (pp. 239–266). Mahwah, NJ: Lawrence Erlbaum Associates, Inc.

Freeman, M., Csikszentmihalyi, M., & Larson, R. (1986). Adolescence and its recollection: Toward an interpretive model of development. *Merrill-Palmer Quarterly, 32,* 167–185.

Friedman, A., & Pines, A. (1991). Sex differences in gender-related memories. *Sex Roles, 25,* 25–32.

Gergen, M. (1994). The social construction of personal histories: Gendered lives in popular autobiographies. In T. R. Sarbin & J. I. Kitsuse (Eds.), *Constructing the social* (pp. 19–44). London: Sage.

Harré, R., & Van Langenhove, L. (1991). Varieties of positioning. *Journal for the Theory of Social Behaviour, 21,* 393–407.

Josselson, R. (1997, June). *Stability and change in early memories over 22 years: Themes, variations, and cadenzas.* Paper presented at the annual meeting of the Society for Personology, Evanston, IL.

Kihlstrom, J. F., & Harackiewicz, J. M. (1982). The earliest recollection: A new survey. *Journal of Personality, 50,* 134–148.

Linton, M. (1978). Real world memory after six years: An *in vivo* study of very long term memory. In M. M. Gruneberg, P. E. Morris, & R. N. Sykes (Eds.), *Practical aspects of memory* (pp. 69–76). London: Academic.

Mackavey, W. R., Malley, J. E., & Stewart, A. J. (1991). Remembering autobiographically consequential experiences: Content analysis of psychologists' accounts of their lives. *Psychology of Aging, 6,* 50–59.

Main, M., & Goldwyn, R. (1996). *Adult attachment interview.* Unpublished manuscript.

Mandler, J. M., & Johnson, N. S. (1977). Remembrance of things parsed: Story structure and recall. *Cognitive Psychology, 9,* 111–151.

McAdams, D. P. (1980). A thematic coding system for the intimacy motive. *Journal of Research in Personality, 14,* 413–432.

McAdams, D. P. (1988). *Power, intimacy, and the life story: Personological inquiries into identity.* New York: Guilford.

McAdams, D. P. (1993). *The stories we live by: Personal myths and the making of the self.* New York: Morrow.

McAdams, D. P. (1995). What do we know when we know a person? *Journal of Personality, 63,* 365–396.

McCabe, A., Capron, E., & Peterson, C. (1991). The voice of experience: The recall of early childhood and adolescent memories by young adults. In A. McCabe & C. Peterson (Eds.), *Developing narrative structure* (pp. 137–173). Hillsdale, NJ: Lawrence Erlbaum Associates, Inc.

McCrae, R. R., & Costa, P. T. (1990). *Personality in adulthood.* New York: Guilford.

Mead, G. H. (1934). *Mind, self, and society.* Chicago: University of Chicago Press.

Miller, P. J., Wiley, A. R., Fung, H., & Liang, C-H. (1997). Personal storytelling as a medium of socialization in Chinese and American families. *Child Development, 68,* 557–568.

Minami, M., & McCabe, A. (1991). Haiku as a discourse regulation device: A stanza analysis of Japanese children's personal narratives. *Language in Society, 20,* 577–599.

Mullen, M. K. (1994). Earliest recollections of childhood: A demographic analysis. *Cognition, 52,* 55–79.

Murray, H. A. (1938). *Explorations in personality.* New York: Oxford University Press.

Murray, H. A. (1943). *Thematic Apperception Test Manual.* Cambridge, MA: Harvard University Press.

Nelson, K. (1993). The psychological and social origins of autobiographical memory. *Psychological Science, 4,* 7–14.

Nishino, R., & Reichle, D. (1996). [Identifying negative and positive memories]. Unpublished raw data.

Pals, J. L., Hendin, H. M., & Beer, J. S. (1998, August). *Self-defining memories in a longitudinal study of the college experience.* Paper presented at the annual meeting of the American Psychological Association, San Francisco, CA.

Park, C. L., Cohen, L. H., & Murch, R. L. (1996). Assessment and prediction of stress-related growth. *Journal. of Personality, 64,* 71–105.

Pennebaker, J. W., & Beall, S. K. (1986). Confronting a traumatic event: Toward an understanding of inhibition and disease. *Journal of Abnormal Psychology, 95,* 274–281.

Pillemer, D. B. (1984). Flashbulb memories of the assassination attempt on President Reagan. *Cognition, 16,* 63–80.

Pillemer, D. B. (1998). *Momentous events, vivid memories.* Cambridge, MA: Harvard University Press.

Rimé, B., Mesquita, B., Philippot, P., & Boca, S. (1991). Beyond the emotional event: Six studies on the social sharing of emotion. *Cognition and Emotion, 5,* 435–465.

Robinson, J. A., & Taylor, L. R. (1998). Autobiographical memory and self-narratives: A tale of two stories. In C. P. Thompson, D. J. Herrmann, D. Bruce, & J. D. Read (Eds.), *Autobiographical memory: Theoretical and applied perspectives* (pp. 125–143). Mahwah, NJ: Lawrence Erlbaum Associates, Inc.

Rogoff, B., & Mistry, J. (1990). The social and functional context of children's remembering. In R. Fivush & J. A. Hudson (Eds.), *Knowing and remembering in young children* (pp. 197–222). New York: Cambridge University Press.

Rubin, D. C., Rahhal, T. A., & Poon, L. W. (1998). Things learned in early adulthood are remembered best. *Memory & Cognition, 26,* 3–19.

Singer, J. A., & Salovey, P. (1993). *The remembered self: Emotion and memory in personality.* New York: Free Press.

Thompson, C. P., Skowronski, J. J., Larsen, S. F., & Betz, A. L. (1996). *Autobiographical memory: Remembering what and remembering when.* Mahwah, NJ: Lawrence Erlbaum Associates, Inc.

Thorne, A. (1987). The press of personality: A study of conversations between introverts and extraverts. *Journal of Personality and Social Psychology, 53,* 718–726.

Thorne, A. (1989). Conditional patterns, transference, and the coherence of personality across time. In D. M. Buss & N. Cantor (Eds.), *Personality psychology: Recent trends and emerging directions* (pp. 149–159). New York: Springer-Verlag.

Thorne, A. (1995). Developmental truths in memories of childhood and adolescence. *Journal of Personality, 63,* 139–163.

Thorne, A. (1998). Using what to remember when: Studies of 450 daily diaries [Review of the book *Autobiographical memory: Remembering what and remembering when*]. *American Journal of Psychology, 111,* 480–485.

Thorne, A., Cutting, L., & Skaw, D. (1998). Young adults' relationship memories and the life story: Examples or essential landmarks? *Narrative Inquiry, 8,* 237–268.

Thorne, A., & Klohnen, E. (1993). Interpersonal memories as maps for personality consistency. In D. Funder, R. D. Parke, C. Tomlinson-Keasey, & K. Widaman, (Eds.), *Studying lives through time: Personality and development* (pp. 223–253). Washington, DC: American Psychological Association.

Thorne, A., & McLean, K. (2000, February). *Contexts and consequences of telling self-defining memories in adolescence.* Paper presented at the Personality Pre-conference, Society for Personality and Social Psychology, Nashville, TN.

Van Langenhove, L., & Harré, R. (1993). Positioning and autobiography: Telling your life. In N. Coupland & J. F. Nussbaum (Eds.), *Discourse and lifespan identity* (pp. 81–99). Newbury Park, CA: Sage.

Webster, J. D. (1995). Adult age differences in reminiscence functions. In B. K. Haight & J. D. Webster (Eds.), *The art and science of reminiscing: Theory, research, methods, and application* (pp. 89–102). Washington, DC: Taylor & Francis.

Winter, D. G., John, O. P., Stewart, A. J., Klohnen, E. C., & Duncan, L. E. (1998). Traits and motives: Toward an integration of two traditions in personality research. *Psychological Review, 105,* 230–250.

Woike, B. A. (1995). Most memorable experiences: Evidence for a link between implicit and explicit motives and social cognitive processes in everyday life. *Journal of Personality and Social Psychology, 68,* 1081–1091.

Personality and Social Psychology Review
2000, Vol. 4, No. 1, 57–75

Plan 9 From Cyberspace: The Implications of the Internet for Personality and Social Psychology

Katelyn Y. A. McKenna and John A. Bargh

Department of Psychology
New York University

Just as with most other communication breakthroughs before it, the initial media and popular reaction to the Internet has been largely negative, if not apocalyptic. For example, it has been described as "awash in pornography," and more recently as making people "sad and lonely." Yet, counter to the initial and widely publicized claim that Internet use causes depression and social isolation, the body of evidence (even in the initial study on which the claim was based) is mainly to the contrary. More than this, however, it is argued that like the telephone and television before it, the Internet by itself is not a main effect cause of anything, and that psychology must move beyond this notion to an informed analysis of how social identity, social interaction, and relationship formation may be different on the Internet than in real life. Four major differences and their implications for self and identity, social interaction, and relationships are identified: one's greater anonymity, the greatly reduced importance of physical appearance and physical distance as "gating features" to relationship development, and one's greater control over the time and pace of interactions. Existing research is reviewed along these lines and some promising directions for future research are described.

The growth of the Internet has been truly exponential over the past decade. Until recently there were relatively few nodes in that network to carry digitized information from one part of the world to another and relatively few people (mainly academics and government workers) accessing that network. Personal computers for the home were expensive and the interface used to view, send, and receive data over the Internet was not user friendly. However, in recent years personal computers have dropped drastically in price. Sophisticated Internet browser software, such as Internet Explorer and Netscape, is now readily available. Although the Internet is not yet a vital utility such as the telephone, it will not be long before having a connection to the Internet will be equally as important. Indeed, in a recent poll of 1,000 Internet users, 64% said that "using an online or Internet service is a necessity to me" (D'Amico, 1998, p. 1).

These developments have made it possible for the average person to become an active user of the Internet. Currently, several hundred million people are connecting themselves and their families to the Internet through their personal computer, telephone line, and portal company (e.g., America Online [AOL™], which has more than 15 million users worldwide). It is projected that 10% of the world's population, 600 million people, will be regularly accessing information on the Internet by the year 2001 ("Making a business," 1997), and that number will certainly grow.

More important, for personality and social psychology, the Internet is a place where people are engaging in social interaction. Indeed, the number one use of the Internet at home is for interpersonal communication (Kraut, Mukopadhyay, Szczypula, Kiesler, & Scherlis, 1998). People are increasingly turning to the Internet as a quick and easy way to maintain contact with family and friends who live far away. In the survey mentioned earlier, fully 94% reported that the Internet made it easier for them to communicate with friends and family, and 87% regularly use it for that purpose (D'Amico, 1998).

There are a wide variety of electronic venues available on the Internet for interpersonal communi-

Preparation of this article was supported in part by a Research Challenge Fund grant from New York University to Katelyn Y. A. McKenna, and National Institute of Mental Health Grant R01–MH60767 to John A. Bargh.

Requests for reprints should be sent to Katelyn Y. A. McKenna or John A. Bargh, Department of Psychology, New York University, 6 Washington Place, Seventh Floor, New York, NY 10003. E-mail: mckenna@psych.nyu.edu and bargh@psych.nyu.edu.

cation. There are thousands of Internet chat rooms, message boards, listservs, and news groups each dedicated to a specific topic or area of interest for those interested in taking part in group interactions. People can also communicate privately through the creation of private chat rooms, personal messaging, and of course electronic mail. Text-based online adventure games called Multi-User Dungeons (MUDs) and their more socially oriented relatives, the Mud Object Orienteds and Multi-User Shared Hallucinations, are attractive venues for many, particularly younger, Internet users.

Fear and Loathing of the Internet

The public, however, is somewhat apprehensive about the changes the Internet may or will bring. This fear of the unknown is to be expected to some extent, and it has been a feature of the introduction of most previous technological breakthroughs that greatly affect nearly everyone's lives. Many people were reluctant to have telephones installed when they first became available because it was rumored that outsiders could listen in on the household through the mouthpiece, even when the phone was on the hook. It was also not uncommon for people to resist the installation of electricity because it might leak out of the outlets. Soon after television was invented and publicly demonstrated around 1930, Bela Lugosi made a horror movie called *Murder by Television* that capitalized on public fears of this emerging technology. More recently, there was an initial negative reaction to the introduction of microwave ovens, because of the possibility of escaping radiation, but today microwave cooking is a mundane feature of modern kitchens.

The Internet has fared no differently. For most of the 1990s most people only heard about the Internet in terms of being a dangerous conveyor of pornography to the unwitting eyes of children, or as causing "Internet addiction" (Young, 1998). Politicians responded to public fears of the uncontrolled dissemination of information on the Internet: The U.S. Congress has repeatedly passed legislation such as the Computer Decency Act (CDA) that seeks to censor or regulate the content of Internet Web sites, only to have such legislation ruled unconstitutional as a violation of the First Amendment by the courts. In fact, the CDA came about largely because of the furor in the media and in Congress caused by the publication, in 1995, of a study by a student at Carnegie Mellon University (Rimm, 1995) that purportedly showed that the Internet was awash in pornography, although this conclusion was "based on false premises and quickly discredited" (Caruso, 1998, p. C5; e.g., the

study was never subjected to peer review; see also Hoffman & Novak, 1995; Rossney, 1995).

More recently, another Carnegie Mellon study received U.S. national media coverage when it concluded that using the Internet leads to significant increases in loneliness and depression (Kraut, Patterson, et al., 1998). The participants in this study were people from the Pittsburgh area who had never been on the Internet before; in fact, most had never before used a computer at home. They were not randomly selected but recruited for the "HomeNet" study because their families included high school students, or an adult who was on a community board of directors. These participants had unusually large social circles at the beginning of the study, an average of 49 friends and associates each. Kraut, Patterson, et al. followed these families for 2 years, measuring among other variables the number of hours each individual was on the Internet per day, their levels of depression and loneliness both at the beginning and at the end of the 2-year period, and the number of people in their social circle at the end of the study.

Kraut, Patterson, et al. (1998) found a small but statistically reliable partial correlation of .15 between amount of Internet use and self-reported loneliness, accounting for less than 1% of the change in loneliness over the 2-year period. They also reported that using the Internet for as little as 2 hours per week over the 2-year period resulted in a reduction in the size of the average participant's *social network*—defined as the number of people in Pittsburgh with whom the participant socialized at least once a month—from 24 to 23 people. The authors also obtained a small but statistically reliable increase in level of self-reported depression (actually, self-reported dysphoric mood) with increased amount of Internet use, again accounting for less than 1% of the change in depression level over the 2-year period. The authors concluded that using the Internet causes increases in loneliness and depression, and this was the "sound bite" conclusion reported widely by the media.

It is one of the standard principles of journalism (and horror films as well) that "scare headlines sell newspapers": A threat, no matter how statistically rare and unlikely, to which nearly everyone is vulnerable, whether it be poisoned Tylenol tablets or mad-cow disease, is sure to capture the public's attention (e.g., Fuller, 1996; Gans, 1979). So the media play given the "Internet causes loneliness" conclusion is understandable; it is doubtful much coverage would have been given a study showing a slight but statistically significant decrease in loneliness and depression level with Internet use.

However, this becomes more than merely a hypothetical question, because such a decrease is, in fact, what the study did find.

For the entire group of participants, the average reported level of depression for participants after 2 years of being on the Internet was less than it had been before being on the Internet, and the average reported level of loneliness for this group was also lower at the end of the study than when the study began. Furthermore, whereas the average number of people in the local social network declined one person over the 2-year period, the size of the average participant's distant social network—defined as the number of people outside of Pittsburgh with whom the participant talked or visited at least once per year—substantially increased after 2 years of using the Internet, from 25 to 32. Thus, the total number of people in the average participant's social network in the Kraut, Patterson, et al. (1998) study actually increased over the 2 years, from 49 to 55. Of course, there could have been many other factors over the course of the 2 years in participants' lives besides Internet use that could have produced these decreases in depression and loneliness, and increases in number of friends and acquaintances, but because the Kraut, Patterson, et al. study did not include a control group of comparable people who were not given and did not use home computers over the same 2-year period,[1] the only known potential causal factor was participants' use of the Internet. The study's design provided no basis for concluding anything other than that the reason for these changes was the introduction of home computers and Internet access into participants' lives.

Unfortunately, the take-home sound bite message reported by the media was the opposite one. For instance, the headline on the front page of the *New York Times* read "Sad, lonely world discovered in cyberspace" (Harmon, 1998), and that on the front page of the American Psychological Association's (APA) *Monitor* for that month was similar ("Isolation increases with Internet use"; Sleek, 1998). Due to the great deal of publicity the study received, both within APA and in the national and international media, it is widely accepted by psychologists and public alike that Internet use leads to depression and social isolation.

In the previous case of the Internet pornography study (Rimm, 1995), the (entirely false) conclusion that 83.5% of pictorial content on the Internet was pornographic (and that much of this was child pornography) received immediate media fanfare (most notably

the cover of *Time* magazine, before the actual article had appeared), and was a major reason for the passage of CDA in 1996. Although that study was quickly debunked for its gross distortions and its extremely inadequate methodology (e.g., Hoffman & Novak, 1995; Rossney, 1995), these problems were not reported in the media (if at all) to anything approaching the extent of the initial (false) report.

It may well be that the "sad, lonely Internet" conclusion will similarly influence public policy decisions about Internet access and regulation. This would be despite the facts that, according to several large-scale national and international surveys of Internet users, the great majority of respondents consider Internet use to have improved their lives (D'Amico, 1998; Katz & Aspden, 1997; McKenna & Bargh, 1999a), that a substantial proportion (over 50%) of over 600 Internet users surveyed had brought an Internet relationship into their real life (i.e., met in person), and that over 20% of those respondents had formed a romantic relationship and were now living with or engaged to someone they met on the Internet (McKenna, 1998).

This article is unlikely to correct public opinion on this important issue, but our goal is nevertheless to set the record straight among personality and social psychologists about the actual social and interpersonal consequences of the Internet—both as to what the existing body of research has found, and as to what further research is likely to find.

The first important point is that there is no simple main effect of the Internet on the average person (e.g., as to make the individual lonelier or more depressed). Like everything else learned in the past 25 years of personality and social psychology research, situational variables such as modes of Internet communication interact with individual differences or "person" variables to produce psychological and behavioral outcomes (e.g., Mischel, 1973). One of the central messages is an old one in communications research (known widely as the *uses and gratifications model*; Blumler, 1979; Blumler & Katz, 1974; Katz, 1959): How a person is affected by a given communications medium depends on that person's reasons and goals for using that medium (Bargh, 1988). People use the Internet for a variety of reasons and motivations (see McKenna & Bargh, 1999b), and will thus use it differently and it will have different effects on them accordingly. There is, in short, no simple sound bite for how using the Internet will affect an individual.

The related second point is that the Internet per se is neither entirely good or entirely bad as to the kinds of interactive social effects it can have on individuals. Although in this article the positive aspects and outcomes are emphasized (but at the same time point to the potential downsides to Internet communication),

---

[1]This is a design problem that, in addition to the nonrepresentative and nonrandomly selected sample of civic leaders and their teenage children (with very few people between the ages of 22–40 years old) who as of 1995 had no computer in the home (Kraut, Kiesler, Mukhopadhyay, Scherlis, & Patterson, 1998), makes it quite difficult to draw any conclusions about the social consequences of Internet use for the general population (see also Caruso, 1998).

this is motivated by the need for a corrective to the overly negative portrayals that have received so much emphasis to date. Television can link a world together and help bring down the Berlin wall (Friedman, 1999), but it is also fertile ground for the cultivation of couch potatoes. The Internet can bring people of like interests and minds together in ways heretofore unseen, but those similarities can range from a past history of sexual abuse among people in great need of anonymous social support, to virulent hatred of other racial groups.

How is the Internet Different?

To personality and social psychological researchers, the Internet as an emerging domain of research creates a situation similar to that of 10 or so years ago, with the emergence of cultural psychology (e.g., Markus & Kitayama, 1991; Shweder, 1990). Theories and models of psychological phenomena that were developed from research performed mainly within a single culture (i.e., North American and Western European societies) were assumed to hold universally, yet this assumption was rarely tested. As the world has grown smaller, cross-cultural research collaborations have multiplied, and much is and will continue to be learned about cultural moderators of important psychological processes (e.g., Brewer & Gardner, 1996; Iyengar & Lepper, 1999; Rhee, Uleman, & Lee, 1996; Rhee, Uleman, Lee, & Roman, 1995). In a similar fashion, the Internet is a virtual world that is the same in some ways but different in others from the one traditionally studied. How well will existing theory apply to the world of the Internet?

We begin, therefore, by considering how communication and interaction on the Internet may be different from that in real life. There are four major differences that are likely to be important moderators. First, it is quite possible to be anonymous while on the Internet. For many of us, our names appear in our e-mail addresses, and even if they do not, our identity (and much other information about us) can be ascertained through "fingering" programs and other means. However, it is quite possible, such as on AOL™ and other Internet service providers, to have an anonymous e-mail name. Moreover, even when using one's real name one is relatively anonymous when interacting with people from other cities and countries.

That physical distance, or propinquity, does not matter on the Internet means that one can interact with, and meet, people from all over the world, at least those who speak the same languages. Physical distance is the major determinant of who one will meet and form relationships with in the real world,

but the Internet vastly expands the range and variety of interaction partners.

Also, unlike in real life, physical appearance and visual cues more generally are not present and not an influential factor on the Internet. As these are powerful determinants of initial attraction and the potential for relationship formation, as well as strong cues for stereotype and other social categorization processes, their absence on the Internet should alter the course of interactions and relationship formation.

Finally, time becomes relatively immaterial on the Internet. Not only can an individual engage in a social exchange without the other person being online at the same time but also he or she has far greater control over his or her side of the interaction than is possible in a conversation by telephone or in person, because there is no need for an instantaneous response. An individual can take all the time he or she needs to formulate a response, perhaps polishing and editing the phrasing until it seems perfect in his or her eyes, rather than having to respond off the cuff.

To summarize, people via the Internet are engaging in largely anonymous but repeated interactions with others who are equally anonymous. They are forming close relationships with others sight unseen. They are also able to construct and reconstruct their identity in numerous ways on the Internet—something not possible for the average individual in non-Internet life. People can and are thus engaging in very different behaviors on the Internet than they do in the real world.

The Effects of Anonymity in Cyberspace

The Internet's nature allows for an individual to be anonymous if he or she wishes, through anonymous remailers, commercial accounts (such as Prodigy™ and AOL™) and anonymity-enabling software. Indeed, even those who interact on the Internet non-anonymously (i.e., "nonymously," with their real names present on their newsgroup posts, or where their identity can be obtained by fingering their nickname on Internet Relay Chat) tend to feel relatively anonymous. When an individual posts an article in a newsgroup or enters a chat room full of strangers, he or she may well feel that his or her actions will be submerged in the hundreds (or thousands) of other actions taking place there. It is not surprising then that deindividuation and the negative results that often accompany it (e.g., Zimbardo, 1970) readily occur on the Internet (see Mendels, 1999). However, other, more positive effects are also produced because of this very same anonymity.

Deindividuation

When an individual's self-awareness is blocked or seriously reduced by environmental conditions (e.g., such as darkness, presence of large numbers of other people), deindividuation can occur (Diener, 1980; Zimbardo, 1970). Anonymity, feelings of close group unity, a high level of physiological arousal, and a focus on external events or goals are conditions that have been shown to encourage, and often produce, deindividuation. Some of the outcomes produced by deindividuation include a weakened ability for an individual to regulate his or her own behavior, reduced ability to engage in rational, long-term planning, and a tendency to react to immediate cues or based largely on his or her current emotional state. Furthermore, an individual will be less likely to care what others think of his or her behavior and may even have a reduced awareness of what others have said or done. These effects can culminate in impulsive and disinhibited behaviors (Zimbardo, 1970).

Among the many interactions and means of communicating on the Internet, such conditions leading to a lessening of an individual's self-awareness occur either singly or in conjunction with one another. For instance, a person may anonymously participate in an Internet newsgroup and come to feel a sense of unity with the other members of the group (see McKenna & Bargh, 1998, Study 1). A situation may then occur that raises his or her physiological arousal (perhaps someone has posted a statement with which this individual strongly disagrees or finds upsetting). He or she then may experience deindividuation and react ferociously—responding in the heat of the moment by attacking the offending statement (and its author) with a highly volatile, angry, and offensive post of his or her own. On the Internet, such newsgroup posts are known as "flames" and, as more people in the group join in, entire "flamewars" can erupt and involve several hundred arguing, largely anonymous, deindividuated participants.

The negative, deindividuating effects of anonymous communication via the Internet have been among the most discussed aspects of computer-mediated communication to date. Researchers have found that people tend to behave more bluntly when communicating by e-mail or participating in other electronic venues such as newsgroups, than they would in a face-to-face situation. Moreover, misunderstandings, greater hostility and aggressive responses, and nonconforming behavior are more likely to occur in computer-mediated interactions than in interactions that take place face to face (Culnan & Markus, 1987; Dubrovsky, Kiesler, & Sethna, 1991; Kiesler, Siegal, & McGuire, 1984; Siegal, Dubrovsky, Kiesler, & McGuire, 1986). Researchers have also found that under some conditions computer-mediated communication can foster an inability to form group consensus, increased verbal hostility and impersonalization, and an inability to become task focused (Siegal et al., 1986).

More alarmingly, racists and members of hate groups have used the cloak of anonymity afforded by the Internet to harass minority group members through sending hateful or threatening e-mail (Mendels, 1999). For example, the perpetrators of the recent shootings at Columbine High School in Colorado had disseminated racist views anonymously on personal Web pages (Clausing, 1999). The publicity and notoriety of such cases of abuse have led to federal and state legislative efforts to outlaw anonymous Internet (e-mail, newsgroup) communications.

At the same time, the anonymity of the Internet played a major role in getting accurate information about the conflict in Kosovo out to the rest of the world despite heavy Serbian government censorship, and many give the Internet credit for the grass roots communication that facilitated the independence movement in Indonesia (Frankel & Teich, 1999). The powerful effects of anonymous communication on the Internet, both positive and negative, resulted in a recent conference on the topic cosponsored by the American Association for the Advancement of Science (AAAS) and the U.S. National Science Foundation (Mendels, 1999). This article returns to their considered assessment of the situation, but first other recent psychological research indicating positive consequences of Internet anonymity are related.

Positive Effects of Anonymity

In the social and personality psychology literature, less research has been done on the positive effects that may result from anonymous communication on the Internet and anonymous communication in general. In part, this lack of research stems from the fact that, prior to the advent of the Internet, anonymous interpersonal communication between individuals (as opposed to individuals interacting as a part of a larger group) tended to occur mainly in fleeting, relatively impersonal exchanges (e.g., conversations with one's unknown seatmate on an airplane or a train, polite—or not so polite—exchanges with the latest telemarketer). Such interactions are generally limited to a one-time occurrence and are of short duration. By contrast, on the Internet, people are commonly communicating with others over time behind the shroud of anonymity.

Deindividuation, as through anonymity, does not by itself produce negative behavior. Rather, it decreases the influence of internal (i.e., self) standards of or guides to behavior, and increases the power of external, situational cues (Johnson & Downing, 1979). If those external cues are associated with negative and antisocial behavior, such as Ku Klux Klan hoods, behavior will be negative (Zimbardo, 1970), but if those same hoods are portrayed as those worn by recovery room nurses, the resultant behavior of the person hidden under it is more positive than normal (Johnson & Downing, 1979). A classic example of the positive effects of anonymity is a study by Gergen, Gergen, and Barton (1973), in which individuals who met and conversed in a situation where they could not see one another, sitting in the dark, disclosed much more intimate details of their lives and of the self than did those who met and conversed in a lighted room. Indeed, those who were in the darkened condition left the encounter feeling more positively about the other person, compared to a control condition in which people interacted with the lights on.

Communicating with another via the Internet is much like being in a darkened room in that one cannot see the other person, nor can one be seen. The relative anonymity of Internet communication may allow individuals to take greater risks in making disclosures to their Internet friends than they would with someone they met in a more traditional, nonymous setting. Under the protective cloak of anonymity users can express the way they truly feel and think (Spears & Lea, 1994). If individuals do share more intimate confidences and do so earlier in a potential Internet relationship than in a potential real-life one, Internet relationships should develop intimacy and closeness more quickly than do offline relationships. As is discussed in a later section, this does seem to be the case.

The assurance of anonymity gives one far greater play in identity construction than is conceivable in face-to-face encounters. One can, for instance, change one's gender, one's way of relating to others, and literally everything about oneself. Even those who do not log in from an anonymous account experience almost as much freedom in identity construction. On the Internet, where one can be anonymous, where one does not deal in face-to-face interactions, where one is simply responding to other anonymous people, the roles and characters one maintains for family, friends, and associates can be cast aside. One very important and interesting direction for future research, then, concerns the implications of this greater freedom in identity construction for the individual. As Turkle (1995) argued, the Internet provides a kind of experimental laboratory in which one can try out various possible selves (Markus & Nurius, 1986) and different roles in a safe and risk-free manner. Would doing so increase self-knowledge, or enable better perspective taking ability for other groups or roles (e.g., a man portraying himself as a woman, and being treated as one, in a chat room or news group)?

Role identity. Individuals define themselves, and are defined by others, by the social roles that they perform (see Burke, 1980; Burke & Tully, 1977; Stryker & Statham, 1985). Considerable research has shown that those individuals who claim multiple roles or aspects of self (i.e., a woman who feels that she is a good wife and mother, is successful professionally, a wonderful gardener, etc.) enjoy many more benefits than do those who have only a few defining identities. Sarbin and Allen (1968), for instance, observed that people who have a larger number of self-defining identities are better prepared to face changes and stresses in life. The "role rich" also experience better health (Linville, 1985; Verbrugge, 1983, 1986) and greater satisfaction with their lives (Spreitzer, Snyder, & Larson, 1979).

Furthermore, other lines of research have shown that it is quite difficult for a person to effect changes in his or her self-concept when the surrounding social environment (i.e., one's network of acquaintances, colleagues, family, and friends) remains static. When an individual attempts to make such changes, his or her peers may be unwilling to accept, acknowledge, and provide validation for these new self-aspects, and unless and until they do so, the new role or identity does not become real for the individual (Gollwitzer, 1986). Moreover, features of one's physical appearance (e.g., gender, age, weight, race) are strongly associated with social categories, roles, and stereotypes (e.g., Bargh, 1994; Brewer, 1988) in the perceiver's mind, and so additionally constrain one's ability to successfully adopt alternative roles or personalities.

Changes in self-esteem, therefore, are most likely to coincide with catastrophic changes in one's social environment such as moving to a new city, going off to college, or changing jobs (Harter, 1993; Ruble, 1994). As has been previously noted, when an individual begins to take part in the social outlets on the Internet (e.g., newsgroups, MUDs, and chat rooms), he or she is acquiring a new peer group that has no ties to his or her offline social group. Thus, interacting with others on the Internet may provide individuals with the opportunity to successfully implement wished for changes in their self-concept, and indeed this has been found to occur and to result in increased feelings of self-worth and acceptance (McKenna & Bargh, 1998, Studies 2–3).

The Internet provides the opportunity for individuals to engage in greater identity and role construction than is possible in the non-Internet world. The identities an individual is able to express and to claim are all, to some extent, constrained by that person's current roles and relationships (Stryker & Statham, 1985). That is, others have certain expectations about the way one will behave and the kinds of identities that one should express based on the roles they perceive one to fill. On the Internet, however, an individual is in effect gaining a new peer group that is unrelated to those he or she knows in the non-Internet world. The members of this new Internet peer group have no prior conceptions or expectations about the kinds of identities or roles to which this person should adhere. Starting out as a blank slate, the individual is then free to construct him or herself in any number of different ways. As Turkle (1995) pointed out, the Internet offers an alternative playground for testing out personality and identity aspects with no fallout for the individual.

This ability to carve out different identities or roles may be particularly important for those who are role poor (i.e., they have few self-defining roles and identities) and for those who feel that important aspects of their identity are constrained in the relationships they maintain in the non-Internet world. People have a need to present their true or inner self to the outside world and to have others know them as they know themselves (e.g., Gollwitzer, 1986; McKenna & Bargh, 1998; Swann, 1983). When an individual is unable to do this in his or her current relationships, there is likely to be a strong motivation to establish relationships in which those needs and preferences can be expressed and accepted. The Internet makes it much easier for an individual to establish such new relationships and express these important aspects of identity without the risk of upsetting the balance of their offline relationships. We therefore expect to observe a great deal of the taking on of inner personae in Internet social interactions.

Numerous case studies demonstrate that individuals do indeed engage in a great deal of role playing and the expression of multiple identities on the Internet (e.g., Rheingold, 1993; Turkle, 1995). In a survey and in in-depth interviews hundreds of Internet participants described how they try on different personalities and aspects of personality on the Internet that they feel are closed to them in their non-Internet relationships and situations (McKenna, 1998). What is not yet known are what possible consequences may result from such expression of multiple roles and identities online. For example, do individuals who express multiple roles and self-aspects on the Internet experience the same benefits of better health, greater life satisfaction, and the ability to better deal with stressful life changes as do those who can do the same in the non-Internet realm? Under what conditions are individuals motivated or willing to incorporate their online identities into their offline world?

In stressing the potential positive effects of anonymity for the expression and development of possible selves, one must also consider the potential negative consequences. For example, if the various aspects of self are not well integrated, there is the possibility of a loss of coherent sense of self, such as in split or multiple personalities (e.g., Donahue, Robins, Roberts, & John, 1993). Fantasy selves may become well developed under safe, online circumstances but without experience in dealing with the possibly negative or distancing reactions that could well occur in real life if such a self were to be expressed. Finally, there is the clear possibility that rewarding experiences with a fantasy online self may become decompartmentalized: generalized to the offline or real world, causing, in the worst case, delusions and unrealistic behavior. (One is reminded of the perhaps apocryphal story of actor George Reeves, who played Superman on the television series, and who jumped to his death from a tall building under the delusion that he really could fly.) The Internet creates a powerful virtual realm in which to experiment with one's self-concept, but the ultimate effects of such experimentation are uncharted territory at present; just as with similar experimentation on the self through use of mind altering drugs in the 1960s, one should proceed with caution. The consequences of persona tryout on the Internet for self-understanding and emotional and mental health is a critically important domain for further research.

Marginalized social identities. The ability to engage in anonymous interactions on the Internet allows individuals to explore aspects of identity and to interact with members of socially sanctioned groups, such as lesbians and gay men or fringe political groups. The most popular method of participating in these groups on the Internet is through newsgroups, in which a person can post their thoughts or feelings for others to read and perhaps reply, within what is called a *topical thread* (see McKenna & Bargh, 1998).

Over 30,000 of these newsgroups on often quite specialized topics and interests now exist, and many concern mainstream and nonstigmatized issues and topics, such as parenting and coin collecting. However, the existence of these groups has proved especially important for individuals who possess concealable stigmatized identities (see Frable, 1993), for whom finding others in real life who share this self-aspect can be difficult, if not impossible. Due to the fact that those with concealable stigmatized identities tend to do just that—conceal the identity at all costs —it is difficult to identify them in society (Frable, 1993), and the potentially embarrassing nature of the identity and fear of the possible consequences of disclosure keep these people from seeking out similar others.

However, under the protective cloak of anonymity on the Internet, individuals can admit to having marginalized or nonmainstream proclivities that they must hide from the rest of the world. Through newsgroups and other venues (Web sites, listservs, and chat rooms) they can find others who share the marginalized identity. By doing so, these individuals are able to reap (for the first time and in the only way possible to them) the considerable benefits of joining a group of similar others (McKenna & Bargh, 1998): feeling less isolated and different, disclosing a long-held secret part of one's identity, and gaining emotional and motivational support (see Archer, 1987; Derlega, Metts, Petronio, & Margulis, 1993; Jones et al., 1984). It was found that active participation in newsgroups (as opposed to passive lurking by reading posts and not contributing oneself) that were concerned with marginalized aspects of identity caused the individual to eventually bring the concealed identities into the open, telling his or her family and friends about it for the first time.

Pennebaker (1989, 1990) found that revealing previously concealed and perhaps shameful aspects of oneself in an experimental session significantly reduced reported health symptoms in a long-term follow-up, even when the confession was entirely anonymous. The parallels between Pennebaker's "confessional" research and the anonymity of Internet newsgroups and chat rooms are obvious. Therefore, would the same benefits of increased health accompany such disclosures if they are made anonymously in a virtual setting?

The downside. As McKenna and Bargh (1998) concluded, what may be beneficial for the individual in terms of self-expression may not be so for society at large. This would certainly seem to be the case for newsgroups and Web sites devoted to the hatred of other ethnic or racial groups, and for the advocation of violence against others (see Clausing, 1999). Not only are one's negative social beliefs reinforced by the positive feedback and support given by others of similar mind but also there is a reasoning fallacy perhaps unique to the Internet that may be termed the *illusion of large numbers*. For example, the fact that 4,000 people visit a particular Web site or subscribe to a given news group seems like a lot of similar others because they are experienced to be at the same place in virtual space (see next section), just as if those 4,000 people showed up in the local park. However, in terms of the actual percentage of Internet users this number represents far less than a tenth of 1%. The result is that individuals may come to grossly overestimate how many other people share their views, and fail to realize just how different and unusual are their beliefs from the mainstream.

Summary. The anonymity of Internet communication is a special and important difference between it and other forms of social interaction. Although some individuals hide behind it to propagate hate, for many others it is a liberating mode of communication, especially where social or government sanctions exist for the expression of those ideas or beliefs. The Internet seems to be a powerful means by which individuals can overcome totalitarian governments' control over communication media, and through which people can gain social support for stigmatized or embarrassing aspects of their identity. At the aforementioned AAAS conference on the consequences and effects of Internet anonymity, the organization's directory of science and policy programs concluded that "while there are clearly ways [anonymity] can be misused, the beneficial uses outweigh the negative uses" (Mendels, 1999, p. 1), and the overall recommendation of the conference participants was that governments not attempt to restrict the anonymity of Internet communication (Frankel & Teich, 1999).

Turning the Tables on Attraction

Considerable research has shown that physical appearance plays a major role in determining whether a relationship will even start between two people. If initial attraction is not there, that is often the end of the story (Hatfield, Aronson, Abrahams, & Rottman, 1966)—not only for potential intimate relationships but also for possible friendships as well (Hatfield & Sprecher, 1986).

On the Internet, however, physical attractiveness cannot be assessed, at least initially. Due to the fact that one cannot see the interaction partner, physical appearance does not stop potential relationships from getting off the ground. Liking, attraction, and friendship on the Internet, therefore, must be based on different grounds, such as similarity, values, and interests, or an engaging conversational style. As these are also powerful determinants of friendship and attraction (Byrne, 1971; Byrne, Clore, & Smeaton, 1986), the Internet may foster the formation of relationships that never would have begun in real life. In fact, relationships formed at these deeper levels may be more durable and important to the individual than those that form based on more superficial physical features, and this is another important issue for further research.

Self-Presentational Consequences of Anonymity and Lack of Physical Cues

Tice, Butler, Muraven, and Stillwell (1995) found that when two strangers meet for the first time and the meeting takes place in the absence of any other friends or acquaintances, they tend to behave with less modesty. That is, they tend to present more of their ideal self-qualities to strangers than they do to their friends. The presence of a friend at the meeting provoked more modest self-presentation. Thus, when the information presented had little chance of being called into question by another person, the tendency was to present an idealized version of self.

When interacting with unknown others on the Internet, individuals also present idealized versions of self. McKenna and Bargh (1999a, Study 2) conducted a laboratory study comparing stranger dyads who communicated either face to face or in an Internet chat room. Those who interacted on the Internet were able to more successfully present their ideal qualities (i.e., those attributes the individual would ideally like to possess) than were those who interacted face to face. When the paired participants were asked to assess one another at the end of the study, they described their partners more in terms of that partner's previously reported ideal self than his or her reported actual self. Those who interacted face to face, on the other hand, provided assessments that dovetailed with the partner's reported actual self. Thus, it seems that on the Internet people are indeed seen as they wish to be seen.

The Internet would seem to open up new and high-quality possibilities for individuals who have the self-presentational motive of "constructing a certain image of self and claiming an identity for oneself" (Baumeister, 1998, p. 704). For instance, those individuals for whom the ideal self is an important self-guide (see Higgins, 1987) will be highly motivated to incorporate these ideal attributes into the actual self. For this to happen, however, an individual must make these attributes a "social reality" (Baumeister, 1998; Gollwitzer, 1986). That is, an individual feels the need to have these attributes acknowledged and affirmed by others before he or she can feel fully convinced that he or she really possesses these ideal qualities. Such an individual is therefore quite likely to adopt a self-presentational strategy that highlights these attributes. As McKenna and Bargh (1999a, Study 2) showed, they are going to have greater success gaining the needed affirmation and acknowledgment through their Internet interactions than they will through face-to-face interactions. Social feedback has been shown to have a great impact on whether or not an individual will be able to succeed in changing his or her self-concept (Harter, 1993; Heatherton & Nichols, 1994).

Liking and Attraction

McKenna and Bargh (1999a, Study 3) found that in first-time encounters an individual will be liked better if the encounter takes place in an Internet chat room than if the two strangers were to meet face to face. Furthermore, this greater liking continued to hold (and indeed significantly increased for those who had first met on the Internet) after the interaction partners met a second time, this time in person. That is, those who first met on the Internet and then talked face to face liked one another more than did those who met face to face in both encounters. Even when participants thought that they had met two different people, one on the Internet and one face to face, they significantly liked the person they talked with on the Internet better: In actuality, these participants had talked with the same person both times.

What causes this increased liking and attraction when people meet on the Internet rather than face to face? Is it simply because physical appearance and nonverbal cues are absent and thus more attention and importance is placed on what the other person says than the way the other person looks? Research has long shown, of course, that first impressions are critical to subsequent interactions and that people are reluctant to change their initial assessment even when presented with new information (Asch, 1946; Belmore, 1987; Higgins & Bargh, 1987). Thus, one may speculate, if physical appearance does not interfere with initial liking and so a positive impression is formed, then once Internet interaction partners meet in person and physical appearance does come into play, it may carry far less weight. However, other factors may contribute or cause this increased liking—for example, the greater intimacy and consequent liking established through self-disclosure (Collins & Miller, 1994) due to the relative anonymity of the Internet relative to the face-to-face initial meeting. Teasing apart the causes for liking and attraction on the Internet will tell us not only about how and why Internet relationships form but also a great deal about the role played by physical attraction for relationships in general.

The Shared Virtual Space of the Internet (The Negation of Physical Proximity)

A considerable body of research has demonstrated that people are much more likely to begin relationships with others who are regularly in close physical proximity, and far less likely to do so with those who are even a short additional distance away (Festinger, 1950; Hays, 1984, 1985; Segal, 1974; Whitbeck &

Hoyt, 1994). Similarly, Brockner and Swap (1976) found that the more a person had seen, but not interacted with, another person, the more likely he or she was to initiate an interaction. Berscheid and Reis (1998) noted that familiarity is the most basic determinant of attraction.

When taking part in social gathering places on the Internet (e.g., newsgroups, chat rooms, and MUDs) a person cannot physically see the other people present, but he or she nonetheless becomes familiar with these people through their nicknames, e-mail addresses, or character names. If one regularly joins a particular chat room or news group, one will begin to notice others who frequently post messages or pop in to chat and in turn will be noticed by others. The mere exposure effect (Zajonc, 1968) would predict that repeatedly being exposed to these Internet personae, perhaps even by just seeing their names again and again in the list of posters, will lead to positive feelings about the person behind the name. Despite the fact that these people may live on the far corners of the earth, when they are all gathered in this shared virtual space they may well be perceived and experienced as being in much closer proximity. After all, people often talk about how they get together to chat in a chat room, and use phrases such as "when I am in the MUD with my friends" as if they were all in one physical locality.

Research has shown that we tend to be more attracted to those who are similar to us and who share our opinions (Byrne, 1971; Newcomb, 1961). Indeed, even within married couples the more similar two people are the more compatible they are (Houts, Robins, & Huston, 1996) and the more likely they are to remain married (Byrne, 1997). When individuals begin to get to know one another in the traditional way, however (i.e., not via the Internet), it generally takes some time for them to establish if they have anything in common and to what extent. Hill, Rubin, and Peplau (1976) followed more than 200 dating couples who stated that they were "in love" for a period of 2 years. By the end of the 2 years, nearly 50% of the couples had broken up and the main reason given for the breakup was that they discovered that they had, in fact, different interests and attitudes.

On the Internet, however, the unique structure of newsgroups and Internet relay chat allows individuals to easily find others who share highly specialized interests. There may be, for example, 50,000 people in the world who share one's special passion, but these people are scattered across all five continents and dispersed among over 5 billion human beings. The Internet enables all of them (who have connections to the Internet) to come together in the same virtual space, transcending the problems of physical distance and wide dispersion, and of finding each other. Espe-

cially in more rural areas, if it were not for the Internet many people would never have the opportunity to share these important interests and passions with another person.

Thus, when a person enters a chat channel devoted to discussions about exotic butterfly collecting, he or she is already aware of sharing a base of knowledge and interest with the others who are on the channel. This allows them to cut to the chase (so to speak). They do not have to spend time discovering if they have any interests in common with the other participants, but rather can move quickly forward to find out what other key interests they may share. As one person who took part in a series of in-depth interviews put it:

> It seems to be easier to recognize who is similar to you and who you'll like on the net. Maybe this is because chat rooms and newsgroups are more personalized (i.e. the "golf room" or "ferret lovers") and so you come into the room knowing you have something in common. (McKenna, 1998, p. 57)

A Time and Pace Unlike Face to Face

The timing and the pacing of social exchanges on the Internet differ from face-to-face and telephone interactions in several ways. First of all, it is not necessary for the other person to be online at the same time for a conversation to take place. Rather than having to engage in a groggy telephone conversation in the middle of the night to reach a friend who lives overseas, for instance, one can simply send an e-mail before going to bed and a reply is likely to be waiting in the morning. It is not unusual when engaging in an exchange via e-mail to wait minutes, hours, or days to receive the next piece in the conversation.

Unlike conversations that take place in person or on the telephone that require immediate and spontaneous responses, an individual can take as much time as he or she needs to respond to another person on the Internet. In an e-mail message or newsgroup post, individuals are able to carefully select what they want to say and how they want to say it. They can change and edit their messages before sending them. In contrast, in verbal exchanges, as soon as someone opens his or her mouth the cat is out of the bag and cannot, at least not easily, be put back in.

Finally, in electronic exchanges, a person can "hold the floor" to an extent quite unusual in verbal conversations. Relatively short explanations are the norm in spoken conversations and people often interrupt one another in midsentence. In e-mail or a newsgroup post, however, an individual can say as much or as little about a subject as he or she pleases, without fear of interruption before being able to fully make his or her point (McKenna, 1998). (This is not to say that the individual always takes advantage of the relative lack of time pressure in making one's points; although the person has greater control over the timing and the expression of content in such Internet communications, another operating force is the anonymity of the communication [see earlier], which can cause the individual to feel more free to react quickly and sometimes angrily, as in "flamewars.")

These differences in timing and pacing provide an individual with a great deal more control over his or her side of a conversation. This higher degree of control, coupled with anonymity, seems to contribute to individuals taking greater risks and chances with making self-disclosures to those with whom they talk on the Internet compared to real life (McKenna, 1998). Moreover, as individuals begin to incorporate their Internet relationships into their non-Internet lives, they engage in a presence-control exchange. That is, they start the relationship from a position of relatively high control over their side of the encounter (via e-mail), and gradually, as their comfort level and greater knowledge of the other person increases, exchange or trade that control gradually for physical closeness in a series of stages (McKenna, 1998).

This seems to be the Internet equivalent of the progression of real-life relationships from superficial acquaintances to close and even intimate relationships, which, according to Altman and Taylor's (1973) social penetration theory, occurs when individuals trade acts of self-disclosure with each other. As real-life relationships develop, the disclosures become more revealing and personal and cover a wider area of each other's lives. The partners are exchanging sensitive information in a gradual way because of their mutual vulnerability. In the same way, on the Internet people tend to trade control over the interaction for greater physical reality of the relationship. Their first offline step is either to write a letter by mail or talk on the telephone. Those who exchange letters then move on to telephone conversations. Only after telephone contact has been made are individuals likely to take the final step of meeting in person (McKenna, 1998).

Individual Differences: Who Is More Likely to Go to the Net?

As mentioned earlier, the Internet does not affect everyone in the same way. People vary as to what goals they have, or needs to be met, while using the Internet. In this focus on social interaction and relationship formation, the question becomes: Who will be more likely than others to seek out interactions and to form relationships with others on the Internet?

Social Anxiety

Forging social connections is quite difficult for those individuals who experience high levels of anxiety when in social situations (see Leary, 1983; Leary & Kowalski, 1995). Those who become anxious when meeting new people, talking to individuals they find attractive, or engaging in social group activities (e.g., parties or work-related social affairs), may be barred from the benefits of close personal relationships and group membership. Their basic needs for belonging and intimacy (Baumeister & Leary, 1995; Brewer, 1991) may therefore go unmet. On the Internet, however, many of the situational factors that foster feelings of social anxiety (e.g., talking to someone face to face, having to respond on the spot with verbal exchanges) are absent. Socially anxious individuals may thus be motivated to turn to the Internet as a means through which they can make social connections and meet these needs. Due to the absence of many of the anxiety-enhancing factors that exist in face-to-face interactions, they may then find it easier to form relationships on the Internet.

Indeed, recent research (McKenna & Bargh, 1999a, Study 1) has found that social anxiety is a strong predictor of who will be likely to form Internet relationships. Those who scored highly on the Interaction Anxiousness Scale (Leary, 1983) were found to be significantly more likely than their more socially comfortable counterparts to form relationships with others via the Internet. Moreover, socially anxious individuals were more likely to have formed very close Internet friendships and romantic relationships as opposed to weaker relationships (e.g., acquaintanceships).

What is not yet known, however, is whether the formation of such close relationships in the "virtual" realm will have the downstream results of lessening feelings of social anxiety in the offline realm. It may be that the successful formation of relationships in an online setting will lead to increases in the individual's feelings of self-confidence and self-efficacy. He or she may then become more confident of his or her social abilities when placed in face-to-face settings. As one participant who took part in a series of in-depth interviews (McKenna, 1998) stated

> I used to be a complete disaster when it came to talking with women. In fact, I was so nervous about it that I would go to great lengths to avoid having to meet or talk with them, especially if I found them pretty or intelligent. On the Internet I discovered that talking with women was much easier and not only that, many of

them seemed to really like me, found me humorous, and sought *me* out to talk to. I have become so much more confident with women and not just on-line. (p. 85)

Concluding that the Internet is a positive source of interactions for those who are socially anxious as a means for overcoming anxiety in meeting people assumes that the individual is still trying (and perhaps often failing) to interact with people in real life, outside of the Internet. As the McKenna and Bargh (1998) and McKenna (1998) research showed, in general people are motivated to bring their newly gained Internet identities and relationships into their real-life world. However, it may prove too seductive for some, perhaps the most socially anxious individuals, to escape the trauma of real-life interactions almost entirely, and live their entire social life on the Internet (see Green & Brock, 1998). Again, here is an important avenue for further Internet social research: Is it the case that for some set of identifiable individuals (e.g., extremely socially anxious) under certain circumstances the Internet becomes an escape from real-life interactions, with the consequence that these individuals do withdraw from their offline social sphere?

Loneliness

Although socially anxious individuals are often also lonely, it is also the case that there are many individuals who are lonely but not socially anxious. In some cases, loneliness may be a temporary condition, occasioned perhaps by changing jobs or moving to a new city. In others, it may be more chronic (e.g., for the homebound, for single working mothers with small children and little or no time left over for socializing). Loneliness is another individual difference that predicts who will form online relationships (McKenna & Bargh, 1999a, Study 1). The Internet would seem to be double edged when it comes to loneliness; lonely people may meet others over the Internet and so decrease their degree of loneliness, but protracted time on the Internet necessarily takes time away from one's existing, non-Internet relationships and could thus impact those, thus increasing loneliness eventually for some individuals (Kraut, Patterson, et al., 1998). This is an important set of issues about the Internet that needs further research. Another critical question concerns the quality of relationships that currently lonely people form on the Internet, and their duration and quality.

Relationship Formation on the Internet

The culmination of these various forces can be found in data on the formation of acquaintanceships, friendships, and even intimate relationships on the Internet. Due to the greater anonymity, differences in self-presentation, lack of physical gating features that prevent people from getting to know each other better, the fact that physical distance is no longer a barrier to meeting someone, and that the virtual shared space of the Internet brings together far-flung individuals with core shared interests and passions, one may expect the Internet to be a fertile ground for the formation and establishment of relationships. It is indeed that (McKenna, 1998; Parks & Floyd, 1995; Parks & Roberts, 1998). Parks and Roberts (1998), for example, found that 94% of surveyed participants in online text-based games had formed close friendships or romantic relationships with other players. A separate survey conducted with 600 randomly selected news group participants also showed that the formation of strong relationships is quite common on the Internet, with 51% reporting that they had formed close friendships and 35% that they had forged romantic relationships with others on the Internet (McKenna, 1998). It is important to note that, fully 79% of the survey respondents considered their Internet relationships to be as close, as real, and as important as their non-Internet relationships.

Two conclusions should be drawn from the aforementioned. First, far from being solely a cause of loneliness and isolation, people can and do use the Internet to meet others with similar interests and values, and get to know them in a safe environment at their own preferred pace. Second, these relationships are not of lesser quality than real-life relationships; instead, they become real-life relationships. People tend to bring their Internet friends and romantic interests into their real life by talking on the telephone, exchanging pictures and letters, eventually meeting many of them in person, and in many cases moving in with them. It is too early in the Internet game to tell, but it is possible that relationships formed on the Internet are deeper, more stable and lasting than those formed in the real-world environment in which physical attractiveness and proximity are such powerful constraining and determining forces. We believe this will be an important question for relationship research in the near future.

Methodological Techniques for Internet Research

How does one go about researching the psychology of the Internet? There are several ways to study social interactions and the other psychological phenomena previously discussed, such as conducting surveys within newsgroups, interviewing people "live" in chat rooms, analyzing readily available archival records of newsgroup posts, qualitative research (e.g., intensive interviews, case histories), and even laboratory experiments. Each of these approaches are later described, but before doing so it is emphasized that each single technique has both strengths and weaknesses. For instance, there may well be a self-selection problem with survey responses, but if a laboratory experiment with random selection and assignment to condition produces converging evidence, this helps to rule out the possible confound. Similarly, it may be problematic to generalize from the behavior of introductory psychology students in a subject pool to Internet users (of all ages), but if broadband surveys and qualitative interviews produce converging evidence, one can feel more comfortable in generalizing from the more controlled laboratory study. Thus, we recommend a metamethodological strategy of "triangulation" in which one uses a variety of approaches in testing a given hypothesis when studying social and psychological phenomena on the Internet.

Natural Experiments and Archival Research

The Internet presents a unique opportunity to study individuals and groups as they interact in a naturalistic setting, without the intrusive presence of a researcher. One can test hypotheses about the behavior of the group or the individual given certain events or occurrences by observing and coding the verbal content of chat room responses or newsgroup posts. For example, in Study 1 of McKenna and Bargh (1998), the hypothesis that the posting frequency of individuals in a particular newsgroup would be affected by the feedback of other group members was tested (i.e., more posting if positive feedback, less if negative), but only if membership in the newsgroup was important to the individual's social identity. Each post was coded over several weeks in terms of the positivity or negativity of the posts of others responding to it, and then the number of subsequent posts by that individual over the next month was counted. Another useful feature of the Internet is that it enables the easy collection of data on individuals' or groups' reactions to naturally occurring historical events, such as the death of John F. Kennedy, Jr., or the war in Kosovo.

One need not wait for events to happen, or wait weeks or months while data is being collected, because there exist archives of newsgroup posts. There is a wealth of data available on the Internet through the DejaNews archive (http://www.dejanews.com). This archive contains hundreds of thousands of posted messages dating back to Spring 1995 and conveniently or-

ganized by the newsgroup, date, and time the article was originally posted. Additionally, these archives are searchable. One can thus find all posts that have been written on a particular topic, by a specific author, or (within a specific newsgroup) that were contributed within a particular time frame. Internet chat rooms can also be studied by logging the publicly made comments (but not those conversations that are being privately made between participants in a chat room through what is called personal messaging) contributed to specific Internet chat rooms; logging chat room conversations is a feature of standard and readily available software needed to access and participate in chat rooms.

It can be argued that because of the anonymity afforded by the Internet, one may gain an understanding of people's real goals, ideas, and behaviors, unmuddied by demand effects that can occur when an individual is aware of being under study, or by self-presentational concerns when his or her public responses are not anonymous. However, it could be counterargued that precisely because of the reduced concern with social sanctions afforded by anonymity, the individual will exert less effort or control over the communication, and so it may be more affected by temporary states such as mood, emotion, or recent experience (e.g., priming effects) and so be less, not more representative of the person's true attitudes and beliefs. The very existence of stable and decontextualized true attitudes is a complex and controversial issue in itself (e.g., Wilson, in press), one beyond the scope of this article; nevertheless, the possibility that Internet communications may be a more accurate or bona fide source of individuals' opinions and beliefs is certainly deserving of further research scrutiny.

Surveys

There are several reasons why one may want to conduct a survey over the Internet. First, one may be interested in studying the characteristics, beliefs, behaviors, and so on of Internet users as such, and it is clearly easier to find them on the Internet than by first having to ask many more people over the telephone or through the mails if they use the Internet. More interestingly, the Internet provides an excellent venue for cross-cultural research, because it obviates the need to travel or to be personally located in each of the countries or cultures studied (also greatly reducing the expenses of such research). By the same token, findings of Internet surveys in general are not as restricted to a given culture or country given that Internet users are worldwide (although one must keep track of respondents' nationalities as the majority of

Internet users at present are North American). This being said, one must take steps to ensure that survey respondents are representative of the country or culture being studied. In many countries today, Internet users are mainly academics or the wealthier citizens. (This is changing, however, with more and more of the general population coming online daily.) Dealing with the problem of sample representativeness is one of several difficulties and disadvantages associated with Internet surveys that is discussed in the next section in the context of each of the Internet venues in which surveys can be conducted (newsgroups, chat rooms, and MUDs).

To conduct survey research on the Internet, one must first identify the population to be studied. Users of newsgroups, chat rooms, and MUDs may differ in important ways from each another and from the average Internet user. For example, if one wishes to generalize findings to the Internet population as a whole, it would be unwise to conduct a survey of just those participants who use MUDs, as they tend to be much younger than the average Internet user and to enjoy cloak and dagger role play. On the other hand, MUD users are an excellent population to study if one is interested in phenomena such as gender bending, fantasy and motivation, and role playing. Therefore, it is recommended to go beyond the notion of the average Internet user and focus instead on the particular Internet communication mode of interest, and if one does wish to generalize across all of these modes, to include each (or at least several) of them in the study, along with a non-Internet control group.

Newsgroups. If one wants to study newsgroups in general (as opposed to groups with a particular content focus, such as parenting or a sports team), then the first step is to randomly select from the population of available newsgroups. There are currently more than 30,000 Internet newsgroups available on the Internet. However, not every Internet provider (e.g., AOL™, Freenets, university servers) gives access to a complete listing of all newsgroups. Providers differ in the kinds and number of newsgroups one can view (e.g., some providers block newsgroups that are not considered suitable for children). One may therefore wish to obtain lists of available newsgroups from two or more servers prior to selecting which newsgroups to study.

Newsgroups themselves often differ in terms of user composition and the kinds of posts that are contributed to them. Some newsgroups are comprised almost entirely of advertisements (called *spam* in the Internet vernacular). It is also often difficult to tell from the subject header of a post if it is a message posted by a legitimate member of that newsgroup or by an advertiser. Newsgroups in the alternative hierarchy are particularly targeted by spammers and many newsgroups have been completely abandoned by their members because of the pervasiveness of the advertisements. Other newsgroups (including many of those in the society or social hierarchy) consist mainly of messages that are simultaneously posted to a large number of different newsgroups at once (called *cross posts*). The replies to the original message (called *threads*) can originate from members in any of the different groups in which it was posted, so that within a particular newsgroup the replies to threads can come from people who have never looked at the particular newsgroup one is studying. Massively cross-posted messages and spam may give the illusion that a particular newsgroup is used by many members who actively post, when the opposite is actually the case. Therefore, when selecting newsgroups to survey—particularly if one is studying group dynamics, social identity, or social interaction processes on the Internet—it is a good rule of thumb to select those groups in which at least 50% of the posts are "on topic" (i.e., made by the members of that particular newsgroup and posted only to that newsgroup).

Once the newsgroups to be studied have been identified and prior to electronically mailing surveys to their members, a message should be posted in each of the selected newsgroups briefly describing the study, informing participants that surveys will be sent out to randomly selected members of that newsgroup and that participation is entirely voluntary. Following Internet etiquette (known, naturally, as *netiquette*) in this way helps to increase response rates and decrease the chances that members will view one's e-mail to them as unsolicited spam. To further increase incentive for participation (and honesty of responses), participants should be informed that results from the study will be made available to them at the conclusion of the study, either directly through e-mail or through posting the results on a specified Web site. Particularly when studying members of groups that are marginalized by society (e.g., lesbians, gay men, epileptics), a researcher may need to take great pains to assure participants that he or she is conducting a legitimate scientific study and that the purpose of the study is not to present these individuals as abnormal or in a negative light (see McKenna & Bargh, 1998, Studies 2 and 3).

Newsgroups may contain hundreds and even thousands of posts each day, so it may not be practical to include all group members in one's survey. One may therefore wish to randomly select a subset of members. When a person contributes a post to a news group, his or her e-mail address appears in the header of the post. Participants can thus be randomly selected (e.g., mailing the survey to every fifth poster). Again to increase response rates, surveys should be sent singly to each participant, not as a carbon copy (or "cc") or as a group mailing; although doing it this way is more time consuming, recipients are less likely to respond if they are treated as just one person in a large group. (They also feel that their responses are more important to the study.) Researchers should be aware that spam is increasingly being sent not only to newsgroups but also to people's e-mail addresses. Over the past few years this has had the unfortunate effect of lowering potential survey participants' willingness to cooperate with a study. Many people now view any unsolicited e-mail as spam and are quite likely to so categorize even a legitimate scientific survey. Under these circumstances, following the aforementioned steps has become even more important to attain a sufficient response rate.

Chat rooms and MUDs. To study chat rooms and MUDs, one first needs an access program (known as a *client*). There are many client software programs available; we recommend mIRC (http://www. greifswald-online.de/vccom/software/32bit.html). Using a client, one can connect to the various nets available (e.g., the Undernet, the Ethernet) and obtain a list of all the available chat rooms in operation at that time (generally several thousand). Each chat room will have an identifying name (e.g., *newbies*). The number of chat rooms vary by the minute as any user can create a temporary chat room at any time, but there are also permanent chat rooms. Some chat rooms are private and "invitation only," however, and researchers will not be able to enter those.

One can randomly select chat rooms to survey from the entire list available at that moment, or identify those chat rooms that revolve around a topic or group one is interested in studying and select from that subsidiary list. Once in a chat room one can see a list of all the participants in that particular room. (Note, however, that because chat rooms operate in real time, the time of day one studies the room matters a great deal as to the characteristics [e.g., age, nationality] of the people one will find there. At 11 a.m. on a school day, one will find few children and teenagers but this changes dramatically once school is out, and in the evenings. At 2 p.m. in New York one will find many Europeans but not at 10 p.m.; by 2 a.m., there are few New Yorkers but many Californians in the chat rooms, and so on.) Unlike in newsgroup posts, chat room users are not identified by their e-mail addresses but rather by a chosen nickname. One must, therefore, contact each potential participant (again, they should be randomly selected from the list of people in the room) with a private

message explaining that a survey is being conducted and asking him or her to provide an e-mail address if they are willing to participate. It is a good idea to simultaneously have a mail program open and to send the survey immediately after obtaining each participant's address, inserting the participant's nickname at the top of the survey.

Lists of MUDs that are currently in operation can be obtained via the World Wide Web (http://mudlist. eorbit.net/~mudlist/). Using telnet or, preferably, a MUD client (ZMUD is recommended, available at http://www.zuggsoft.com/zuggsoft/index.cfm), one can enter each of the MUDs selected for study from the MUD list by connecting to the given Internet address. In each MUD one must go through the character generation process and create a character before being able to obtain a list of those who are playing at that time. As with chats, MUD users are identified by the name of the character he or she is currently playing. It is not possible to obtain a list of all the players in a particular MUD, but only those players who are currently online. MUDs differ in the commands one needs to use to talk with other players or to obtain a list of those playing, although typing the word *who* will generally provide a list of the current players. Each MUD has a list of help files providing information on the social mores of the MUD and commands to use and it is strongly recommended that these help files be read prior to contacting any potential participants. (It should be noted that a growing trend in many MUDs is to do away with the "who" command so that one is not able to detect what players are currently online, to increase the sense of realism within the MUD.) As with the chat room users, a researcher should plan on approaching each MUD user separately to explain the study and to obtain his or her e-mail address.

A note on participant observation. When conducting surveys on the Internet it is often beneficial to participate for a while oneself in some of the newsgroups, chat rooms, or MUDs selected for study. Taking part in the groups under study aids in gaining the trust of the members of the group, and can substantially increase response rates. This potential gain must be weighed against some negatives, however, when deciding whether or not to participate. First of all, one must be careful not to influence or otherwise affect the responses participants may make to the survey by one's own postings and contribution to the group. This possibility can be checked to some extent by comparing survey results between groups in which one did versus did not participate.

A second problem is ethical. For instance, to increase the near-zero initial survey response rate in the study of conspiracy and White supremacist newsgroups (McKenna & Bargh, 1998, Study 3), participation took place for a time to convince group members researchers were not government law enforcement officers. The participation significantly increased the response rate to a respectable final 34%. In doing so, any statements making or expressing agreement with racist remarks were avoided, but instead only statements neutral in tone and content were contributed, usually on neutral group discussion topics.

Experimental (Laboratory) Studies

There is no reason that the Internet cannot be studied under the controlled conditions of the experimental laboratory. This approach to the study of the social and personality aspects of the Internet has all of the traditional advantages of controlled experiments—random assignment of individuals to conditions, the inclusion of control conditions to rule out alternative explanations, and so forth. All that is needed are computers in the experimental rooms with separate direct connections to the Internet. This enables one, for example, to study behavior within chat rooms by logging each participant into the same chat room. One could compare relationship formation in chat rooms to real life in this way, by having pairs of participants meet initially one way or the other, and then collect the outcome variables of interest (e.g., impressions of each other, degree of liking; McKenna, 1998). The important methodological point is that any manipulation that can be performed in a real-life or face-to-face social interaction or group behavior study can also be used to study the same phenomenon on the Internet. One could (explicitly or implicitly through priming) give participants expectations or interpersonal goals regarding the upcoming interaction, could manipulate participants' moods, and so on.

In-Depth Interviews

In-depth interviews of Internet users about their experiences, particularly when used in conjunction with one or more of the methodologies discussed previously, can provide valuable insight and rich data about the given phenomenon. Interviews enable more free responding than do preconfigured surveys and thereby provide information that surveys and the other data collection methods might miss. To give one example, it was not foreseen prior to conducting in-depth interviews that single working mothers with young children—because of their often extreme shortage of time for socializing outside of work and the home—would be prime candidates for turning to the Internet to make and maintain friendships and romantic relationships (McKenna & Bargh, 1999b). This interview finding was later confirmed through inclusion of questions concerning marital status and ages of children in an Internet survey (McKenna & Bargh, 1999a).

Conclusions

Plan 9 From Outer Space was Bela Lugosi's final movie (actually, he died while making it). Its rather simple plot was that aliens were trying to conquer the earth by turning freshly deceased humans into zombies that they could control by remote control (thanks to their advanced technology). What does this have to do with this article? Simply that the Internet does not, contrary to current popular opinion, have by itself the power or ability to control people, to turn them into addicted zombies, or make them dispositionally sad or lonely (or, for that matter, happy or popular), and neither does the telephone, or television, or movies. Rather, the Internet is one of several social domains in which an individual can live his or her life, and attempt to fulfill his or her needs and goals, whatever they happen to be (see McKenna & Bargh, 1999b).

We sought in the first part of this article to identify and highlight the key situational variables that make the Internet a unique and special social domain: anonymity, the mitigation of physical proximity, and physical attractiveness as gating features to relationship formation, and the enhanced personal control over the time and pacing of interpersonal interactions and communications. These are important situational variables but they do not operate in isolation, as main effects on all Internet users; rather, they have their effect in interaction with the individual's needs and purposes. So that is where Internet social research will be most profitably directed—toward identifying the critical individual differences that will mediate and moderate the Internet's powerful situational forces to determine whether the effect on the self, social identity, relationship formation and maintenance, social interactions, organizational functioning, and mental health will be positive and fulfilling or negative and destructive. Like the communications advances before it, the Internet will always and only be what individuals make of it.

References

Altman, I., & Taylor, D. A. (1973). *Social penetration: The development of interpersonal relationships.* New York: Holt, Rinehart & Winston.

Archer, R. L. (1987). Commentary: Self-disclosure, a very useful behavior. In V. L. Derlega & J. H. Berg (Eds.), *Self-disclosure: Theory, research, and therapy* (pp. 329–342). New York: Plenum.

Asch, S. E. (1946). Forming impressions of personality. *Journal of Abnormal and Social Psychology, 41,* 258–290.

Bargh, J. A. (1988). Automatic information processing: Implications for communication and affect. In L. Donohew, H. E. Sypher, & E. T. Higgins (Eds.), *Communication, social cognition, and affect* (pp. 9–32). Hillsdale, NJ: Lawrence Erlbaum Associates, Inc.

Bargh, J. A. (1994). The four horsemen of automaticity: Awareness, intention, efficiency and control in social cognition. In R. S. Wyer & T. K. Srull (Eds.), *Handbook of social cognition* (2nd ed., pp. 1–40). Hillsdale, NJ: Lawrence Erlbaum Associates, Inc.

Baumeister, R. F. (1998). The self. In D. T. Gilbert, S. T. Fiske, & G. Lindzey (Eds.), *Handbook of social psychology* (4th ed., pp. 680–740). New York: McGraw-Hill.

Baumeister, R. F., & Leary, M. R. (1995). The need to belong: Desire for interpersonal attachments as a fundamental human motivation. *Psychological Bulletin, 117,* 497–529.

Belmore, S. M. (1987). Determinants of attention during impression formation. *Journal of Experimental Psychology: Learning, Memory, and Cognition, 13,* 480–489.

Berscheid, E., & Reis, H. T. (1998). Attraction and close relationships. In D. T. Gilbert, S. T. Fiske, & G. Lindzey (Eds.), *Handbook of social psychology* (4th ed., pp. 193–281). New York: McGraw-Hill.

Blumler, J. (1979). The role of theory in uses and gratifications studies. *Communication Research, 6,* 9–33.

Blumler, J., & Katz, E. (1974). *The uses of mass communications.* Thousand Oaks, CA: Sage.

Brewer, M. B. (1988). A dual process model of impression formation. In T. K. Srull & R. S. Wyer, Jr. (Eds.), *Advances in social cognition* (Vol. 1, pp. 1–36). Hillsdale, NJ: Lawrence Erlbaum Associates, Inc.

Brewer, M. B. (1991). The social self: On being the same and different at the same time. *Personality and Social Psychology Bulletin, 17,* 475–482.

Brewer, M. B., & Gardner, W. (1996). Who is this "we"? Levels of collective identity and self representations. *Journal of Personality and Social Psychology, 71,* 83–93.

Brockner, J., & Swap, W. C. (1976). Effects of repeated exposure and attitudinal similarity on self disclosure and interpersonal attraction. *Journal of Personality and Social Psychology, 33,* 531–540.

Burke, P. J. (1980). The self: Measurement requirements from an interactionist perspective. *Sociometry, 43,* 18–29.

Burke, P. J., & Tully, J. (1977). Reconstructing social identity. *Personality and Social Psychology Bulletin, 19,* 4–5.

Byrne, D. (1971). *The attraction paradigm.* New York: Academic.

Byrne, D. (1997). An overview (and underview) of research and theory within the attraction paradigm. *Journal of Social and Personal Relationships, 14,* 417–431.

Byrne, D., Clore, G. L., & Smeaton, G. (1986). The attraction hypothesis: Do similar attitudes affect anything? *Journal of Personality and Social Psychology, 51,* 1167–1170.

Caruso, D. (1998, September 14). Critics pick apart study on Internet and depression. *New York Times,* p. C5.

Clausing, J. (1999, May 20). Congressional Internet debate turns to issues of violence. *New York Times* [Internet edition], p. 1.

Collins, N. L., & Miller, L. C. (1994). Self-disclosure and liking: A meta-analytic review. *Psychological Bulletin, 116,* 457–475.

Culnan, M. J., & Markus, M. L. (1987). Information technologies. In F. Jablin, L. L. Putnam, K. Roberts, & L. Porter (Eds.), *Hand-book of organizational communication* (pp. 420–443). Newbury Park, CA: Sage.

D'Amico, M. L. (1998, December 7). Internet has become a necessity, U.S. poll shows. *CNNinteractive* [Internet magazine], p. 1. Retrieved June 20, 1999 from the World Wide Web: http://cnn.com/tech/computing/9812/07/neednet.idg/index.htm

Derlega, V. L., Metts, S., Petronio, S., & Margulis, S. T. (1993). *Self-disclosure.* London: Sage.

Diener, E. (1980). De-individuation: The absence of self-awareness and self-regulation in group members. In P. Paulus (Ed.), *The psychology of group influence* (pp. 1160–1171). Hillsdale, NJ: Lawrence Erlbaum Associates, Inc.

Donahue, E. M., Robins, R. W., Roberts, B. W., & John, O. P. (1993). The divided self: Concurrent and longitudinal effects of psychological adjustment and social roles on self-concept differentiation. *Journal of Personality and Social Psychology, 64,* 834–846.

Dubrovsky, V. J., Kiesler, S. B., & Sethna, B. N. (1991). The equalization phenomenon: Status effects in computer-mediated and face-to-face decision-making groups. *Human–Computer Interaction, 6,* 119–146.

Festinger, L. (1950). Informal social communication. *Psychological Review, 57,* 271–282.

Frable, D. E. S. (1993). Being and feeling unique: Statistical deviance and psychological marginality. *Journal of Personality, 61,* 85–110.

Frankel, M. S., & Teich, A. (Eds.). (1999). Anonymous communication on the Internet [Special issue]. *Information Society, 15*(2).

Friedman, T. L. (1999). *The Lexus and the olive tree.* New York: Farrar, Straus & Giroux.

Fuller, J. (1996). *News values.* Chicago: University of Chicago Press.

Gans, H. J. (1979). *Deciding what's news: A study of CBS Evening News, NBC Nightly News, Newsweek, and Time.* New York: Random House.

Gergen, K. J., Gergen, M. M., & Barton, W. H. (1973). Deviance in the dark. *Psychology Today, 7,* 129–130.

Gollwitzer, P. M. (1986). Striving for specific identities: The social reality of self-symbolizing. In R. Baumeister (Ed.), *Public self and private self* (pp. 143–159). New York: Springer.

Green, M., & Brock, T. (1998). Trust, mood, and outcomes of friendship determine preferences for real versus ersatz social capital. *Political Psychology, 19,* 527–544.

Harmon, A. (1998, August 30). Sad, lonely world discovered in cyberspace. *New York Times,* p. A1.

Harter, S. (1993). Causes and consequences of low self-esteem in children and adolescents. In R. Baumeister (Ed.), *Self-esteem: The puzzle of low self-regard* (pp. 87–116). New York: Plenum.

Hatfield, E., Aronson, E., Abrahams, D., & Rottman, L. (1966). The importance of physical attractiveness in dating behavior. *Journal of Personality and Social Psychology, 4,* 508–516.

Hatfield, E., & Sprecher, S. (1986). *Mirror, mirror: The importance of looks in everyday life.* Albany: State University of New York Press.

Hays, R. B. (1984). The development and maintenance of friendship. *Journal of Social and Personal Relationships, 1,* 75–98.

Hays, R. B. (1985). A longitudinal study of friendship and development. *Journal of Personality and Social Psychology, 48,* 909–924.

Heatherton, T. F., & Nichols, P. A. (1994). Personal accounts of successful versus failed attempts at life change. *Personality and Social Psychology Bulletin, 20,* 664–675.

Higgins, E. T. (1987). Self-discrepancy theory. *Psychological Review, 94,* 1120–1134.

Higgins, E. T., & Bargh, J. A. (1987). Social cognition and social perception. *Annual Review of Psychology, 38,* 369–425.

Hill, C. T., Rubin, Z., & Peplau, L. A. (1976). Breakups before marriage: The end of 103 affairs. *Journal of Social Issues, 32,* 147–168.

Hoffman, D. L., & Novak, T. P. (1995, July 2). *A detailed analysis of the conceptual, logical, and methodological flaws in the article: "Marketing pornography on the information superhighway"* Available: http://ecommerce.vanderbilt.edu/cyberporn.debate.html

Houts, R. M., Robins, E., & Huston, T. L. (1996). Compatibility and the development of premarital relationships. *Journal of Marriage and the Family, 58,* 7–20.

Iyengar, S. S., & Lepper, M. R. (1999). Rethinking the value of choice: A cultural perspective on intrinsic motivation. *Journal of Personality and Social Psychology, 76,* 349–366.

Johnson, R. D., & Downing, L. L. (1979). Deindividuation and valence of cues: Effects on prosocial and antisocial behavior. *Journal of Personality and Social Psychology, 37,* 1532–1538.

Jones, E. E., Farina, A., Hastorf, A. H., Markus, H., Miller, D. T., & Scott, R. A. (1984). *Social stigma: The psychology of marked relationships.* Thousand Oaks, CA: Sage.

Katz, E. (1959). Mass communication research and the study of culture. *Studies in Public Communication, 2,* 1–6.

Katz, J. E., & Aspden, P. (1997). A nation of strangers? *Communications of the ACM, 40,* 81–86.

Kiesler, S., Siegal, J., & McGuire, T. (1984). Social psychological aspects of computer-mediated communication. *American Psychologist, 39,* 1123–1134.

Kraut, R., Kiesler, S., Mukhopadhyay, T., Scherlis, W., & Patterson, M. (1998). Social impact of the Internet: What does it mean? *Communications of the ACM, 41,* 21–22.

Kraut, R., Mukopadhyay, T., Szczypula, J., Kiesler, S., & Scherlis, W. (1998). Communication and information: Alternative uses of the Internet in households. In *Proceedings of the CHI 98* (pp. 368–383). New York: ACM.

Kraut, R., Patterson, M., Lundmark, V., Kiesler, S., Mukopadhyay, T., & Scherlis, W. (1998). Internet paradox: A social technology that reduces social involvement and psychological well-being? *American Psychologist, 53,* 1017–1031.

Leary, M. R. (1983). Social anxiousness: The construct and its measurement. *Journal of Personality Assessment, 47,* 66–75.

Leary, M. R., & Kowalski, R. M. (1995). *Social anxiety.* New York: Guilford.

Linville, P. W. (1985). Self-complexity and affective extremity: Don't put all your eggs in one cognitive basket. *Social Cognition, 3,* 94–120.

Making a business of the bit buffet. (1997, March 8). *The Economist, 158,* p. 81.

Markus, H. R., & Kitayama, S. (1991). Culture and the self: Implications for cognition, emotion, and motivation. *Psychological Review, 98,* 224–253.

Markus, H. R., & Nurius, P. (1986). Possible selves. *American Psychologist, 41,* 954–969.

McKenna, K. Y. A. (1998). *The computers that bind: Relationship formation on the Internet.* Unpublished doctoral dissertation, Ohio University.

McKenna, K. Y. A., & Bargh, J. A. (1998). Coming out in the age of the Internet: Identity "de-marginalization" through virtual group participation. *Journal of Personality and Social Psychology, 75,* 681–694.

McKenna, K. Y. A., & Bargh, J. A. (1999a). *Can you see the real me? Relationship formation and development on the Internet.* Manuscript submitted for publication.

McKenna, K. Y. A., & Bargh, J. A. (1999b). Causes and consequences of social interaction on the Internet: A conceptual framework. *Media Psychology, 1,* 249–270.

Mendels, P. (1999, July 21). The two faces of on-line anonymity. *New York Times* [Internet edition]. Available: http://www.nytimes.com/library/tech/99/07/cyber/articles/21anonymity.html

Mischel, W. (1973). Toward a cognitive social learning reconceptualization of personality. *Psychological Review, 80,* 252–283.

Newcomb, T. M. (1961). *The acquaintance process.* New York: Holt, Rinehart & Winston.

Parks, M. R., & Floyd, K. (1995). Making friends in cyberspace. *Journal of Communication, 46,* 80–97.

Parks, M. R., & Roberts, L. D. (1998). "Making MOOsic": The development of personal relationships on line and a comparison to their off-line counterparts. *Journal of Social and Personal Relationships, 15,* 517–537.

Pennebaker, J. W. (1989). Confession, inhibition, and disease. In L. Berkowitz (Ed.), *Advances in experimental social psychology* (Vol. 22, pp. 211–244). New York: Academic.

Pennebaker, J. W. (1990). *Opening up: The healing power of confiding in others.* New York: Morrow.

Rhee, E., Uleman, J. S., & Lee, H. K. (1996). Variations in collectivism and individualism by ingroup and culture: Confirmatory factor analyses. *Journal of Personality and Social Psychology, 71,* 1037–1054.

Rhee, E., Uleman, J. S., Lee, H. K., & Roman, R. J. (1995). Spontaneous self-concepts and ethnic identities in individualistic and collectivistic cultures. *Journal of Personality and Social Psychology, 69,* 142–152.

Rheingold, H. (1993). *The virtual community: Homesteading on the electronic frontier.* New York: Harper & Row.

Rimm, M. (1995). Marketing pornography on the information superhighway. *Georgetown Law Review, 83,* 1839–1934.

Rossney, R. (1995, July 13). *Time*'s story on cyberporn of questionable validity. *San Francisco Chronicle,* p. C3. Available: http://www.sfgate.com/net/rossney/0713.htm

Ruble, D. N. (1994). A phase model of transitions: Cognitive and motivational consequences. In M. P. Zanna (Ed.), *Advances in experimental social psychology* (Vol. 26, pp. 163–214). New York: Academic.

Sarbin, T., & Allen, V. L. (1968). Role theory. In G. Lindzey & E. Aronson (Eds.), *Handbook of social psychology* (2nd ed., Vol. 2, pp. 223–258). Reading, MA: Addison-Wesley.

Segal, M. W. (1974). Alphabet and attraction: An unobtrusive measure of the effect of propinquity in a field setting. *Journal of Personality and Social Psychology, 30,* 654–657.

Shweder, R. A. (1990). Cultural psychology: What is it? In J. W. Stigler, R. A. Shweder, & G. Herdt (Eds.), *Cultural psychology: Essays on comparative human development* (pp. 1–46). New York: Cambridge University Press.

Siegal, J., Dubrovsky, V., Kiesler, S., & McGuire, T. W. (1986). Group processes in computer-mediated communication. *Organizational Behavior and Human Decision Processes, 37,* 157–187.

Sleek, S. (1998). Isolation increases with Internet use. *American Psychological Association Monitor, 29,* 1.

Spears, R., & Lea, M. (1994). Panacea or panopticon? The hidden power in computer-mediated communication. *Communication Research, 21,* 427–459.

Spreitzer, E., Snyder, E., & Larson, D. (1979). Multiple roles and psychological well-being. *Sociological Focus, 12,* 141–148.

Stryker, S., & Statham, A. (1985). Symbolic interaction and role theory. In G. Lindzey & E. Aronson, (Eds.), *Handbook of social psychology* (3rd ed., pp. 311–378). New York: Random House.

Swann, W. B. (1983). Self-verification: Bringing social reality into harmony with the self. In J. Suls & A. G. Greenwald (Eds.), *Psychological perspectives on the self* (Vol. 2, pp. 33–66). Hillsdale, NJ: Lawrence Erlbaum Associates, Inc.

Tice, D. M., Butler, J. L., Muraven, M. B., & Stillwell, A. M. (1995). When modesty prevails: Differential favorability of self-presentation to friends and strangers. *Journal of Personality and Social Psychology, 69,* 1120–1138.

Turkle, S. (1995). *Life on the screen: Identity in the age of the Internet.* New York: Simon & Schuster.

Verbrugge, L. M. (1983). Multiple roles and physical health of women and men. *Journal of Health and Social Behavior, 24,* 16–30.

Verbrugge, L. M. (1986). Role burdens and physical health of women and men. *Women and Health, 11,* 47–77.

Whitbeck, L. B., & Hoyt, D. R. (1994). Social prestige and assortitative mating: A comparison of students from 1956 and 1988. *Journal of Social and Personal Relationships, 11,* 137–145.

Wilson, T. D. (in press). Dual model of attitudes. *Psychological Review.*

Young, K. (1998). *Caught in the net: How to recognize the signs of Internet addiction and a winning strategy for recovery..* New York: Wiley.

Zajonc, R. B. (1968). Attitudinal effects of mere exposure. *Journal of Personality and Social Psychology Monograph, 9* (Pt. 2).

Zimbardo, P. (1970). The human choice: Individuation, reason, and order versus deindividuation, impulse, and chaos. In W. J. Arnold & D. Levine (Eds.), *Nebraska symposium on motivation* (Vol. 17, pp. 237–307). Lincoln: University of Nebraska Press.

Personality and Social Psychology Review
2000, Vol. 4, No. 1, 76–94

Complementarity Theory: Why Human Social Capacities Evolved to Require Cultural Complements

Alan Page Fiske
Department of Anthropology
University of California, Los Angeles

This article introduces complementarity theory, which explains the psychology of cultural diversity as a product of evolved social proclivities that enable—and require—people to coordinate action in culture-specific ways. The theory presents evolutionary processes and psychological mechanisms that may account for the cultural variability of social coordination devices such as language, relational models, rituals, moral interpretations of misfortune, taboos, religion, marriage, and descent systems. Human fitness and well-being depend on social coordination characterized by complementarity among the participants' actions. This complementarity is based primarily on coordination devices derived from the conjunction of cultural paradigms and specific, highly structured, evolved proclivities. The proclivities have no adaptive value without the paradigms, and the paradigms have no meaning without the proclivities. They are coadapted to function together. Operating in conjunction with each other, proclivities and paradigms jointly define the generative structures for meaningful coordination of social interaction in each particular culture.

My aim in this article is to describe the natural selection of universal psychological mechanisms that result in cultural diversity. Complementarity theory posits that human social coordination is the product of structured psychological proclivities linked to corresponding cultural paradigms. Using innate expectations about the ways in which people encode and conduct social relations, children take primary responsibility in actively searching for the relevant cultural paradigms they need. Putting proclivities together with congruent paradigms, children learn to construct culture-specific coordination devices that enable them to interact in locally meaningful ways. The evolved proclivities and cultural paradigms are complementary: Both are necessary but neither is sufficient to permit complex social coordination. People cannot use either their socially transmitted paradigms or their evolved proclivities independently of each other. Combining them, humans devise and depend on diverse, flexible social adaptations.

These coordination systems make possible a second kind of complementarity: the complementarity of the respective actions of the participants. To cooperate, contest, or defect, it is extremely advantageous to know what other people want, judge, feel, think, and will do. Moreover, many kinds of complex mutually beneficial cooperation require this kind of complementarity: communication, exchange, division of labor, joint action, meeting at a known time and place, planning a schedule for the flow of work, conducting a complex ritual, making joint decisions and committing to collective behavior, acting in concert in relation to outsiders, or cooperating to sanction someone—any action whose outcome depends on cooperation based on shared understandings.

This complementarity in human interaction is usually made possible by participants' joint use of shared coordination devices to construct their own actions and to interpret others' actions. Moreover, unlike social insects and most eusocial mammals, humans are capable of generating an infinite number of social coordination devices based on each evolved social proclivity. They do this by combining an evolved social proclivity with different cultural paradigms. Furthermore, people can generate endless additional possibilities by combining multiple coordination devices. This generativity makes coordination devices uniquely versatile, permitting humans to use a limited num-

I am very grateful for the support of National Institutes of Mental Health Grant MH 43857, which made this research possible. I thank Robert Boyd, Marilynn Brewer, Roy D'Andrade, Francisco Gil-White, and Nick Haslam for their extremely helpful comments on an earlier draft.

Requests for reprints should be sent to Alan Fiske, Department of Anthropology, University of California, Los Angeles, Box 951553, Los Angeles, CA 90095-1553. E-mail: afiske@ucla.edu.

ber of evolved proclivities to construct a multitude of varied, complex, yet flexible, rapidly mutable, and locally specialized social adaptations. This generativity results from the indeterminacy of the evolved proclivities that permits them to be combined with any congruent socially transmitted paradigms, but this indeterminacy has another consequence. It makes social coordination dependent on cultural paradigms: Virtually all human social coordination is organized with reference to culture-specific coordination devices. This is a primary source of cultural diversity.

However, although humans can construct innumerable devices for social coordination, these devices are not arbitrary or unconstrained. Structured psychological proclivities facilitate the invention, learning, use, social transmission, and transformation of congruent cultural paradigms. Conversely, humans slowly evolve structured psychological proclivities to learn to construct adaptive coordination devices using all the diverse paradigms that people transmit over the long run and across diverse cultures. These proclivities evolve much, much more slowly than cultures change and they cannot track cultural ephemera. However, there is strong selection—weighted according to the frequency, duration, and adaptive value of the set of previous cultural paradigms—for universal capacities to construct culture-specific coordination devices based on just the set of diverse paradigms that people transmit. In turn, these paradigms, although diverse and potentially infinite in number, are substantially constrained by existing proclivities. Nevertheless, there is latitude for humans to invent and learn new paradigms. Some of these paradigms may diffuse widely, endure over many generations, and permit people to construct fitness-enhancing coordination devices. When this occurs there is strong selection for psychological proclivities to evolve to facilitate reliable learning of these paradigms and versatile, proficient utilization of them to construct adaptive coordination devices. Hence, proclivities and paradigms are symbiotically coadapted to fit each other and to require each other.

The Natural Selection of Generative Proclivities for Social Coordination

Cultural coordination devices (CCDs) are cognitive, motivational mechanisms that permit complementarity of social action. By definition, a CCD is determined by a specialized evolved proclivity in conjunction with one or more complementary paradigms. In the simplest case, a CCD is the product of a proclivity conjoined with one congruent cultural paradigm, but most proclivities require linkage with multiple paradigms. Most complex CCDs represent combinations of proclivities together with their corresponding paradigms. CCDs include language, relational models, rituals, religion, many taboos, systems of punishment, moral interpretations of misfortune, and kinship systems for forming groups according to descent and marriage. Probably many other universal yet culturally diverse practices and institutions are CCDs, including shame, jealousy, joking relationships, and music (although the adaptive value of the latter two is uncertain). Humans are exceptional in the extent of their adaptive exploitation of CCDs, their extreme reliance on CCDs, and the extraordinary number, complexity, and intergroup variability of these CCDs. CCDs are usually based on a shared model or schema (cf. D'Andrade & Strauss, 1992), or a syntax, paradigm, prototype, artifact, architecture, or landscape. Participants use this model to understand, anticipate, evaluate, facilitate, forestall, resist, or sanction other participants' actions and to construct their own actions. The paradigm or syntax—and the social coordination resulting from such an artifact—is often inaccessible to reflection and incapable of being articulated; people do not know how they coordinate, plan, construct their action, or interpret each other's action.

Most CCDs probably result from an evolutionary sequence that is described in detail later in this article. In outline, this sequence of adaptations begins when people invent a system for coordinating behavior (e.g., a form of communication, a system of exchange, a method for dividing labor, a ritual that defines social status, or a taboo that regulates sexuality). The invention is the product of an unusual, accidental experience, or results from individual or group creativity and learning. The innovation or modification in a previous system may be very small, but if it enhances fitness then natural selection will favor those who learn the invention most reliably and most rapidly and are most adept at using it. Natural selection will operate on ontogeny, attention, learning, primary reinforcers, emotions, memory, cognition, and motoric systems to strengthen all proclivities to consistently develop and effectively utilize this learned innovation. People are most likely to invent new cultural systems for coordinating behavior that take advantage of—that are facilitated by—the evolving psycho–social–developmental specializations. If these additional cultural coordination devices enhance fitness, are widely diffused, and persist for many generations, then natural selection will further expand the adaptive specializations so that they enable people to learn and use the new devices effectively as well. Thus, within the constraints of the psycho–social–developmental proclivities required to become proficient using a set of socially transmitted coordination devices, natural selection will favor the widest range of adaptive uses of these specialized adaptive proclivities.

In humans, natural selection has gone beyond facilitating individual learning and use of social coordination systems. People cannot use such systems alone. Hence, there is strong selection for the capacity to learn such systems from others—and to convey them to potential partners, especially close kin. There are tremendous advantages in learning all kinds of adaptive behaviors from others, although it is surprising that no other animal has a very versatile capacity to do this (see following). Such capacities may begin to evolve primarily because of their advantages for profiting from other's experiences and fortuitous discoveries, whether cumulated or not, and whether social or nonsocial: The aggregate knowledge and skills of the local population must always exceed what any individual can learn for itself in one lifetime. Or such capacities may have begun to evolve because of their advantages for learning local devices for coordinating social interaction. In either case, once people begin to evolve such capacities, they are tremendously advantageous both for nonsocial learning and for learning social coordination devices.

Thus, culture builds on psychological proclivities, constructing and reproducing coordination devices congruent with human psyches; natural selection assimilates in the genome the psychological potential to reliably learn and effectively utilize the full range of adaptive CCDs enduring in the population. Natural selection simultaneously fosters capacities to learn from others and cumulate socially transmitted knowledge and skills over successive generations. Indeed, natural selection favors the evolution of capacities to link these two sets of skills, resulting in the evolution of specialized capacities to learn local forms of basic systems for social coordination.

So at some point, *Homo* evolved to the point where people could learn social coordination devices from each other. Building on this, there was another evolutionary step, based on two factors. First, there are constraints on the number of adaptive specializations that can evolve for learning social coordination devices. Adaptive specializations for learning can require a lot of energetically expensive neurological capacity. They may be very slow to evolve, so that they lag far behind the creation of individually learned and socially constructed innovations. They may be difficult to isolate in their proper domains, interfering with each other so that domain-specific cognition is constrained and the evolution of domain-specific learning faculties is impeded. This means that it is functionally advantageous to develop learning proclivities that somehow combine two seemingly incompatible features: (a) the high degree of structure needed to enable people to reliably and quickly learn

and proficiently utilize complex capacities and (b) great flexibility of functional applications. This means that if there are principles of learning and cognition that are powerful for solving diverse problems, they be will extremely advantageous.

A second factor contributes even more to this next evolutionary step. People have two complementary preadaptations: capacities to learn from others and capacities to learn some set of social coordination devices. There is a way to link these that enhances both and at the same time provides a powerful structure for learning functionally diverse capacities. This is to evolve the capacity to construct generative systems that define basic structure, relational principles, and operations that work well in diverse contexts but leave key determining paradigms or prototypes open to be learned from others. The great adaptive advantage of generative structures is their unique combination of versatility, learnability, and coordinative potential.

This is an evolutionary step with a great adaptive advantage for two reasons. First, the most valuable things to learn from other people are devices for getting along with them—for understanding their motives, emotions, evaluations, cognition, and probable actions. To construct effective complementary action (to cooperate, avoid, or contest others' action) one needs to discover the structures used to organize their social action. So capacities to learn from others will be especially advantageous if they evolve to include specializations for learning social coordination devices. This will permit complementarity in diverse, locally adapted, rapidly mutable social systems. Second, it is virtually impossible to inductively construct a model that predicts the actions of a complex organism without extensive prior knowledge of its motives and strategies; this prediction is feasible only if most of the structure of that action is known a priori, so that there are only a few points of indeterminacy. To obtain the great benefits of coordinating social action—including the benefits of strategies for coordinating either conflict or cooperation—people must evolve psychological structures that they use jointly to construct action and to interpret it. For example, I can generally understand your action and know that you will generally understand mine if we both use the same device for constructing our respective actions and for interpreting each other's actions. It is possible to do this and still construct innumerable coordination devices if much of the structure of those devices is innately shared but certain paradigms are left open for learning and mutual social determination—if natural selection can construct mechanisms for this learning and joint determination of paradigms. A plausible mechanism is sketched in the section on ontogenetic externalization.

The Functional Interdependence of Evolved Proclivities and Cultural Paradigms

The key concept in complementarity theory is that people have highly structured, evolved (predominately universal), attentional, motivational, cognitive, and developmental proclivities for discerning congruent cultural paradigms and using them to construct and utilize local cultural coordination devices. I have coined the term *mod* for such a proclivity. (The term is based on the Indo European root for *mediate, mold, accommodate, modify, mode, model,* and the Latin *modus—measure, standard, size, limit, manner, harmony, melody*). Mods have three defining features. First, they are innate proclivities for learning and performing structured behaviors, and in this respect they are more or less similar to (and build on) a number of important concepts in the existing literature: adaptive specializations for learning (Gallistel, 1995; Rozin, 1976), learning programs (Pulliam & Dunford, 1980), transmission coefficients for cultural selection of traits (Cavalli-Sforza & Feldman, 1981), epigenetic rules that affect usage bias curves for culturgens (Lumsden & Wilson, 1981), direct biases or evolved predispositions guiding the adoption of cultural practices (Boyd & Richerson, 1985, 1989), functional modules (Fodor, 1983; Hirschfeld & Gelman, 1994; Tooby & Cosmides, 1992), or primary values (Durham, 1991).

Second, mods are incomplete without a congruent socially transmitted complement. That is, a mod is insufficient for structuring action until it is linked with appropriate cultural paradigms that specify how, when, and where it operates. Third, a mod in conjunction with congruent cultural paradigms constitutes a cultural coordinating device that permits complementarity of action, cognition, emotions, motives, and evaluations. In short, a mod is a structured proclivity for learning and action that, when conjoined with the necessary type of cultural complement, permits culture-specific forms of social coordination based on complementarity of action. These last two features differentiate mods from the concepts cited in the preceding paragraph: Mods are not simply tendencies to learn selectively. Mods are adaptations for coordinating social interaction with reference to local cultural paradigms or prototypes. Mods are proclivities to learn from other people how to get along with them.

The theory is called *complementarity theory* for two reasons. First, it posits close complementarity between mods and socially transmitted cultural paradigms. This complementarity is hypothesized to consist of close historically causal linkages between mods and corresponding cultural paradigms that have coevolved. A mod can be adaptively expressed in the behavioral phenotype only in conjunction with one or more congruent cultural paradigms.

A second, closely linked dimension of complementarity is both cause and effect of the first type of complementarity. Humans create extraordinarily complex and diverse social practices, relationships, groups, and institutions in which the action of each person only makes sense in terms of the actions of the other participants and observers. Participants' actions are often mutually presupposing and mutually completing: The fulfillment of the participants' intentions depends on the congruence of others' actions. This is essential for large-scale cooperation, especially when it goes beyond immediate face-to-face responses. This social complementarity results from joint usage of the coordination devices that people construct by joining a mod with a congruent cultural paradigm.

Research on the coevolution of human psyches and cultures shows that social inventions form an important aspect of the environment that shapes natural selection and evolved psyches form an important component of the selective environment for cultural transmission (Boyd & Richerson, 1985; Caporael, 1997; Durham, 1991; Lumsden & Wilson, 1981; Pulliam & Dunford, 1980; Rozin, 1982). The human invention, retention, use, transformation, acquisition and interest in cultural practices, artifacts, symbols, and institutions depends on the compatibility of these cultural paradigms with mods. Lumsden and Wilson (1981) described this as the *bias curves* that represent the translation of epigenetic rules into ethnographic curves. Boyd and Richerson (1985) called this *direct bias* in the adoption of cultural variants. Atran (1998) made a similar point with regard to adaptive habits of mind that universally shape folk biological classification, and Sperber (1996) took an analogous perspective when he described culture as infectious ideas to which human psyches are susceptible (cf. Boyer, 1994). Complementarity theory goes beyond this to posit that human social coordination is based primarily on cultural coordination devices that people construct by putting mods together with corresponding cultural paradigms. Mods cannot function and are not adaptive until conjoined with congruent socially transmitted complements. Conversely, mods permit humans to learn and to use cultural paradigms to construct culture-specific coordination devices. Thus, complementarity theory posits that natural selection, ontogeny, psychology, social organization, and culture are mutually potentiating and mutually determining. To delineate the theory there are four basic concepts that need to be considered more fully: (a) cultural coordination devices, (b) mods, (c) preos, and (d) ontogenetic externalization.

Concepts

Cultural Coordination Device (CCD)

In essence, CCDs are the core of the phenomena the theory attempts to explain. CCDs exhibit both universal fundamental principles and diversity across cultures. This is evident in relational models, rituals, religion, taboos, systems of punishment, moral interpretations of misfortune, kinship and marriage systems, perhaps language, and probably many other practices and institutions.

Relational models are CCDs (Fiske, 1991, 1998: Fiske & Haslam, 1996). Relational models are universal structures that people implement in culture-specific ways to organize mutually intelligible social interactions: making group decisions or moral judgments; organizing labor; exchanging, distributing, and contributing; using objects, time, or space to mediate social interaction; or coordinating conflict and aggression. There are four relational models that people in all cultures apparently use to cognize, construct, comprehend, coordinate, and evaluate most social interactions, groups, and institutions. These models are communal sharing, authority ranking, equality matching, and market pricing (Fiske, 1992). Each model defines a set of relations and operations that are socially meaningful. For example, in aspects of an interaction organized with reference to communal sharing, people divide the world into social categories that are equivalence classes. With regard to the given aspect of the interaction, people within each category are not differentiated but each category is entirely distinct. For example, when people organize labor according to communal sharing, the task is a joint, shared responsibility of the participants and it does not matter which of them does what. If people consume something (e.g., food) according to communal sharing, then they just dig in and help themselves without being concerned about the amounts each person consumes: "What is mine is yours." Other models define additional relations and operations. For example, if people work according to equality matching, they divide the work up, being concerned about whether each person's tasks are equal, or they take turns at each task. People consuming a resource in an equality matching mode match their shares so they correspond one to one; if one person gets more than another, all participants know what they need to do to make things even.

The mod that is fundamental to each relational model specifies the meaningful kinds of relations and operations but is incomplete: The mod does not delineate when, how, or with whom to implement it. To use a model to coordinate a social interaction, participants need shared cultural paradigms, precedents, or principles that indicate some way to use the abstract structure. In communal sharing, for example, there must be a process that assigns persons to social categories: by descent, by contract, by residence, by gender, or whatever. To implement equality matching, people need cultural practices that define what tasks to organize this way, what counts as a turn, and what operations to use to compare shares. For example, to operationalize equality matching as a form of exchange, the participants must have a shared understanding of what kinds of entities can be exchanged in this manner, what constitutes an offer and acceptance of something proffered, what constitutes a return of the "same" thing or value, what is the proper interval between receiving and giving a return, permissible limits to imbalance, and so forth. Without these shared understandings to coordinate interaction, it is impossible to generate the complementarity of action necessary for effective social relationships. If a Fulani man gives you a cow, even if you guess correctly that the framework is equality matching, there is a lot more you need to know to figure out how to respond.

Language appears to be a CCD. Most linguists and psychologists have long accepted Chomsky's (1959, 1988) argument that a child could not learn a language without prior knowledge of a universal grammar and innately structured language acquisition device. No one speaks universal grammar (UG) and, according to the theory, it cannot be used to communicate until a finite number of parameters are set to specific values; to specify a particular language, each parameter must be set to one of a small number of possibilities (perhaps two). If this theory is correct, then UG together with the child's language acquisition device is a mod. However, the theory of UG and parameter setting remains controversial (e.g., Deacon, 1998; Elman, Bates, & Johnson, 1996; Tomasello, 1998). Furthermore, there is no stable consensus on how to characterize universal grammar, its parameters, or the language acquisition device; and after 40 years there is little or no empirical evidence that directly supports the existence of a UG. Nevertheless, humans seem to have species-specific capacities that presumably evolved because of the enormous adaptive advantage conferred by linguistic abilities.

Another CCD is *ritual.* People engage in rituals for certain well-delineated purposes: to transform social status, mark life transitions, constitute social relationships and group membership, to cure ills, to redress wrongdoing or protect against misfortune. Rituals all over the world are composed primarily from a very limited, well-specified, contextually distinctive repertoire of actions, ideas, and emotions (Dulaney & Fiske, 1994; Fiske & Haslam, 1997). Among the most common of these are (a) repetition of the same action, word, song, or sound; (b) a focus on special numbers and colors; (c) concerns about pollution and purity and consequent washing or other purification; (d) contact avoidance; (e) special ways of touching; (f) fears about immanent, serious sanctions for rule violations; (g) a focus on boundaries and thresholds; and (h) symmetrical arrays and other precise spatial patterns. Yet, the rituals that people compose from these elements are infinitely varied and unique to each culture. Evidently the psyche resonates with certain ideas and actions, providing a repertoire for composing rituals. The specific content, the arrangement of components, and the precise uses of this repertoire are open and must be culturally determined.

Another major CCD consists of *beliefs, fears, and practices related to the moral interpretation of misfortune.* People everywhere commonly assume that when something very bad happens, someone must have done something bad. That is, in every culture, people attribute many or all deaths and much suffering to wrongdoing: by the victim or against the victim. For example, the Tumbuka of northern Malawi attribute severe and persistent coughs such as tuberculosis to adultery—adultery committed by a parent, if the patient is a child (personal observations). In the biblical story of Job, Job's neighbors assume that his misfortunes and the suffering of his family must be due to his having angered God. Among the Moose (pronounced *MOH-say*) of Burkina Faso, people consult diviners whenever anyone falls ill and they interview the deceased, seeking to determine the moral meaning of the illness or death. They assume that such suffering could result from violation of a taboo (violation committed by the sufferer or by a kinsperson or spouse), witchcraft or sorcery against the victim, or the anger of the ancestors or other beings who have not received their due sacrifices (personal observations). As in every other culture, these attributions about misfortune focus overwhelmingly on a search for some kind of transgression of a social relationship with another person, spirit, ancestor, or god.

People seek this kind of explanation even if they are satisfied that they fully understand the biomechanical or material causes of their suffering: They want something more. What they seek is not just any explanation that would give them some sense of predictability and meaning: In every culture people focus predominately on social transgressions. Nonsocial interpretations are always less prevalent and less emotionally satisfying. (People may also use astrological or numerological accounts, but moral explanations are almost always much more important.) In a great many cultures after a major misfortune, people attempt to redress the moral disequilibrium by making some kind of sacrifice that consists of a gesture of obeisance to gods, ancestors, or other superior beings and an attempt to renew solidarity with them. This basic approach to making sense of misfortune is universal, yet cultures vary greatly in their attribution of suffering to specific transgressions and relationships with specific types of beings, as well as the oracular processes they use to determine who has committed what transgression. To know what to do when you fall ill among the Azande, you have to know the culture.

Sex and food taboos with a certain characteristic structure represent another CCD. There is evidence that in every culture where there are important, institutionalized communal sharing relationships, these relationships entail a strong taboo concerning food, sex, or both (Fiske, 2000). Participation in the communal sharing relationship is contingent on observing the taboos: Observance is partially constitutive of the relationship. For Western readers, the most obvious examples are the incest taboos inherent in familial relationships, and the celibacy and food proscriptions entailed by joining a monastery or marrying God (becoming a nun). South Asians will immediately think of their caste rules. For Africans, totemic taboos associated with clans and protective associations, and the sex and food taboos associated with blood brotherhood will spring to mind. Readers from the Mediterranean and Central America will recognize their strongest taboos: against sexual relationships with the spouse of a trusted *compadre.* Traditional Melanesians will reflect on the numerous intense food and sex taboos incumbent on initiated males in a communal long house. There are innumerable other examples. All share certain remarkable structural features. The most notable feature is that the taboos proscribe a combination of three or more relationships that are innocuous in isolation from each other. It is taboo to engage in one or more particular triadic configuration of these relationships. For example, Americans value romantic sexual relationships, marriage, and parenthood, but it is taboo to combine these three relationships—it is not good to have a sexual relationship with the daughter of your spouse. Despite these common structural features, the examples demonstrate the diversity of the particular communal sharing relationships and specific food and sex interactions that are taboo in different cultures. The universality of taboos with this distinctive structure reflects the underlying mod; the necessity for completing these mods with specific cultural paradigms is evident in cultural specificity of the constellations that are taboo.

Religion, another CCD, consists partly of ritual, moral interpretation of misfortune, and taboos. Religion also involves two other elements: some kind of deferential (authority ranking) relationship with one or more immaterial superior beings and a desire to develop a relationship of solidarity or oneness (communal sharing) with the immaterial being or beings, with some ultimate essence, with the congregation as a whole, or all of these. Needless to say, these features are present in virtually all cultures, yet the world's religions have many distinctive features (cf. Boyer, 1994).

There appear to be many other CCDs; in any event, researchers need to further analyze these CCDs and search for more.

Mod

A *mod* is an innate proclivity to coordinate social interaction in a universally structured yet culturally organized way. It is an evolved but incomplete attentional–cognitive–learning–motivational system for organizing social interaction that cannot function without a congruent cultural complement. Many (although not necessarily all) of the following characteristic features should be present before something is called a mod:

• A quasi-universal socially transmitted coordinative practice (CCD) with a distinctive, consistent structure; coupled with a generative capacity to construct indefinitely many culture-specific systems, group- or dyad-specific practices, and unique interactive events.
• Virtually universal adult social competence for participating effectively in a given type of CCD despite vast differences in general intelligence and individual experience.
• A highly structured learning mechanism that results in competence that would be difficult to learn on the basis of individual experience without strong innate expectations (Bayesian prior hypotheses), yet that works very reliably with a distinctive kind of highly variable and imperfect cultural input.
• A sensitive period during maturation in which competence in the CCD can be acquired and retained much more readily, fully, and precisely than at any subsequent time.
• Perceptual capacities, attentional filters, and motivational effects tuned to a distinctive semiotic modality (sign system, communicative channel, or social medium) for learning, marking, and constituting a particular type of CCD (e.g., creating communal sharing relationships by eating and drinking together).
• Well-structured enactive and performative capacities that are partially preformed and emerge with minimal practice; performative capacities are linked to selective perceptual capacities, attentional filters, and constitutive modality.
• Focused, directive motives for acquiring and participating in a specific type of coordinative structure,

sometimes overriding simple reinforcers, distraction, and fatigue.
• Active search initiated by the child, who experiments and innovates in ways not readily induced from the input stimuli and who makes constructive mistakes that could not result from simple associative induction.
• Signs of the unrealized potential of the mod in cultures in which the competence is not valued or not manifestly elaborated on the surface. For example, children may inventively initiate utilization of the CCD, which may subsequently be lost, channeled into something else, or suppressed. Perhaps repression is evident: In dreams or fantasy, adults may exhibit covert signs of the cultural loss or mental suppression of the mod.
• Distinctive combinatorial properties: characteristic tendencies to combine to form CCDs with certain other mods, to remain independent of other mods, or to oppose certain other mods (cf. the related concept of cultural selection according to secondary values; Durham, 1991).
• Crucial role in coordinating human sociality: Important kinds of social complementarity depend on it.
• Significant adaptive advantage resulting from plausible process of natural selection.
• Homologous (albeit much simpler) social behavior in great apes and possibly other highly social primates and mammals.
• Functional neurological modularity, indicated by capacity to solve relevant problems in parallel (without interference) with other cognitive tasks, distinctive memory systems, problem-solving procedures, or types of errors.
• (?) Anatomical localization, as evinced by imaging, by phylogenetic anatomical comparisons, and by specific dysfunctions resulting from delimited lesions.[1]

Note that many evolved, function-specific mental modules are not mods because their function does not depend on being conjoined with any particular type of congruent cultural complement. For example, neither the adaptive specializations for recognizing faces, nor for distinguishing material objects and interpreting motions, are mods. Nor is cultural variation in some domain of behavior indicative of a mod. By definition there is no mod unless the proclivity re-

---

[1]There are somewhat modular neurocultural systems such as language that are clearly based on mods. However, some neurological modules, such as reflex arcs or facial recognition (if that is a module), are not mods because they do not presuppose culture or depend on any culture to be fully functional. Conversely, it is also quite possible that there are mods that cannot be isolated in any region of the brain, and that do not correspond with any discrete neurological circuits. For example, some mods may have evolved as interactions or co-adaptations of multiple neurological systems, each of which also has other, only indirectly related functions.

quires a cultural complement to function. Hence, although food and sexual attraction are susceptible to cultural influence, aversion to chili peppers (Rozin, 1982) and male attraction to youthful women with regular features (Buss, 1994) are not mods. However, the proclivity for shame probably is a mod because the factors eliciting shame and the practices for dealing with it must be provided by the culture.

One of the central hypotheses of complementarity theory is that these 15 features are systematically related and hence should be highly correlated, but it does not follow that they should always occur together. Mod is a polythetic concept. Much further research will be needed to determine the extent to which these features do co-occur. Due to the fact that cultural reproduction and diffusion, natural selection, cognition, development, and social relations are dynamic processes acting on each other in a continuously shifting balance that never reaches equilibrium, it seems likely that "modity" will be a matter of degree: There may be intermediate types of adaptive specializations that substantially shape some aspects of social interaction and are amenable to substantial cultural molding, amplification, or inhibition, yet do not require one particular, distinctive type of cultural complement to operate. There is a need to reanalyze from this perspective infant and parental attachment, male proprietary sexual jealousy, and aversion to sexual relations with persons who were intimate coresidents during childhood.

The existence of a mod does not invariably result in the construction of a corresponding CCD and the fact that a certain type of CCD is not universal does not imply that there is no corresponding mod. Bear in mind that mods may push in diverse directions, may counteract each other, and can interact to produce cultural coordination devices that are not additive sums of the proclivities that potentiate them. There are cultures with little or no hierarchy, groups without religion, and individuals sexually attracted to animals. However, hypothesizing a mod requires explaining cases where it is not directly expressed.

Preo

To implement a mod to construct meaningful, coordinated interaction, people need shared indicators for how, when, and with whom to use the mod. We call such an indicator a *preo* because preos take the form of precedents, prototypes, paragons, precepts, propositions, practices, and paradigms. (Up to this point in the text, the term *paradigm* has been used instead of *preo* to avoid defining a new term before it was necessary.) A preo is the complement to a mod, completing the mod by specifying how to implement

it as a particular CCD. Like a key or catalyst, a preo has to correspond to the nature of the indeterminacy of the mod. For example, in a given context the implementation of authority ranking may be modeled on representations of the comportment of a cultural paragon: a hero, media star, mythical figure, or god. Balancing shares in equality matching may be based on a process—a concrete operation that determines what counts as equal (e.g., weighing amounts in a pan balance, counting out items or aligning them in one-to-one arrays, or having the person who divides the shares take the share left over after others take their pick). According to the Chomskian view, the setting of parameters turns universal grammar into a particular syntax. People often construct and legitimate ritual performances to perpetuate their identity-defining traditions by reproducing "what we have always done." Other rituals are defined as reenactments of a prototypical event.

Complementarity theory suggests that cultural reproduction, diffusion, and acquisition of CCDs consist of the transmission of preos; likewise, cultural transformation consists of modification of preos. Hence, it is not a religion that is transmitted but only the paragons and practices that orient the relevant mods and permit children to shape their dispositions to be congruent with the particular local practices. Children do not "learn" the sexual disgust, disinterest, and fear that is the core of incest taboos: They learn whom to avoid and some ideas about what kind of misfortune may befall transgressors.

Ontogenetic Externalization

Complementarity theory suggests that children become cultural in large part at their own initiative. Children learn their culture because they there are insatiably social: They want to communicate and participate in relationships and daily activities (see Trevarthen, 1988). To coordinate with the people around them, children (or immigrants or anthropologists) need to determine the preos that will permit them to transform their mods into the CCDs that people in their community use to construct, comprehend, and evaluate actions. Rather than describing norms as being internalized by children who utilize social relationships as means to asocial ends, complementarity theory describes inherently sociable children who externalize their mods to connect with their families and communities. Children actively (though unreflectively) attempt to use their mods to interpret and to evaluate what goes on around them and construct relationships with those they encounter. Guessing and attempting to discern the correct preos to complete their mods, children try out various implementations

83

of their mods in the hopes of coordinating interaction successfully. They initiate interactions, seeking to discover the preos that will complete their mods and satisfy their social appetites.

There are infinitely many preos for implementing any mod; hence, there are infinitely many possible CCDs. This creates a considerable problem for the child, the immigrant, or the anthropologist in learning a culture. Indeed, the problem appears as though it may be insoluble. How could a naïve person recognize the preos for implementing any mod? One seemingly insuperable difficulty is that the naïf has to guess which mod is operative before discovering which preo is being used to implement it. That is, the naïve individual has to decipher combinations of mods and preos without initially knowing what either of them is. How do we do this?

Mods, preos, and CCDs generally are not readily accessible to reflective understanding or articulate expression. Who can explain the phonetic system, let alone the syntax, of their own language? Who can describe the operations and relations defined in everyday market pricing interactions such as buying groceries? (Who can describe the distributive law that partially defines an ordered field, or the necessary Archimedian property?) People do not learn most CCDs by instruction; for example, no one explains most of what you know about how to interpret misfortune. If someone tries to explain why it is wrong to have sex with one's mother, they cannot really explain why it just feels disgusting or awful. Adults do not have the capacity to teach CCDs and in most cultures adults and older children provide very little or no instruction to children (Fiske, 1999; Lancy, 1996). However, children do not need instruction to become competent in most aspects of most cultures.

Children learn most of what they need to know by observation, imitation, and incremental participation (Fiske, 1999). In general, children establish their first relationships by imitating each other (Eckerman & Didow, 1996) and become proficient cultural participants by observing and then gradually participating more competently in more of the everyday practices of older children and adults (Greenfield, Maynard, Boehm, & Yut-Schmidtling, in press; Lancy, 1996; Lave & Wenger, 1991; Rogoff, Baker-Sennett, Lacasa, & Goldsmith, 1995). Even technical skills are typically learned primarily by observation and apprenticeship involving guided participation or legitimate peripheral participation. Imitation may seem simple, but in fact only humans have evolved very sophisticated capacities to observe others, understand the functional relations of means to ends, and imitate the purposeful sequence (Nagel, Olguin, & Tomasello, 1993; Tomasello & Call, 1997; Tomasello, Kruger, & Ratner, 1993; but see Whiten & Custance, 1996).

We know very little about the cognitive processes involved in imitation, and almost nothing about the hypothesized specializations for learning preos. This crucial aspect of complementarity theory remains to be worked out—as it does for all other theories of evolution, psychology, culture, and development. The hypothesis, based on ethnographic evidence, is that children and adults arriving in novel cultures have strongly focused prior expectations about the ways in which people signal the social actions based on particular proclivities (see Fiske, 1991, pp. 148–149, 203–207). Apparently, mods are conjoined with focused prior expectations about the specific modality of the corresponding preos and default domains in which they are most likely to be utilized. For example, children expect communal sharing relationships to be constituted in part by breast-feeding and by commensality (eating and drinking the same substances together from the same vessels). Although this cue is not invariably correct, in every culture consistent commensality—especially ceremonially highlighted sharing of food, drink, and other comestibles—indexes all or most of the important communal sharing relationships (see Sahlins, 1972, pp. 215–219). Furthermore, suppose that children expect communal sharing also to be indexed by birth, by sleeping in the same space, by coresidence, and by similarity in appearance, dress, and adornment. These expectations do not fully determine or absolutely limit the possible preos for communal sharing, but if some of the local mod–preo linkages do correspond to a priori expectations they make it possible for naïfs to bootstrap themselves enough to learn the other, culture-specific mod–preo combinations for which they are not innately prepared.

In contrast, children expect that when people are marking hierarchical positions, superior people will be higher up, assume more upright postures, assume positions in front, have the right to act first or go ahead, be accorded more personal space, wear accoutrements that make them appear bigger and higher, be accorded bigger shares and bigger items, be treated as if they were plural (e.g., royal *we* and respectful *vous*), be regarded as if they were more powerful, stronger, and more forceful, and be entitled to speak louder. Although not all of these expectations will fit every hierarchy in every culture, many of them will fit most of the important hierarchies in every culture. In any culture, one can reliably bootstrap the fundamental hierarchies, discovering who occupies what ranks, and when and where and how authority ranking operates with respect to what social domains. From these initial clues the naïf can discover unique cultural cues such as the chiefly prerogative to construct rectangular houses, place ostrich eggs at the roof corners, and be greeted with an expression that means, "May your place be beautiful" (traditional norms of the Moose of Burkina Faso).

If people signal the paradigms and prototypes for different proclivities in distinctive modalities (if people conduct different CCDs in different interactive media and use these media in predictable ways) this enormously simplifies the problem of discerning the locally shared paradigms. However, we still need to learn much more about learning.

Natural Selection for Ontogenetic Strategies

Why do humans depend so extensively on learning coordination devices from other humans? To answer this question one needs to consider a broader issue, the evolution of ontogeny. When does natural selection result in genotypically fixed behaviors or plasticity, and how does it produce any given learning strategy?

Baldwinian Adaptation

A century ago Baldwin (1896), Morgan (1896), and Osborn (1896a, 1896b) simultaneously proposed a theory connecting learning to natural selection. What follows is a modern restatement of their idea. Within any population there is genotypic variation affecting the behaviors that different organisms exhibit in given conditions. When a population encounters new conditions, there will inevitably be differences among individuals in the behaviors they display. A behavioral adaptation can originate as a learned behavior that provides the learners with a selective advantage compared to nonlearners. Animals more likely to learn the adaptation reliably and rapidly have greater fitness than animals less prone to learn it. If the environmental conditions are relatively uniform and constant over a number of generations, the likelihood of any animal displaying the adaptive behavior increases. Within the often significant constraints imposed by the developmental and neurological costs of canalization, natural selection will produce animals that display adaptive traits most rapidly and reliably under the widest variety of experiential conditions. The behavioral adaptation can become fixed so that the animals display it even prior to any relevant experience. The behavior that was originally learned has become assimilated into the genome.

Baldwinian adaptation enables organisms to evolve complex combinations of interdependent traits that only enhance fitness in conjunction with each other. Furthermore, as Hinton and Nowlan (1987) first simulated, and Mayley (1997) and others further demonstrated theoretically, Baldwinian processes make it possible to evolve complex adaptations that are only functional when perfected: Maladaptive chasms between fitness peaks in the adaptive landscape may be bridged by plasticity in learning that permits animals to discover these complex adaptations without persistently exhibiting maladaptive intermediate phenotypes (cf. Laland, Richerson, & Boyd, 1993).

Waddington (1975) confirmed empirically that such a process can occur. In a series of experiments on Drosophila beginning in 1956, Waddington artificially selected animals that acquired certain anatomical traits under specified environmental conditions. He showed that after a number of generations many of these traits appeared under a wider range of conditions: the Drosophila developed to display the trait reliably in the absence of the conditions that were originally necessary to induce its ontogenetic acquisition. Waddington called this process of narrowing the range of variability and increasing the probability of a given adaptive endpoint of ontogenetic development "canalization." Waddington thus proved that under strong selection it was possible for a trait acquired developmentally in earlier generations to become genetically assimilated. Although Waddington was aware of Baldwin (1896) and Morgan (1896), he analyzed this process only with regard to anatomical traits and did not explore learning or behavior in any detail.

Baldwin (1896), Osborn (1896a, 1896b), and Morgan (1896) assumed that learning of adaptive behavior would inevitably pave the way for assimilation that fixed the behavior more rigidly in the genotype. The crucial point that they ignored was that under many conditions the adaptive advantages of learning would lead to more effective and more specialized learning, rather than a genetically fixed action pattern. The equilibrium point of selection is somewhere in between random unstructured learning, at one extreme, and behavior rigidly canalized by the genotype, at the other extreme. That is, the function that maps experience onto behavior is itself an adaptation. Natural selection can move ontogenetic strategies in either direction and, at the plastic end of the continuum, can shape domain-specific learning strategies to fit adaptive contingencies (Boyd & Richerson, 1985; Gallistel, 1990, 1995; Lumsden & Wilson, 1981; Pulliam & Dunford, 1980; Rozin, 1976; Tooby & Cosmides, 1992).

When is Learning Adaptive?

There is some optimum degree and form of plasticity for a given organism inhabiting a given range of environments (see Scheiner 1993). If the environment is uniform and constant, then it is adaptive for the population to fix innately the behavior that arose through ontogenetic plasticity: Complete genetic assimilation avoids the considerable costs of the time it takes to learn the behavior, the costs of errors along the way, and the costs of not learning the behavior at all under some conditions (see, e.g., Boyd & Richerson, 1985; Scheiner, 1993; Wcislo, 1989). The organism can adapt to temporal and spatial heterogeneity in the environment in two ways. The genotypes of all living things specify contingent responses determined by genotypically delineated cues. A seed germinates only under certain conditions, then sends its roots in the direction of gravitational attraction while its leaves grow upward. Many organisms reproduce asexually under optimal conditions and sexually under more adverse conditions. In these cases, the organism's behavior is plastic but not learned: The function that relates environmental conditions to behavior is predetermined by the genotype. An organism can evolve genetically predetermined responses to any number of specified environmental conditions, making its phenotype adaptively responsive to diverse environments. This does not require learning and indeed, if a given environmental cue reliably predicts a given optimal response, it is a liability for the organism to have to discover the correlation for itself in its own lifetime experience. If a given cue predicts the same adaptively relevant condition in most environments that an organism encounters, then natural selection should tend to produce rigid genotypic determination of the function relating cue to response. However, as phenotypic plasticity decreases, the range of niches to which the organism can adapt narrows and the speed of its reaction to environmental changes slows.

Learning is adaptive and should be selected if there is variability in the patterns of co-occurrence of cues and optimally adaptive responses, or if a limited set of fixed responses is less advantageous than the generation of an (indefinitely) abundant set of constructed responses based on an effective strategy. So, for example, if a smile on the face of a male adult stranger toward an isolated female adult always predicts friendly behavior that the perceiver should respond to with trusting affiliation, then natural selection will tend to hardwire this response into the mind. If, however, male smiles can signal many different meanings that cannot be predicted without local experience, then it is adaptive to learn from experience, imitation, or instruction. Learning always has a cost and is selected to the extent that the experience of the population over many generations cannot be effectively used to predict the adaptive response.

Learning is also adaptive when the necessary information is reliably available in the environment and readily accessible by a learning mechanism that can evolve more easily than a genetic mechanism for storing the same information. This is probably part of the reason that the lexicons of human languages are not innate. (Another reason must be that it is highly adaptive to be able to learn new words for referring to new things and performing new speech acts.)

Learning is only possible when the organism has a genotypically structured strategy that enables it to (a) focus attention on potentially relevant cues, (b) evaluate plausible functions connecting these cues to a repertoire of potentially appropriate responses, and (c) effectively deploy organized adaptive actions. This was Chomsky's (1959, 1988) message when he argued for the existence of a language acquisition device; Seligman (1970) when he argued for functional preparedness to learn in certain ways; Rozin (1976; Rozin & Kalat, 1972) when he showed that there must be adaptive specializations for learning; Garcia (Garcia & Ervin, 1968) when he demonstrated specialized capacities to make associations relevant to the animal's niche; Boyd and Richerson (1985) when they analyzed the conditions selecting, respectively, for individual learning, cultural inheritance, or genetic inheritance of behavior; and Tooby and Cosmides (1992) when they posited adaptive cognitive modules (see also Hinde & Stevenson-Hinde, 1973). Pure unstructured plasticity that calculated all correlations among all features of the environment and randomly explored all possible responses would not be adaptive: It would only very slowly and rarely arrive at adaptive responses. In any event, such a mechanism would be computationally impossible.

Using this foundation, consider how humans could have evolved mods that depend on cultural complements.

The Human Adaptations for Social Cumulation, Complementation, and Generativity

Often the evolution of a new adaptation results in a change in selection that leads to the evolution of other adaptations, which in turn produce selection for the evolution of further adaptations in a process of "sequential evolution" (Seaborg, 1999). Sometimes the second- or third-order adaptations have strong effects on the selection that shapes the first adaptation, resulting in evolutionary feedback. This kind of sequential evolution and evolutionary feedback can result in the relatively sudden and dramatic adaptive shifts that appear as punctuated evolutionary change (Seaborg, 1999). Complementarity theory posits a process of sequential evolution with feedback that led to the culturally organized eusociality of *Homo sapiens* (cf. Campbell, 1983, for another account).

Cumulation

Humans are characterized by three connected adaptations: (a) socially transmitted knowledge and therefore cumulative learning, (b) extremely complex social coordination, and (c) highly varied social systems that are adapted to specific ecologies and social environments. Taken together, these three adaptations are called *culture*, but it is analytically useful to separate them. Consider first the importance of socially transmitted skills that accumulate across generations. As previously noted, humans have evolved a set of uniquely powerful capacities for transmitting knowledge and skills; the most important of these capacities is the collection of skills called *imitation* (see Fiske, 1999). In addition, the social construction of spaces and artifacts facilitates the transmission of knowledge and practices. Tools, especially, guide action and are a powerful medium of social inheritance in conjunction with imitation. Humans have language and other symbol systems, permitting them to store all kinds of knowledge and competence in propositional and narrative form. In addition, humans often issue commands to younger or subordinate persons that more or less incidentally permit the latter to learn new skills. In some cultures people sometimes instruct others. These adaptations must have coevolved with the long dependency and delayed sexual maturation that are distinctive of *Homo*.

Once humans began to be able to learn from each other, the accumulating knowledge and skills available would have placed a tremendous premium on the capacity to learn, remember, and apply such capacities. Each individual would have had the opportunity to acquire and utilize far more skills than any individual could ever acquire on its own in one lifetime. In principle, the knowledge and skills available to any individual could grow exponentially if each individual could learn from several ancestors and peers. Special cognitive capacities would be needed to store such a vast body of knowledge and use such a vast array of skills. In this context, those individuals who exhibited the best social learning would have a tremendous advantage, leading to a very intense selection for the genotypic proclivity to learn from others. The more varied the environmental contingencies and the greater the cost of individual learning, the greater the benefits of capacities for learning socially transmitted knowledge (Boyd & Richerson, 1985). The value of such learning would be enhanced if the most competent learners could parlay their knowledge into social sta-

tus, offering access to their knowledge in return for other benefits.

Humans have uniquely powerful capacities for learning from others, in conjunction with ancillary memory and performance capacities (cf. Donald, 1991). To distinguish this adaptation from individual learning, let us call it *cumulation*. (Other terms, such as *social learning*, have also been used in somewhat different theoretical frameworks.) Note that cumulation does not require any high degree of social cooperation beyond that which is involved in merely permitting others to observe and imitate. Capacities for cumulation must have evolved gradually from simpler observational capacities that modern apes currently possess (Tomasello & Call, 1997; Whiten & Custance, 1996). A recent analysis of the variability of behavior of seven chimpanzee groups suggests that *Pan troglodytes* apparently has some capacity for cumulation. Whiten et al. (1999) identified 39 socially transmitted behaviors that do not appear to be explained by individual learning in response to differing ecologies. Most of these involve ways of using tools. My interpretation is that these cumulated practices may be transmitted by stimulus enhancement rather than sophisticated functional imitation. (That is, observation facilitates associations that provide shortcuts to learning: Once chimpanzees observe an association between a tool and a reward, they are capable of exploring individually and eventually learning for themselves how to use the tool to get the reward.)

Complementation

Cumulation is the capacity to learn what others have learned (e.g., how to build a fire, cook, make a tool, track an animal, or find tubers), but what is learned by cumulation consists of skills that can be used alone, without further interaction with the people from whom one has learned. Building on this imitative capacity, humans evolved a step further: the capacity to learn coordination devices from each other. Among toddlers, imitating another person is often the first step in developing an interaction with them (Eckerman & Didow, 1996). One hypothetical process leads to a communal sharing relationship: Imitating another person results in a sense of similarity (i.e., imitation becomes conformity and identification). Another process leads to equality matching via turn taking (e.g., he does it; her imitation of him becomes taking a turn), matching (she does it, he matches her action; she takes one and then, by his taking one for himself, he keeps even), or in-kind reciprocation (A hits B and then B hits A, or A helps B and then B helps A). Similarly, ritual could evolve from a repetitive reflection of each other's actions:

Imitation becomes reenactment. Indeed, people performing rituals often explain their action as the reproduction of previous performances: "It is what we found when we were born and what we leave behind when we die," say the Moose.

Thus, it is a smooth but significant step to go from learning a technique to coordinating an interaction. This adaptive step may build on the fact that imitating another person's action potentially leads to understanding their point of view. Suppose A takes something from B, then B takes something from A; now each may begin to understand the other's perspective. In human children, we see this kind of imitation: role playing in which the child plays the part of the parent (i.e., from the point of view of the parent). When the child does this kind of role playing, the child may act as mother while a doll or sibling occupies the role that the child normally plays.

We call this adaptation *complementation*; it entails cumulation but in addition consists of the capacity to use the acquired device to mediate a coordinated interaction. What is learned is not simply knowledge or a skill—it is a device for constructing action that complements the action of the people from whom one has learned. Complementation is learning from another person a model, schema, or artifact that they are using to organize their action; this model or artifact then mediates the mutual construction and interpretation of each other's action.

Coordinated social interaction can be achieved by genetic adaptation to the social actions of other members of the species, as social insects do, without complementation (Wilson, 1974). Among close kin, selection can facilitate coordination when the behavior of all is genotypically fixed: Social insects can coadapt to relatively unchanging, invariant, hence predictable behavior by others in the colony. In this case, the cognitive structures used to produce an action may be entirely distinct from those used to respond to it. Nonhuman primates apparently lack much sense of what others are thinking: They do not have a subtle theory of mind, if they have any at all. They may coordinate interaction using a set of social coadaptations in which the cognitive structures for constructing behavior are distinct from those used to respond to others, or they may use simple shared models (Haslam, 1997). Social coordination through genetically fixed behavior eliminates the difficult learning problem that complementation poses for the individual, eliminating the costs of delays, initial errors, and failures to learn in the face of novel conditions. Strategies for independent individual learning of social skills permit some coordination as well, but only to a limited extent. Neither direct genotypic control nor individual learning permit complex, flexible complementarity. Complementation makes the learn-

ing and mutual adjustment problems very difficult, but if natural selection solves these problems, complementation permits individuals to vary their forms of coordination to adapt to local conditions. It also permits rapid collective changes from one coordination device to another.

Generativity

Complementation is the capacity to learn coordination devices one by one. For example, at this evolutionary stage, the individual can observe others and learn to share meat or learn from others how to take turns using a tool to dig for tubers. Complementation can develop into something further if the coordination devices can be generalized to other situations by freeing them of their specific content and context. Complementation is the adaptation that enables individuals to learn to share meat, but at this stage learning to share meat does not enable the learner to share responsibility for providing the meat or to make a decision by consensus. Complementation enables the individual to observe, imitate, and learn to take turns using a digging tool, but having learned this the individual still does not know how to take turns cooking, how to exchange a tuber received today for a tuber returned tomorrow, or how to conduct a fair lottery. This is the next step.

This adaptive step gradually results from natural selection for proclivities to learn coordination devices. Certain kinds of coordination devices are versatile and effective: They permit complementation that offers adaptive advantages to participants coordinating an infinite variety of contextually diverse interactions. Relational models, for one example, are structures that have exceptionally powerful fundamental properties. These structures remain the same under important types of transformation (a property called *uniqueness* in measurement theory) and every element has the same relational properties (*homogeneity*; see Fiske, 1991, p. 229). This makes these four structures effective for organizing almost any social activity.

Consequently, natural selection would favor capacities to generalize such coordination devices beyond the context in which they were initially learned. For example, an individual would benefit greatly if, after learning the basic structure and operations of an ordered Abelian group in the form of turn taking, it subsequently developed any capacity to use ordered Abelian groups for balanced reciprocity or evenly dividing tasks (Fiske, 1991, pp. 207–223). This assumes, of course, that people associated preferentially with close kin likely to share the same mutations. Similarly, an individual who imitated others and learned to use equivalence relations to share shellfish would benefit greatly from any proclivity to apply equivalence relations to sharing pine nuts or taking joint responsibility for tending the fire. In general, an increase in fitness would be conferred by any mutation that facilitated the invention of new uses for a relational model; reliable, rapid learning of a relational model; or proficient use of one. By small increments, Homo sapiens must have acquired greater and greater faculties for learning to use relational models. In much the same manner, natural selection would steadily increase proclivities to learn and use other valuable coordination devices. These devices were devised by processes of individual learning and transmitted initially by complementation capacities such as imitation. Once this social transmission was pervasive and enduring, the coordination devices become part of the environment to which *Homo* adapted genetically in subsequent generations.

By the logic we reviewed previously in the section on natural selection for ontogenetic strategies, this process of natural selection should continue up to the point at which further genetic assimilation reduces adaptively advantageous versatility, flexibility, and capacity to change quickly in response to environmental changes and new opportunities. Furthermore, natural selection should construct a limited number of proclivities that each facilitate the widest functionally possible range of most beneficial coordination devices. This led by small increments to the evolution of proclivities that consisted of those structures specifying all of the relations and operations that are functionally valuable in diverse contexts for a wide variety of adaptive coordinations. However, these structures would become liabilities if they evolved beyond this point and began to be specialized for particular, limited contexts in ways that interfered with a range of numerous other potentially more beneficial uses. In short, what evolved were cognitive developmental proclivities innately defining coordination structures and processes of wide adaptive value but leaving open the specification of how, when, with whom, and with respect to what aspects of social life they are used. In other words, *Homo sapiens* evolved generative mods requiring preos.

Mods linked with preos are generative at approximately three levels: using a mod with a set of preos generates a social institution (e.g., marriage); further precision in specifying preos, or additional preos, generates a particular relationship (e.g., my own marriage); and applying these preos to particular circumstances generates specific interactive events (I bathe the children tonight). In language, this is evident in the variety of languages purportedly generated by universal grammar, the variety of dialects and styles within each language, and the innumerable utterances that a speaker can produce and comprehend. This generativity makes human sociality uniquely adaptive in two respects.

First, people within a community or interaction network can use the same mod with different preos to generate innumerable cultural institutions, particular relationships, and specific interactions (Fiske, 1991). Thus, equality matching can be used to make group decisions (e.g., by voting), to organize exchange (e.g., by even, in-kind reciprocation), to structure violence (an eye for an eye, a tooth for a tooth), to make moral judgments (equal treatment and equal opportunity), to divide work (take turns), and so forth, indefinitely. Using it to organize exchange, we can construct rotating credit associations in which participants meet weekly, each bringing $100 and one member taking home the entire pot each week. We can conduct exchanges in which you invite me to dinner and I owe you a dinner in return. We can exchange baby-sitting in a cooperative in which the medium is coupons. Your baby-sitting coop may count each hour for each child as one coupon, while my coop exchanges a night out for another night out, regardless of the number of hours and children. Thus, a very small set of mods permit people to easily coordinate innumerable activities with mutual understanding: All you have to do is perceive what mod is being used with what preos.

Second, this kind of generativity makes it possible for people to use the same CCDs to generate highly varied behavior in different circumstances: Different cultures can generate different systems of marriage in different ecological and political–historical contexts; different dyads can generate marriages appropriate to their pair of personalities and their social circumstances; dyads or groups can generate distinct actions that take into account the immediate situation. So in one culture, marriage is governed primarily by communal sharing, in another by authority ranking, by equality matching in a third culture, and market pricing in a fourth. If equality matching is the prescriptive CCD for marriage in one culture, that still leaves room to decide whether to take turns cooking dinner alternate nights or to split the cost of eating out. If a marriage is mediated by equality matching implemented as cooking alternate nights, one still has lots of room for interpretation, improvisation (and perhaps conflict) each night over what constitutes "cooking dinner" (e.g., ordering pizza), and who should cook the night after a dinner party. This makes a few generative mods capable of adapting to all kinds of conditions. In effect, the process is recursive: The conjunction of a mod and a preo generates a CCD that operates globally to define a system, but that CCD must be applied with further preos to define a specific relationship and with still more preos to construct each particular interaction.

This is *generativity*: the capacity to construct social coordination in indefinite ways using a finite set of mods (concatenated and nested) with an indefinite set of socially transmitted, shared preos. Humans gain enormous fitness advantages through the evolution of mods and the social transmission of complementary preos that enable them to generate indefinitely many implementations of the same model—*implementations that are unique but coordinated with sets of local partners.* Humans are culturally social animals whose fitness depends on coordinating in culturally and situationally varied ways: There is no an advantage in being able to speak a language if it is not the language the other people around you speak. Nor is there any advantage in constructing novel utterances if the listeners do not understand them. Generativity is the extraordinarily beneficial adaptive capacity to combine productivity and creativity with social coordination based on complementarity. Generativity results from combining genotypic inheritance of universal mods with social transmission, local diffusion, ad hoc negotiation, and extemporization of preos. Mods and preos complete each other, permitting complementarity of action in indefinitely many, varied, and novel institutions, relationships, and interactions.

Natural selection for open-ended—hence generative—mods is also the result of the quantitative limitations of the information that the genome can encode directly compared to the enormous capacity of the brain and its cognitive processes. The genome can encode the design for a brain that can learn far more than the genome can encode directly. For example, the available portion of the genome cannot encode the lexicon of a human language, knowledge of all social arrangements, or competence with all technologies that can be adaptive under all environmental conditions. However, the genome can encode mods for assimilating cumulated local preos and then generating any human lexicon, technology, or social system.

A third factor favoring natural selection of generative mods coupled with socially transmitted preos is speed of adaptive response. Creative invention coupled with social transmission result in cultural evolution that is much more rapid than genetic evolution (Boyd & Richerson, 1985). Baldwinian adaptation cannot track and genetically assimilate cultural inventions whenever they are adaptive fast enough to keep up with cultural evolution. This is approximately the temporally extended equivalent of cultural diversity at one point in time: Just as genetic evolution within one gene pool cannot assimilate the diversity of cultural inventions in different groups and networks, so the genotype cannot respond very rapidly with fixed action patterns to adaptive opportunities and hazards (see Boyd & Richerson, 1995). Hence, there is strong selec-

tion to evolve mods that permit rapid transition to new CCDs in response to environmental changes—including novel cultural inventions.

A fourth aspect of generativity is the ability to combine CCDs to construct complex forms of social coordination. The same CCD can be nested or concatenated with itself recursively, or people can link and nest multiple CCDs. For example, a group decision can be made by consensus (communal sharing) that a king should be elected (equality matching) to rule arbitrarily over us (authority ranking) because it is the most efficient, cost-effective system of government (market pricing). This is a basic principle of syntax but it operates in other forms of generative social complementation as well.

Cumulation, complementation, and generativity are synergistic adaptations: The adaptive advantages of each are greatly amplified when linked to the others. In addition, each of these three adaptations must have been greatly facilitated by and in turn provided opportunities for further adaptations based on inclusive fitness (Frank, 1998; Hamilton, 1964) and reciprocal altruism (Trivers, 1971). Both inclusive fitness and reciprocal altruism are functions of the ratio of benefits conferred to another divided by the costs to the actor. Cumulation, complementation, and generative CCDs provide uniquely powerful opportunities for conferring major benefits at little cost to the donor. Consequently, natural selection for adaptations based on the mechanisms of inclusive fitness and reciprocal altruism greatly enhances and in turn is greatly enhanced by the adaptive value of cumulation, complementation, and generative CCDs. Thus, they mutually facilitate each other's evolution. (I shall defer more detailed discussion of this complementarity to a subsequent publication.)

Symbiosis Between Mods and Preos

The complementarity of the reproductive processes of mods and preos can readily result in a kind of symbiosis between them. To reproduce, the mods need the social transmission of compatible preos that result in the construction of adaptive CCDs. Conversely, the preos and the cultural coordination devices based on them need compatible mods; the only niche in which preos can reproduce is a social system comprised of humans with congruent mods. Thus, mods may often evolve so as to support as effectively as possible the most extensive social transmission and greatest expression of the largest number of genotypically adaptive congruent cultural paradigms. This does not mean total plasticity: The mod is only adaptive to the extent that it channels the generation of cultural paradigms in fitness-enhancing directions. It does mean, however, that a mod that originally evolved because it facilitated one type of congruent cultural construct may further evolve to more effectively facilitate diverse adaptive expressions of that mod and to facilitate many others. That is, the mod evolves to ensure the reliable social transmission of any preos that are necessary or sufficient to translate the mod into adaptive CCDs. Conversely, cultural paradigms reproduce most prolifically when the population contains the greatest number of humans with the necessary potentiating mods. Hence, cultural paradigms should gradually transform—evolve—to maximally enhance the inclusive genotypic fitness of the mods that facilitate the social reproduction of those paradigms.

However, this mutual enhancement is a function of the symbiosis of a mod with a preo; it obtains to the extent that the reproduction of either depends entirely on the other. Preos will tend to transform so as to become congruent with mods other than their original complements: This makes such paradigms multiply potentiated. To the extent that a preo comes to depend on the conjunction of a set of mods, requiring Mod A, Mod B, *and* Mod C (etc.), this will limit the further transformations that it can undergo because few transformations will retain congruence with all the potentiating mods. This kind of coevolutionary feedback may lead to adaptive stasis (Seaborg, 1999). However, if a preo becomes transformed so that it is congruent with Mod A, Mod B, *or* Mod C (etc.), then it can be socially reproduced independently of any one of these mods. This makes the preo's reproductive potential partially independent of any one mod and hence its interests diverge from each one. The preo can therefore become less symbiotic and more parasitic, exploiting a mod in ways that are not necessarily entirely conducive to the fitness of the mod.

Conversely, a mod will tend to evolve so as to facilitate the production of additional adaptive cultural paradigms beyond the one in conjunction with which it originally evolved. The greater the number and the greater the adaptive value of the cultural paradigms that any one mod facilitates, the greater the fitness of the mod. However, once again, a mod that evolves to potentiate multiple cultural paradigms will become constrained in ways that limit its further evolution: Subsequent modifications will be less likely to be congruent with all of the cultural paradigms that it already supports. A mod that is congruent with multiple adaptive cultural paradigms no longer depends exclusively on any one of them, and hence natural selection of this mod will become less closely linked to its potentiation of each one of the congruent constructs. This weakens the mod's symbiotic support of the reproductive interests of any one of its congruent cultural paradigms.

Natural selection operates on culturally mediated phenotypes (cf. Caporael, 1997). On the scale of one life span—for the individual—it is adaptive to coordinate according to local cultural norms, to participate in the accessible communities and networks, regardless of whether the local CCDs are optimal in the abstract. An individual is at a great disadvantage if he or she is the only speaker of a language that would be optimal if everyone spoke it. Similarly, there are great costs to the sole person who shares generously—despite the fact that it may be beneficial to all participants if only they all conducted their transactions in such a manner. Humans depend fundamentally on their social relationships for most of their basic needs and, therefore, must generally conform to most of the important CCDs that prevail in their own communities and networks. This means that humans must be tuned to their own particular cultures. They must be adept at learning the particular CCDs through which their own culture implements, elaborates, transforms, and connects the generic human potentials. Meanwhile, over the long run, natural selection shapes the psyche to be capable of learning and motivated to utilize the full cultural diversity of CCDs that have been adaptive in the population. This means that natural selection slowly tracks the historical assortment of adaptive cultural inventions. On the other side, over the long run, the kinds of cultural innovations that resonate most strongly with evolved psychological proclivities will most readily diffuse and persist. So culture adapts to human mods. Overall, these capacities facilitate new kinds of adaptation, including the possibility of a single gene pool—*Homo sapiens*—developing very diverse, highly specialized, yet socially coordinated, adaptations to specific local conditions along with rapid responses to environmental changes.

Conclusions

The theory outlined in this article suggests that cultural transmission; social coordination; cognitive, emotional, and developmental psychology; and natural selection are so highly interdependent in *Homo sapiens* that they cannot be understood separately. These systems have become complementary, and each requires the others to complete it. Natural selection takes advantage of cultural innovations, and culture capitalizes on evolved potentials. The psyche exploits cultural tools, and social relations build on culturally constituted implementations of evolved psychological proclivities. It is not that human cultural transmission, social processes, human psychology, and natural selection influence each other. They rely on each other, presuppose each other, operate by virtue of each other, and are functionally incomplete without each other. The human psyche has evolved to function as a cultural psyche, dependent on cultural precedents, prototypes, and paradigms that make social coordination possible. Conversely, human cultures have adapted themselves to the evolved psychological proclivities that reproduce them. Human nature is cultural and humans are cultural by nature.

Conjoining Preos and Mods to Construct CCDs

Complementarity theory suggests that there are a number of important cultural coordinating devices that require specific evolved psychological proclivities. These cultural coordinating devices are essential for meaningful complementarity in human sociality: They are necessary for the construction and conduct of human social practices, relationships, organized groups, institutions, and societies. These CCDs mediate communicative action, permitting people to generate actions that others can anticipate and understand. People must use one or more CCDs to jointly construct social practices that consist of coordination in which the actions of each person presuppose and make sense only with reference to complementary actions of other participants. The cultural reproduction and systematic transformation of CCDs is made possible because humans have evolved corresponding mods that dispose them to learn and interact in certain specific ways. Conversely, mods evolve when people devise, share, and transmit preos for adaptive CCDs. In this sense, mods are products of a distinctive culturally potentiated sequence of adaptation: first, cumulation of skills across generations, then complementation of actions, and finally, generativity of CCDs. Thus, cultural coordination devices such as language, relational models, rituals, moral interpretations of misfortune, taboos, and religion are the product of evolved, universal psychological proclivities conjoined with socially transmitted, culture-specific complements.

Implications For Social Psychological Research

Complementarity theory implies that researchers analyzing social psychological processes should consider how these processes

- Have shaped natural selection and culture;
- Are potentiated and channeled by evolved proclivities;
- Are developed by inherently sociable children because they desire to relate;

- Are learned by very structured processes; and
- Are intrinsically (not incidentally) variable across cultures.

Complementarity theory reminds social psychologists that culture is not an exogenous variable: The generativity that results in cultural diversity is built into many basic developmental, cognitive, and social psychological processes. Complementarity theory highlights the idea that humans generally do not think about each other primarily as objects with features: People do not focus on others' individual attributes. The crux of social psychology is the coordination of motives, emotions, evaluations, cognitions, and actions. People organize their action in ways that are complementary to the actions of their partners, opponents, and observers in social relationships and groups. When people think about each other they may ask, "What kind of person is this?" However, they ask this question with reference to the possibilities the person offers—and the problems the person poses—for coordinated interaction: for communication, for relationships, and for participating in potentially complementary roles. People consider each other in terms of the congruity or incongruity of their motives, emotions, evaluations, cognitions, and actions.

Complementarity theory focuses on the adaptive specializations that characterize us as eusocial, ultracultural, culturally social animals. Our fitness and our everyday well-being depend on our culturally organized sociality. That sociality is not based primarily on general purpose cognitive processes. It is not based on rigid fixed action patterns that dictate identical genotypically controlled social behavior that is invariant in every community around the world. Nor is our sociality the product of incomparable, arbitrary cultural constructions generated idiosyncratically in each community or each interaction. Humans are social beings who have evolved a finite set of psychological proclivities that are capable of being completed by an infinite number of congruent socially transmitted prototypes and principles, enabling us to construct devices to coordinate with each other. Consequently, we can coordinate in innumerable mutually intelligible, mutually meaningful, culturally distinct yet universally structured institutions, particular relationships, and specific social acts.

References

Atran, S. (1998). Folk biology and the anthropology of science: Cognitive universals and cultural particulars. *Behavioral and Brain Sciences, 21,* 547—609.

Baldwin, J. M. (1896). A new factor in evolution. *The American Naturalist, 30,* 441–451, 536–553.

Boyd, R., & Richerson, P. J. (1985). *Culture and the evolutionary process.* Chicago: University of Chicago Press.

Boyd, R., & Richerson, P. J. (1989). The role of evolved predispositions in cultural evolution. *Ethology and Sociobiology, 10,* 195–219.

Boyd, R., & Richerson, P. J. (1995). Why does culture increase human adaptability? *Ethology and Sociobiology, 16,* 125–143.

Boyer, P. (1994). *The naturalness of religious ideas: A cognitive theory of religion.* Berkeley: University of California Press.

Buss, D. M. (1994). *The evolution of desire: Strategies of human mating.* New York: Basic Books.

Campbell, D. T. (1983). Two distinct routes beyond kin selection to ultrasociality: Implications for the humanities and social sciences. In D. Bridgeman (Ed.), *The nature of prosocial development: Theories and strategies* (pp. 11–41). New York: Academic.

Caporael, L. (1997). The evolution of truly social cognition: The core configurations model. *Personality and Social Psychology Review, 1,* 276–298.

Cavalli-Sforza, L. L., & Feldman, M. W. (1981). *Cultural transmission and evolution: A quantitative approach.* Princeton, NJ: Princeton University Press.

Chomsky, N. (1959). A review of B. F. Skinner's "Verbal Behavior." *Language, 35,* 26–58.

Chomsky, N. (1988). *Language and problems of knowledge: The Managua lectures.* Cambridge, MA: MIT Press.

D'Andrade, R. G., & Strauss, C. (Eds.). (1992). *Human motives and cultural models.* New York: Cambridge University Press.

Deacon, T. W. (1998). *The symbolic species: The co-evolution of language and the brain.* New York: Norton.

Donald, M. (1991) *Origins of the modern mind: Three stages in the evolution of culture and cognition.* Cambridge, MA: Harvard University Press.

Dulaney, S., & Fiske, A. P. (1994). Cultural rituals and obsessive–compulsive disorder: Is there a common psychological mechanism? *Ethos, 22,* 243–283.

Durham, W. H. (1991). *Coevolution: Genes, culture, and human diversity.* Stanford, CA: Stanford University Press.

Eckerman, C. O., & Didow, S. M. (1996). Nonverbal imitation and toddlers' mastery of verbal means of achieving coordinated action. *Developmental Psychology 32,* 141–152.

Elman J. L., Bates, E. A., & Johnson, M. H. (1996). *Rethinking innateness: A connectionist perspective on development.* Cambridge, MA: MIT Press.

Fiske, A. P. (1991). *Structures of social life: The four elementary forms of human relations.* New York: Free Press (Macmillan).

Fiske, A. P. (1992). The four elementary forms of sociality: Framework for a unified theory of social relations. *Psychological Review, 99,* 689–723.

Fiske, A. P. (1998). Human sociality. *International Society for the Study of Personal Relationships Bulletin, 14*(2), 4–9.

Fiske, A. P. (1999). *Learning culture the way informants do: Observation, imitation, and participation.* Unpublished manuscript.

Fiske, A. P. (2000). *Taboo.* Manuscript in preparation.

Fiske, A. P., & Haslam, N. (1996). Social cognition is thinking about relationships. *Current Directions in Psychological Science, 5,* 143–148.

Fiske, A. P., & Haslam, N. (1997). Is obsessive–compulsive disorder a pathology of the human disposition to perform socially meaningful rituals? Evidence of similar content. *Journal of Nervous and Mental Disease, 185,* 211–222.

Fodor, J. A. (1983). *The modularity of mind.* Cambridge, MA: MIT Press.

Frank, S. A. (1998). *Foundations of social evolution.* Princeton, NJ: Princeton University Press.

Gallistel, C. R. (1990). *The organization of learning.* Cambridge, MA: MIT Press.

Gallistel, C. R. (1995). The replacement of general-purpose theories with adaptive specializations. In M. S. Gazzaniga (Ed.), *The cognitive neurosciences* (pp. 1255–1267). Cambridge, MA: MIT Press.

Garcia, J., & Ervin, F. R. (1968). Gustatory-visceral and telereceptor-cutaneous conditioning—Adaptation to internal and external milieus. *Communications in Behavioral Biology, A1,* 389–415.

Greenfield, P. M., Maynard, A. E., Boehm, C., & Yut-Schmidtling, E. (in press). Cultural apprenticeship and cultural change: Tool learning and imitation in chimpanzees and humans. In S. T. Parker, J. Langer, & M. L. McKinney (Eds.), *The evolution of behavioral ontogeny.* Santa Fe, NM: School of American Research Press.

Hamilton, W. D. (1964). The genetical evolution of social behavior. *Journal of Theoretical Biology, 7,* 1—52.

Haslam, N. (1997). Four grammars for primate social relations. In J. Simpson & D. Kenrick (Eds.), *Evolutionary social psychology* (pp. 293–312). Mahwah, NJ: Lawrence Erlbaum Associates, Inc.

Hinde, R. A., & Stevenson-Hinde, J. (Eds.). (1973). *Constraints on learning: Limitations and predispositions.* New York: Academic.

Hinton, G. E., & Nowlan, S. J. (1987). How learning can guide evolution. *Complex Systems, 1,* 495–502.

Hirschfeld, L. A., & Gelman, S. A. (Eds.). (1994). *Mapping the mind: Domain specificity in cognition and culture.* New York: Cambridge University Press.

Laland, K. N., Richerson, P. J., & Boyd, R. (1993). Animal social learning: Toward a new theoretical approach. *Perspectives in Ethology, 10,* 249–277.

Lancy, D. F. (1996). *Playing on the mother-ground: Cultural routines for children's development.* New York: Guilford.

Lave, J., & Wenger, E. (1991). *Situated learning: Legitimate peripheral participation.* Cambridge, England: Cambridge University Press.

Lumsden, C. J., & Wilson, E. O. (1981). *Genes, mind, and culture: The coevolutionary process.* Cambridge, MA: Harvard University Press.

Mayley, G. (1997). Landscapes, learning costs, and genetic assimilation. *Evolutionary Computation, 4,* 213–234.

Morgan, C. L. (1896). On modification and variation. *Science, 4,* 733–740.

Nagel, K., Olguin, R. S., & Tomasello, M. (1993) Processes of social learning in the tool use of chimpanzees (Pan troglodytes) and human children (Homo sapiens). *Journal of Comparative Psychology, 107,* 174–186.

Osborn, H. F. (1896a). A mode of evolution requiring neither natural selection nor the inheritance of acquired characters. *Transactions of the New York Academy of Science, 15,* 141–142, 148.

Osborn, H. F. (1896b). Ontogenetic and phylogenetic variation. *Science, 4,* 786–789.

Pulliam, H. R., & Dunford, C. (1980). *Programmed to learn: An essay on the evolution of culture.* New York: Columbia University Press.

Rogoff, B., Baker-Sennett, J., Lacasa, P., & Goldsmith D. (1995). Development through participation in sociocultural activity. In J. J. Goodenow, P. Miller, & F. Kessel (Eds.), *Cultural practices as contexts for development* (pp. 45–66). San Francisco: Jossey-Bass.

Rozin, P. (1976). The evolution of intelligence and access to the cognitive unconscious. In J. M. Sprague & A. E. Epstein (Eds.), *Progress in psychobiology and physiological psychology, 6,* 245–280.

Rozin, P. (1982). Human food selection: The interaction of biology, culture, and individual experience. In L. M. Barker (Ed.), *The psychobiology of human food selection* (pp. 225–254) Westport, CT: AVI Publishing.

Rozin, P., & Kalat, J. (1972). Learning as a situation-specific adaptation. In M. E. P. Seligman & J. Hager (Eds.), *The biological boundaries of learning* (pp. 66–97). New York: Appleton-Century-Crofts.

Sahlins, M. (1972). *Stone age economics.* New York: Aldine.

Scheiner, S. M. (1993). Genetics and evolution of phenotypic plasticity. *Annual Review of Ecology and Systematics, 24,* 35–68.

Seaborg, D. M. (1999). Evolutionary feedback: A new mechanism for stasis and punctuated evolutionary change based on integration of the organism. *Journal of Theorertical Biology, 198,* 1–26.

Seligman, M. E. P. (1970). On the generality of the laws of learning. *Psychological Review, 77,* 406–418.

Sperber, D. (1996). Anthropology and psychology: Towards an epidemiology of representations. In D. Sperber (Eds.), *Explaining culture: A naturalistic approach* (pp. 56–76). Oxford, England: Blackwell.

Tomasello, M. (Ed.). (1998). *The new psychology of language: Cognitive and functional approaches to language structure.* Mahwah, NJ: Lawrence Erlbaum Associates, Inc.

Tomasello, M., & Call, J. (1997). *Primate cognition.* New York: Oxford University Press.

Tomasello, M., Kruger, A. C., & Ratner, H. H. (1993). Cultural learning (with commentaries and reply). *Behavioral and Brain Sciences, 16,* 495–552.

Tooby, J., & Cosmides, L. (1992). Psychological foundations of culture. In J. H. Barkow, L. Cosmides, & J. Tooby (Eds.), *The adapted mind: Evolutionary psychology and the generation of culture* (pp. 19–36). New York: Oxford University Press.

Trevarthen, C. (1988). Universal co-operative motives: How infants begin to know the language and culture of their parents. In G. Jahoda & I. M. Lewis (Eds.), *Acquiring culture: Cross-cultural studies in child development* (pp. 37–91). London: Croom Helm.

Trivers, R. L. (1971). The evolution of reciprocal altruism. *The Quarterly Review of Biology, 46,* 35–57.

Waddington, C. (1975). *The evolution of an evolutionist.* Edinburgh, Scotland: Edinburgh University Press.

Wcislo, W. T. (1989). Behavioral environments and evolutionary change. *Annual Review of Ecology and Systematics, 20,* 137–169.

Whiten, A., & Custance, D. (1996). Studies of imitation in chimpanzees and children. In C. M. Heyes & B. G. Galef, Jr. (Eds.), *Social learning in animals: The roots of culture* (pp. 291–318). San Diego: Academic.

Whiten, A., Goodall, J., McGrew, W. C., Nishida, T., Reynolds, V., Sugiyama, Y., Tutin, C. E. G., Wrangham, R. W., & Boesch, C. (1999). Cultures in chimpanzees. *Nature, 399,* 682–685.

Wilson, E. O. (1974). *The insect societies.* Cambridge, MA: Harvard University Press.

Personality and Social Psychology Review
2000, Vol. 4, No. 1, 95–105

The Study of Groups: Past, Present, and Future

Joseph E. McGrath
Department of Psychology
University of Illinois at Urbana–Champaign

Holly Arrow
Department of Psychology
University of Oregon

Jennifer L. Berdahl
Haas School of Business
University of California, Berkeley

A century of research on small groups has yielded bountiful findings about many specific features and processes in groups. Much of that work, in line with a positivist epistemology that emphasizes control and precision and favors the laboratory experiment over other data collection strategies, has also tended to treat groups as though they were simple, isolated, static entities. Recent research trends that treat groups as complex, adaptive, dynamic systems open up new approaches to studying groups. In line with those trends, a theory of groups as complex systems is offered and some methodological and conceptual issues raised by this theory are identified. A 3-pronged research strategy based on theory development, computational modeling, and empirical research that holds promise for illuminating the dynamic processes underlying the emergence of complexity and the ongoing balance of continuity and change in groups is proposed.

As the 20th century ends and the 21st begins, we look back on a century of research on groups, take stock of where the accumulated work of the century has brought us, and look ahead to a possible future for the study of small groups. It is time to reorient our thinking about small groups to make it fundamentally dynamic, to refocus group research on the group as a distinct level of analysis in interaction with other levels, and to take time and history in groups seriously. To reground the study of groups in the reality of group life as it occurs in the world, we must acknowledge and study groups as embedded not only within a hierarchy of levels, from the individual to the interpersonal to the embedding contexts of organizations, networks, and institutions, but also within the passage of time.

We view groups as bounded, structured entities that emerge from the purposive, interdependent actions of individuals. Groups bring together individuals who carry their pasts with them, and groups create

their own history, guided by members' sense of the future, as they operate in time. This is not, however, the conception of groups that has guided most research in the past century. It is also not the conception that one would deduce by reviewing most current published studies in social psychology that purport to study groups.

Social psychologists have learned much about phenomena relevant to groups, and also quite a bit about groups, in the past century. However, conceptual and methodological traditions, which in the past have supported advances in our knowledge about groups, have now begun to constrain progress in small-group research. This article adds voice to a persistent chorus of doubts about the current state of small-group research, identifies specific shortcomings grounded in the past that impede advances in the field, and outlines an approach toward setting group research on what is viewed as a more promising path.

To this end, we outline our theory of groups as complex adaptive systems, discuss some of the conceptual and methodological challenges this approach entails, and note some ways of tackling these challenges using new approaches, such as computational

Requests for reprints should be sent to Joseph E. McGrath, Department of Psychology, University of Illinois, 603 E. Daniel Street, Champaign, IL 61820–6267. E-mail: jmcgrath@s.psych.uiuc.edu.

modeling, established but seldom used research strategies (e.g., experimental simulation), and new approaches within the prototypical research strategy of laboratory experiments. First, however, we discuss in more detail what we see as the challenges posed by the current state of the field, shaped by earlier work in this century.

The Study of Groups in the Past

Small groups have been a topic of interest to social psychologists in both psychology and sociology and to scholars in other social and behavioral sciences for the past century (for recent reviews, see Levine & Moreland, 1990; McGrath, 1997; Moreland, Hogg, & Hains, 1994; Sanna & Parks, 1997). Research in Europe and North America during the 1890s and early 1900s looked at group task performance (Triplett, 1898) and at "coalitions in triads" (Simmel, 1902). A flurry of work in the 1920s investigated social facilitation (e.g., Allport, 1920) and related topics. The field really blossomed, however, in North American social psychology of the 1940s, 1950s, and 1960s, which brought a flood of research on leadership, communication, social influence, conflict, norms, and many other aspects of groups (for reviews of work in this period see Cartwright & Zander, 1953, 1960, 1968; Hare, 1976; McGrath & Altman, 1966). Research on groups within psychology declined dramatically in the late 1960s and 1970s (Steiner, 1974), although related fields such as organizational behavior, communication studies, clinical and educational psychology, and political science remained interested in small groups (Levine & Moreland, 1990).

Contributions and Limitations of Past Research

This body of research on groups contains a wealth of studies and considerable theoretical insight. The field has made great progress in mapping the relative strengths and weaknesses of individuals and groups on different types of tasks, and has developed strong theory and effective techniques of measurement for understanding the transformation of individual inputs into group outputs, focusing on how inputs are combined (Steiner, 1972), how group judgments can be predicted from individual preferences (Davis, 1973, 1982), and why groups often fail to capitalize on the potential resources of members, whether these are creative ideas (Diehl & Stroebe, 1991), unique information (Stasser & Titus, 1985, 1987), or divergent opinions (Asch, 1951).

Social psychologists from the sociology tradition have extended our understanding of power and status relationships in groups (Lovaglia, 1994; Ridgeway & Berger, 1986). We have a better understanding of what creates conflict both within groups (e.g., Jehn, 1995, 1997; O'Connor, Gruenfeld, & McGrath, 1993) and among groups (e.g., Blake & Mouton, 1984; Insko et al., 1992; Sherif, Harvey, White, Hood, & Sherif, 1961). We have attended to cognitive and affective forces, such as identity and cohesion that hold groups together (e.g., Bouas & Arrow, 1996; Hogg, 1987). We have studied how groups influence members, how members influence groups through the leadership process, and how members influence one another (e.g., Bass, 1997; Hackman, 1992; Sherif, 1936).

These insights have been applied to improve group performance in organizations (e.g., Hackman, 1990; for a recent review, see Guzzo & Dickson, 1996), and to change individual attitudes, behavior, and psychological functioning through group discussion, support groups such as 12-step programs, and group therapy (e.g., Kaplan & Sadock, 1993; Yalom, 1995). Studies that have focused on dynamic patterns in group interaction over time have led to formulations about microlevel interaction patterns in communication (Bales, 1950), phase patterns in problem solving and decision making (Bales & Strodtbeck, 1951; VanLear & Mabry, 1999), and developmental patterns reflecting the life course of a group (Gersick, 1988, 1989; Tuckman & Jensen, 1977; Worchel, 1994).

At the same time, the field has been limited by the conceptual and methodological paradigms underlying most of those studies. A large proportion of the research on groups throughout the past century, in social psychology and other fields, has been carried out within a strongly positivistic paradigm. That paradigm emphasizes laboratory experimentation as the privileged research strategy. Much of the work has been laboratory research on ad hoc groups working for short periods of time on tasks arbitrarily assigned to them for experimental purposes. Field studies on "real-life" groups have provided a useful complement, but most field studies have also studied groups as isolated entities and for only short time periods. Social psychologists have typically paid little attention to the groups' embedding contexts. Some recent work in organizational behavior is more sophisticated in this regard (e.g., Morgeson & Hofmann, 1999; Sundstrom, DeMuese, & Futrell, 1990; see Ilgen, 1999, for a good review).

Much of the work that studies interacting groups—especially laboratory experiments—is characterized by four factors that impose serious limitations on the meaning and generality of findings:

1. Groups are studied as if they were simple systems composed of chain-like, unidirectional, cause–effect relations.
2. Groups are studied as if they were isolated from their embedding contexts.
3. Groups are studied as if they were static entities, with no past, no future, and only an input–output present.
4. Groups are studied as generic entities made up of generic people, as though all people and all groups are interchangeable.

By concentrating our empirical research (and our subsequent theoretical formulations) on studies with these features, we have denied ourselves the opportunity to envision groups in ways that more accurately reflect our own experiences in groups—namely, that groups are complex, adaptive, and dynamic systems—and to find ways to incorporate such a viewpoint in our empirical and theoretical research.

The Present

The 1980s and 1990s have seen a resurgence in research on group-related topics in social psychology, inspired by social categorization theory, minority influence theories, and social cognition approaches (Moreland et al., 1994). This stream of research typically focuses on individual cognition about groups or about attitudes ascribed to groups. The group is often an abstraction in the minds of individuals, rather than a collective entity composed of interacting members.

Kurt Lewin is often regarded as the father of small-group research. Yet, in analyzing the impact of Lewin on later group research, Moreland (1996) suggested that Lewin's theoretical emphasis on the individual's subjective perceptions promoted an interest on the individual as a focus within a group setting, drawing attention away from the group as a distinct entity of interest. Hogg (1987) discussed how concepts that were originally thought of as fundamentally group-level constructs, such as cohesiveness, have in practice been reduced to the interpersonal level.

In a thoughtful piece reflecting on the status of experimental research conducted by social psychologists, Månson (1993) concluded that many group experiments actually study something that does not exist: a methodological abstraction that has no equivalent among naturally occurring groups (pp. 274–275). In other words, they study hypothetical entities. Taking this abstraction to a logical extreme, a substantial portion of group studies published in social psychology journals in recent years do not study the behavior of any groups, but focus instead on how people think about hypothetical groups (Moreland et al., 1994). Another subset of studies purport to be about groups, but are actually studies of social interaction or conversation by people who would not define themselves as acting in a group (e.g., Bordia, DiFonzo, & Chang, 1999). In such cases, the group exists not in the concrete operation of a bounded system, or even in the minds of the participants, but only in the mind of the experimenter.

Although studies of actual intragroup processes have become rare in mainstream social psychology journals, such work appears increasingly in organizational psychology and management journals (Sanna & Parks, 1997). Much of this research focuses on extant groups operating in an organizational context, such as cockpit crews, management teams, and quality improvement groups (e.g., Hackman, 1990; Ilgen, Major, Hollenbeck, & Sego, 1995). This work does pay attention to the embedding context of groups and to changes over time, and shows an attention to compositional issues such as gender and ethnic diversity that is lacking in most experimental research. Much of this work focuses on teams, which are defined in contrast to groups in general as having a common group goal.

This work is often informed by a systems metaphor for groups, and a number of organizational researchers have tried to delineate dimensions that distinguish groups or provide a typology of groups. Some have incorporated an "over time" feature of groups as an important feature of their analyses (e.g., Hackman, 1990, 1992). Still, there is not yet a clear and shared theoretical conception about the fundamental properties of small groups in either the organizational literature or the social psychological literature on groups.

Recent work also presents encouraging evidence that dynamic approaches to groups, and to processes that are important to groups, such as social influence, are reemerging in the work of scholars in social psychology (e.g., Latané's 1996 dynamic social impact theory; Nowak, Szamrej, & Latané, 1990), sociology (Polley's 1989 Group Field Dynamics approach), communications (Poole & DeSanctis's 1989 adaptive structuration theory), and organizational behavior (Guastello, 1995). Although dynamical systems and chaos and complexity theory are increasingly providing a source of inspiration and new metaphors for group scholars (e.g., Baron, Amazeen, & Beek, 1994; Latané & Nowak, 1994), the ideas and concepts they are borrowing have not yet been widely and systematically integrated and adapted for application to collective human systems such as groups. Our work (Arrow, McGrath, & Berdahl, 2000) is an attempt to create an integrative, broad theory that can provide a grounding for more work of this nature, so that the trickles of new work can merge into a stream.

Groups As Complex Adaptive Systems

We see groups as complex, adaptive, dynamic systems. Rather than simple, groups are complex entities embedded in a hierarchy of levels and characterized by multiple, bidirectional, and nonlinear causal relations. Rather than isolated, groups are intricately embedded within, and have continual mutual adaptation with, a number of embedding contexts. Rather than static, groups are inherently dynamic systems, operating via processes that unfold over time, with those processes dependent both on the group's past history and on its anticipated future. Groups develop as systems over time, and change as a function of changing conditions over time.

Our approach to studying groups as complex, adaptive, dynamic systems (Arrow et al., 2000; McGrath & Argote, in press; McGrath, Arrow, & Berdahl, 1999) draws on concepts from general systems theory (von Bertalanffy, 1968), from dynamical systems theory (Abraham, Abraham, & Shaw, 1990), and from complexity and chaos theory (Casti, 1992; Kelso, 1995; Prigogine & Stengers, 1984). We present our theory of groups here in skeleton form. We then discuss the implications of this theory for conducting research and describe a combination of research strategies that together hold promise for studying groups in a way that views complexity, adaptation, and dynamic cross-level interaction as essential characteristics of groups.

We regard groups as open and complex systems that interact with the smaller systems (i.e., the members) embedded within them and the larger systems (e.g., organizations, communities) within which they are embedded. Groups have fuzzy boundaries that both distinguish them from and connect them to their members and their embedding contexts.

Throughout a group's life, three levels of causal dynamics continually shape the group. Local dynamics involve the activity of a group's constituent elements: members engaged in tasks using tools and resources. Local dynamics give rise to group-level or global dynamics. Global dynamics involve the behavior of system-level variables—such as norms and status structures, group identity and group cohesiveness, leadership, conflict, and task performance effectiveness—that emerge from and subsequently shape and constrain local dynamics. Contextual dynamics refer to the impact of system-level parameters that affect the overall trajectory of global group dynamics over time, and whose values are determined in part by the group's embedding context. Levels of organizational support, supply of potential members, demand for group outputs, and other extrinsic factors, for example, shape and constrain the local and global dynamics of a group.

All groups act in the service of two generic functions: (a) to complete group projects and (b) to fulfill member needs. A group's success in pursuing these two functions affects the viability and integrity of the group as a system. Thus, system integrity becomes a third generic group function, emergent from the other two. A group's system integrity in turn affects its ability to function effectively in completing group projects and fulfilling member needs, and to adapt to changes in demands and opportunities presented by the environment and by the group members.

Groups include three types of elements: (a) people who become a group's members, (b) intentions that are embodied in group projects, and (c) resources that comprise the group's technologies. Group members vary in what they bring to the group in terms of skills, values, attitudes, personalities, and cognitive styles. They also differ in demographic attributes, and in the needs they seek to fulfill via group membership. Group projects vary in the opportunities for and requirements imposed on members for various kinds of activities. Technologies, which include the "software" tools of norms and procedures as well as "hardware" tools (e.g., hammers, computers, trucks, and musical instruments) differ in what kinds of activity and instrumental functions they facilitate.

Groups pursue their functions by creating and enacting a coordinated pattern of member–task–tool relations that are called the coordination network. The full coordination network includes six component networks: (a) the member network (member–member relationships such as friendship, hostility, and influence); (b) the task network (task–task relations such as their sequencing relations); (c) the tool network (tool–tool relations, such as the need for clustering of particular hardware and software tools); (d) the labor network (member–task relations, which specify who is to do what); (e) the role network (member–tool relations, which specify how members will do their tasks); and (f) the job network (task–tool relations, such as what tools are required to complete particular tasks effectively).

The life course of a group can be characterized by three logically ordered modes that are conceptually distinct but have fuzzy temporal boundaries: formation, operation, and metamorphosis. As a group forms, people, intentions, and resources become organized into an initial coordination network of relations among members, projects, and technology that demarcates that group as a bounded social entity. As a group operates in the service of group projects and member needs, its members elaborate, enact, monitor, and modify the coordination network established during formation. Groups both learn from their own experience and adapt to events occurring in their embedding contexts. If and when a group undergoes metamorphosis, it dissolves or is transformed into a different social entity.

All three levels of causal dynamics operate, simultaneously and continuously, in all three modes of a group's life. Local dynamics are manifested in a group's coordination processes, global dynamics reflect a group's developmental processes, and contextual dynamics underlie a group's adaptation processes.

Issues and Opportunities Raised by the Theory

Conducting research on the basis of such a conception of groups raises questions about the logic of inquiry, the nature of cause, the role of time in our logic of inference, and the underlying meaning and purpose of empirical studies.

A Different Logic of Inquiry

Our theory, derived by applying concepts in general systems, dynamical systems, and complexity theories to small groups, implies not only a different conceptual perspective but also a different logic of analysis. To summarize, we posit that groups are complex systems. In small groups, local action consists of recursive, nonlinear interaction among many elements. Local group processes create, activate, replicate, and adjust dynamic links in a coordination network. Our conceptualization treats this as an interaction among many local variables. From local action, global-level patterns emerge—behavioral and cognitive patterns (e.g., group norms, cohesion, division of labor, a role system and influence structure) and temporal patterns (e.g., cycles of conflict and consensus, regularities in changing group performance, and the ebb and flow of communication). These global-level patterns are conceptualized as global variables that emerge from the interaction of local variables and then structure subsequent local action.

We can expect local action for any given group to show at least some regularities, which can be modeled as a set of rules that the system follows. Although the interaction among local-level elements may be highly complicated, the rules governing the action and interaction of group elements may be quite simple (e.g., Latané & Nowak, 1994). Which rules guide local action, however, and which global patterns emerge from the operation of these rules, depends on initial conditions and on subsequent situational factors and external conditions, conceptualized here as contextual parameters. This is not the

kind of relationship traditionally modeled by independent and dependent variables. Rather, we are talking about contextual factors that constrain the operation of local-level rules without determining the outcome. The whole pattern of global dynamics that emerges from this local action may shift when a contextual parameter shifts to a different value, or it may remain unchanged. This depends on where in the range of possible values the shift occurs.

For example, the overall rate of production of group products (a global variable) may remain constant under a range of external incentives for the group products, but at some point along a continuum of external incentives (the contextual parameter) group members may change their actions, resulting in a shift to a much higher or lower global production rate. Allmendinger and Hackman's (1996) study of East German orchestras, for example, found that differences in local cultures were associated with differences in the orchestras' sex composition, which in turn was associated with differences in member satisfaction and system performance. Their results can be interpreted as showing that local dynamics in the orchestras were shaped in part by the contextual variable of its sex composition, and that there are ranges in composition within which those dynamics are unaffected but also points beyond which a small change (e.g., moving from 30% to 40% women) leads to qualitatively different outcomes.

Given the range of potential interactions among local variables, it is not possible to predict the individual and joint values of these variables accurately, even if their values are known with high accuracy at a particular point in time. Complex systems whose behavior depends largely on interactions among local elements (e.g., the pattern of flight delays at major airports during holiday periods) are only predictable in the short run, and these predictions are for global variables, not local variables. Patterns of key global variables, however, do show substantial regularities over time. The qualitative pattern of these regularities may differ for groups under different operating conditions, or for the same group if the value of a contextual parameter changes beyond some critical threshold. The pattern over time of a given global variable such as the division of labor, for example, may be qualitatively different (e.g., centralized or decentralized), depending on the setting of a contextual parameter (e.g., the level of external threats to the group).

In the language of dynamical systems, global variables settle over time into relatively small regions in state space (the space of possibilities for that variable). These regions, called *attractors,* vary in type. One focus of research in this approach is to identify the attractor or attractors into which a global variable will settle over time. Those attractors may be single or multiple, stable or unstable, fixed point or periodic, or some other form. The configuration of attractors is also likely to vary at different levels of key contextual parameters. For example, if conflict is taken as a global variable, one group (the alpha team) may have a single, stable, fixed point attractor of moderate conflict. This is the value for conflict the group settles into and maintains. This configuration holds over a range of values for external stress (a contextual parameter) on the group. At very high levels of stress, however, a new pattern may emerge, with two unstable attractors of either very high conflict or very low conflict. Another group (the beta team) may have a stable periodic attractor for conflict—a consistent pattern of increasing, then decreasing, conflict—that persists over a wide range of stress levels. At very high stress, however, the beta team shifts to a single, stable, fixed point of high conflict.

It is not the aim of this approach, therefore, to predict average levels of specific local variables, either at a given time or aggregated over time. Rather, the aim is to track the characteristic evolution of the system through different system states, as reflected in the pattern of global variables over time, and to investigate which contextual parameters affect this pattern of evolution, and how.

Temporal Issues

Groups are characterized by the simultaneous operation of multiple temporal processes, with potentially different cadences and cyclic forms. Some of those group processes may operate differently depending on where the group is in its historical life cycle. So, too, many extrinsic contextual factors may have different effects depending on where in the group's life they occur. Some of the temporal processes that underlie group operations may arise from the nature of the projects the group is undertaking. These, of course, will differ for groups of different kinds. At more microlevels, executing the tasks that make up group projects often requires precise synchronization of the timing of different actions by the same member and of actions of different members. Consider, for example, that the actions of every member of an orchestra must be synchronized at the temporal level of a 16th note!

Such synchronization requirements suggest that the concept of entrainment of multiple cyclical processes is useful not only for studying biological systems but also for analysis of social systems such as groups. Entrainment refers to the synchronization, in phase and periodicity, of multiple cyclical processes or behaviors. At the biological level, the most well-known set are the circadian rhythms, multiple biological and chemical processes that become synchronized with one another and with the day–night cycle of the planet. At the individual and group behavior level, researchers have found evidence for entrainment in task production rates, interaction patterns, communication timing, and even breathing patterns, for interacting partners and groups (e.g., Ancona & Chung, 1996; Karau & Kelly, 1992; Kelly, 1988; Kelly & McGrath, 1985; McGrath & Kelly, 1986; Warner, 1979). Such complex synchronization also suggests the need to develop methods for data collection, analysis, and interpretation that will let us tease apart such multiple overlapping rhythmic processes and assess their effects.

Causal Issues

A complexity theory view also invites us to raise questions about the nature of causality. Traditionally, small-group research, like most work done in the positivistic tradition, has primarily focused on efficient (also called mechanical) cause. Moreover, it has treated that form of causation as consisting of a series of directional, linear, chain-like cause–effect connections between two (or very few) specific variables. The very idea of complex systems carries with it the implication that the causal connections (at the level of local dynamics) are multivariate, bidirectional, and nonlinear relations. Moreover, the emphasis in complexity theory on developmental processes suggests the importance of formal cause—the way in which process constrains or determines structure. Furthermore, human systems—such as groups—are strongly characterized by the operation of *intentionality*: Individuals and groups do what they do, sometimes and to some extent, because they intend to do so. This is a kind of final cause.

Some Methodological Issues

Not only does a complex system view of groups carry with it a different logic of analysis but also argues for changes in the traditional methods of studying groups. This approach calls for greater use of within-group designs, along with (or really, nested within) our more customary between-group designs. It also suggests the need to change our view of some of the features of designs that have traditionally been considered methodologically problematic (e.g., threats to internal validity, such as history and maturation; Cook & Campbell, 1979). These are, instead, inherent features of groups that persist as systems over time; hence, they are aspects of the phenomena to be studied rather than threats to be eliminated via design and analysis.

The complexity theory view of groups also raises some further methodological issues. It tends to blur the distinctions between nomothetic and ideographic purposes, as well as the distinction between prediction and control versus description and understanding as the bedrock purposes of science. It also invites questions about whether our practice of aggregation and averaging a series of successive measurements as a means for elimination of random error of measurement is in fact a practice that discards information about the functioning of the measured systems over time.

The Future: Where Will We Go From Here?

As is apparent from the previous discussion, it is one thing to talk about a new theoretical view of groups, one that questions some of the field's most entrenched operating assumptions, but it is quite another to formulate a viable and useful research program by which to explore, test, and modify that theory. We suggest that, in the future, effective research on small groups will require major shifts in methodological preferences within our current paradigm (e.g., shift to more emphasis on research dealing with "natural groups" over extended periods of time), as well as major extensions or modifications of that research paradigm (e.g., to shift the object of analysis from average differences in aggregated scores between conditions to tracking the trajectory of global variables over time for groups operating under comparable initial conditions). Such shifts in preferences and paradigms imply major change in our methodology at strategic levels.

This prescription poses enormous challenges for those who wish to extend and redirect future research on small groups. By no means do we believe that we have adequate answers to those challenges at this time. We do, however, have some suggestions for a systematic effort toward meeting those methodological challenges, stemming in part from experience gained and lessons learned in our own research endeavors.

Specifically, we suggest that one can make a good beginning toward meeting these methodological challenges by adopting a tripartite research strategy, consisting of (a) a comprehensive theory of groups as complex adaptive systems, (b) an eclectic and flexible approach to empirical research, informed by theory and by existing empirical findings, and (c) computational models that connect theory and empirical research by enabling researchers to develop complex

sets of theoretical relations and explore their implications over time. Results from work on each of these three fronts—theory, empirical research programs, and computational modeling—should inform further developments in the other two, with a continual need to adjust all three. The theory should be based at the outset on the body of extant empirical evidence and should provide the basis for both the design of new empirical studies and the development of computational models. The theory needs to be reexamined and modified continuously, in light of empirical findings about how people behave in groups and on the basis of computational model output that reveals how the theory behaves when translated into a set of rules and formulas and run over time.

The body of extant empirical evidence offers both the basis for initial theorizing and for setting initial parameters and variables for computational models. New empirical evidence, derived from studies designed to explore the implications of the theory and to verify the output of the computational models, can serve as the crucible in which both theory and model are assessed. Some of this data may be generated by experiments in familiar laboratory settings, looking at dynamics over the short term. Some may be generated by extended experimental simulations, such as the semester-long JEMCO studies (for overviews, see Arrow et al., 1996; McGrath, Arrow, Gruenfeld, Hollingshead, & O'Connor, 1993), which examined the patterns of behavior for multiple groups over time. Some may be generated by comparative field studies of naturally occurring groups over time, as exemplified by the comparative case studies published in Hackman (1990).

Laboratory Experiments

Certain criteria are crucial for studying groups as complex dynamic systems using laboratory experimentation. In those studies it is essential that (a) groups consist of real people interacting over time, rather than isolated individuals making judgments about hypothetical others or groups; (b) key local and global variables are tracked over time rather than measured once or twice; and (c) the researcher examines the trajectories of global variables for each group to look for dynamic patterns, rather than aggregating across groups on the presumption that any variations among those groups are random error masking a single true trajectory for all groups. If we take group composition and group history seriously, we must acknowledge that all real human groups, whether formed in the laboratory or sought out in the field, differ in initial conditions because they are made up of different people, and that as each group develops, it acquires a history that distinguishes it to some extent from other groups of similar membership composition, task, and tools. Studying interacting groups requires the abandonment of some of the control and precision that is a hallmark of experimental research, while preserving the ability to manipulate some of the variables that will affect dynamic processes in groups.

An example of this approach, which looks at short-term dynamics in the laboratory, is a paradigm developed by Arrow and colleagues (Arrow, Bennett, Crosson, & Orbell, 1999) to study the self-organized formation of groups. In contrast to the typical approach to composing groups, in which participants are randomly assigned to groups, participants in the "social poker" paradigm are assembled together, given resources (playing cards) and information about the resources of other players (the cards other players have received) and then must form groups and pool their cards to make a standard card hand such as four-of-a-kind. Different hands earn different amounts of money, and group members must decide how to divide up the proceeds. After groups are formed, players turn in their cards, receive new cards, and must again form groups.

This paradigm is designed to study the stream of individual choices and the intersection and coordination of those choices in a dynamic environment, which results in the formation of ephemeral coalitions (short-lived acting groups) and, if the same members repeatedly seek one another out, the emergence of standing groups and group structures such as allocation norms. Once the range of dynamic patterns is identified for repeated replications in the same condition, extrinsic parameters believed to affect the emergence of relatively stable groups (e.g., the stability of the incentive structure and the demographic composition of the pool that members are drawn from) can be systematically varied to see if different sets of trajectories emerge for global variables such as the rate of membership change, allocation norms, and status hierarchies among players.

Computational Modeling

Computational models, based initially on the premises of a theory and the evidence from extant empirical data, can test a very wide range of possibilities implied by the theory that would be difficult to test empirically (e.g., Carley & Svoboda, 1996; Drogoul & Ferber, 1994; Gordon, Goodwin, & Trainor, 1992). They can do so both with large samples of runs that have identical initial conditions and with large samples of runs that start with different initial conditions. Inclusion of stochastic events in the computational model

will allow simulated groups starting from identical initial conditions to develop different histories, and thus the range of plausible trajectories given a particular set of starting conditions can be mapped.

For example, Berdahl (1998, 1999) developed a computational model of a general, dynamic, and testable theory of small groups that drew on past group research (e.g., Moreland & Levine, 1982; Steiner, 1972). The model was designed in particular to study demographic diversity in groups by exploring the implications of different theories regarding whether and how initial evaluations of members' skills are influenced by demographic cues (Berdahl, 1996). In its current form, the model simulates one fully staffed, four-person group for 20 time periods, whose members remain in the group and do not recruit new members. Several parameters can be manipulated, including (a) group project types; (b) member skills, needs, and demographics; (c) members' initial evaluations of each other's skills; and (d) the degree to which skills, needs, and evaluations change over time. The model makes predictions for group performance, divisions of labor, member commitment to groups, group commitment to members, and member power.

In an initial study, Berdahl (1999) ran thousands of cases of four-person groups, varying how members initially evaluated each other's skills, the demographic composition of the groups, and the procedure for developing a division of labor within the group. The runs contained stochastic elements, including random variation in members' skills from case to case (as though groups were staffed from a population with normal distributions of skills).

Several results from the initial runs highlighted the utility of computational modeling for combining several group parameters into one theoretical treatment, and for illustrating counterintuitive consequences of the complex interaction of several simple but simultaneous rules for group interaction. For example, initial evaluations of member skills had less of an impact than suggested by traditional theories of diversity that fail to incorporate other member characteristics and group processes into their predictions. In addition, groups using an equity norm for allocating assignments and opportunities to their members had significantly worse outcomes than groups using an equality norm. Results also helped highlight problematic implications of the conception of member power used in the model.

These runs systematically mapped a portion—although only a small portion—of the total conceptual space defined by all the combinations of all possible values of the variables of the computational model. Data generating on this scale simply cannot be accomplished by empirical studies of any kind, although empirical studies are essential to investigate whether dynamic patterns that emerge in the computational runs will also appear in real groups. Computational modeling can also be used to assess the theoretical consequences of some possibilities that could not be put to empirical test at all for ethical or practical reasons.

The discussion and examples given in this article are focused on agent-based computational models. Much of our argument applies, as well, to computer simulations more generally. Such simulations often model the operation of the system as a whole directly. It seems, however, that agent-based, object-oriented computational models offer an especially useful tool for modeling the emergence of system level properties from the simulation of local level agents and relations.

Concluding Comments

In sum, future research on small groups would profit if scholars in that area were to adopt the following perspectives on their work:

1. Take into account the idea that groups are dynamic, adaptive, complex systems with multiple forms and levels of causality operating simultaneously, and choose and develop research strategies and tactics appropriate to that recognition.

2. Study groups both at the group system level, and at the level of interchanges between groups and their embedded systems (members) and among groups and their embedding systems (e.g., organizations, communities).

3. Accept the idea that not all entities that fit a general definition of groups are alike, and develop useful classification and taxonomic systems that permit us to make useful distinctions among different types of groups. Work is needed at intermediate levels (not so particular that each group is a separate type, but not so general that families, boards of directors, basketball teams, friendship groups, and steel puddling crews are expected to be responsive to the same general laws).

4. Take variation in member characteristics seriously, and adopt conceptual and methodological strategies that can deal effectively with simultaneous patterning on multiple attributes. Learn to study effects of homogeneity and various patterns of diversity on multiple attributes, at different levels of accessibility.

5. Take into account that much that is interesting about groups develops over time, and with time comes changes in members, projects, technology, and context. Develop both conceptual and methodological tools to study systems that are undergoing change. Recognize the importance both of the past and of the future on group structure and behavior, and learn to study groups that are not static and unchanging systems.

Small groups will continue to be the context for much of human social experience, in families and in organizations, at work and play. Hence, they will be important topics of study for social psychology and for other social and behavioral sciences. Although a lot has been learned in the past century, the heavily positivistic experimental approach that has driven much of that work, and the body of theory and evidence derived from that work, is largely based either on the implicit premise that groups are simple, separate, static entities, or on the premise that social interaction and interpersonal processes in general subsume all that is interesting about groups. The field seems to have reached the limits of what one can learn without developing a unifying conception of the group that recognizes the complex adaptive nature of groups, attends to phenomena that arise from but are not reducible to individual and interpersonal processes, and draws on methodology appropriate for exploring that dynamic, adaptive nature.

References

Abraham, I. D., Abraham, R. H., & Shaw, C. D. (1990). *A visual introduction to dynamical systems theory for psychology.* Santa Cruz, CA: Ariel Press.

Allmendinger, J., & Hackman, J. R. (1996). Organizations in changing environments: The case of East German symphony orchestras. *Administrative Science Quarterly, 41,* 337–369.

Allport, F. H. (1920). The influence of the group upon association and thought. *Journal of Experimental Psychology, 3,* 159–182.

Ancona, D. G., & Chung, C. (1996). Entrainment: Pace, cycle, and rhythm in organizational behavior. In B. Staw & L. L. Cummings (Eds.), *Research in organizational behavior* (pp. 251–284). New York: JAI.

Arrow, H., Bennett, R. E., Crosson, S., & Orbell, J. (1999). *Social poker: A paradigm for studying the formation of self-organized groups* (Tech. Rep. No. 99–101). Eugene: University of Oregon, Institute for Cognitive and Decision Sciences.

Arrow, H., Berdahl, J. L., Bouas, K. S., Craig, K. M., Cummings, A., Lebie, L., McGrath, J. E., O'Connor, K. M., Rhoades, J. A., & Schlosser, A. (1996). Time, technology and groups: An integration. *Computer Supported Cooperative Work, 4,* 253–261.

Arrow, H., McGrath, J. E., & Berdahl, J. L. (2000). *Small groups as complex systems: Formation, coordination, development, and adaptation.* Thousand Oaks, CA: Sage.

Asch, S. (1951). The effects of group pressure upon the modification and distortion of judgment. In H. Guetzkow (Ed.), *Groups, leadership, and men* (pp. 177–190). Pittsburgh, PA: Carnegie Press.

Bales, R. F. (1950). *Interaction process analysis: A method for the study of small groups.* Cambridge, MA: Addison-Wesley.

Bales, R. F., & Strodtbeck, F. L. (1951). Phases in group problem solving. *Journal of Abnormal and Social Psychology, 46,* 485–495.

Baron, R. M., Amazeen, P. G., & Beek, P. J. (1994). Local and global dynamics in social relations. In R. R. Vallacher & A. Nowak

(Eds.), *Dynamical systems in social relations* (pp. 111–138). New York: Academic.

Bass, B. M. (1997). Does the transactional–transformational leadership paradigm transcend organizational and national boundaries? *American Psychologist, 52,* 130–139.

Berdahl, J. L. (1996). Gender and leadership in work groups: Six alternative models. *Leadership Quarterly, 7,* 21–40.

Berdahl, J. L. (1998). The dynamics of composition and socialization in small groups: Insights gained from developing a computational model. In M. A. Neale, E. A. Mannix, & D. H. Gruenfeld (Eds.), *Research on managing groups and teams* (Vol. 1, pp. 209–227). Greenwich, CT: JAI.

Berdahl, J. L. (1999). *Power, perceptions, and performance in small groups: Insights gained from a computational model.* Unpublished doctoral dissertation, University of Illinois, Urbana–Champaign.

Blake, R. R., & Mouton, J. S. (1984). Solving costly organizational conflicts: Achieving intergroup trust, cooperation, and teamwork. San Francisco: Jossey-Bass.

Bordia, P., DiFonzo, N., & Chang, A. (1999). Rumor as group problem solving: Development patterns in informal computer-mediated groups. *Small Group Research, 30,* 8–28.

Bouas, K. S., & Arrow, H. (1996). The development of group identity in face-to-face and computer-mediated groups with membership change. *Computer Supported Cooperative Work, 4,* 153–178.

Carley, K. M., & Svoboda, D. M. (1996). Modeling organizational adaptation as a simulated annealing process. *Sociological Methods and Research, 25,* 138–148.

Cartwright, D., & Zander, A. (Eds.). (1953). *Group dynamics: Research and theory.* Evanston, IL: Row, Peterson.

Cartwright, D., & Zander, A. (Eds.). (1960). *Group dynamics: Research and theory* (2nd ed.). Evanston, IL: Row, Peterson.

Cartwright, D., & Zander, A. (Eds.). (1968). *Group dynamics: Research and theory* (3rd ed.). Evanston, IL: Row, Peterson.

Casti, L. (1992). Recent developments and future perspectives in dynamical systems theory. *SEAM Review, 24,* 302–331.

Cook, T. D., & Campbell, D. T. (1979). *Design and analysis of quasi-experiments for field settings.* Chicago: Rand McNally.

Davis, J. H. (1973). Group decisions and social interaction: A theory of social decision schemes. *Psychological Review, 80,* 97–125.

Davis, J. H. (1982). Social interaction as a combinatorial process in group decisions. In H. Brandstatter, J. H. Davis, & G. Stocker-Kreichgauer (Eds.), *Group decision making* (pp. 27–58). London: Academic.

Diehl, M., & Stroebe, W. (1991). Productivity loss in idea-generating groups: Tracking down the blocking effect. *Journal of Personality and Social Psychology, 61,* 392–403.

Drogoul, A., & Ferber, J. (1994). Multi-agent simulations as a tool for studying emergent processes in societies. In N. Gilbert & J. Duran (Eds.), *Simulating societies: The computer simulation of social phenomena* (pp. 127–142). London: University College of London Press.

Gersick, C. J. G. (1988). Time and transition in work teams: Toward a new model of group development. *Academy of Management Journal, 31,* 9–41.

Gersick, C. J. G. (1989) Marking time: Predictable transitions in task groups. *Academy of Management Journal, 32,* 274–309.

Gordon, D. M., Goodwin, B. C., & Trainor, L. E. H. (1992). A parallel distributed model of the behavior of ant colonies. *Journal of Theoretical Biology, 156,* 293–307.

Guastello, S. J. (1995). *Chaos, catastrophe, and human affairs. Application of non-linear dynamics to work, organizations, and social evolution.* Mahwah, NJ: Lawrence Erlbaum Associates, Inc.

Guzzo, R. A., & Dickson, M. W. (1996). Teams in organizations: Recent research on performance and effectiveness. *Annual Review of Psychology, 47,* 307–338.

Hackman, J. R. (Ed.). (1990). *Groups that work (and those that don't).* San Francisco: Jossey-Bass.

Hackman, J. R. (1992). Group influences on individuals in organizations. In M. D. Dunnette & L. M. Hough (Eds.), *Handbook of industrial and organizational psychology* (Vol. 3, 2nd ed., pp. 199–268). Palo Alto, CA: Consulting Psychologists Press.

Hare, A. P. (1976). *Handbook of small group research* (2nd ed.). New York: Free Press.

Hogg, M. A. (1987). Social identity and group cohesiveness. In J. C. Turner, M. A. Hogg, P. J. Oakes, S. D. Reicher, & M. S. Wetherell, (Eds.), *Rediscovering the social group: A self categorization theory* (pp. 89–116). Oxford, England: Blackwell.

Ilgen, D. R. (1999). Teams embedded in organizations. *American Psychologist, 54,* 129–139.

Ilgen, D. R., Major, D. A., Hollenbeck, J. R., & Sego, D. J. (1995). Team research in the 90's. In M. M. Chemers & R. Ayman (Eds.), *Leadership theory and research: Perspectives and directions* (pp. 245–270). New York: Academic.

Insko, C. A., Schopler, J., Kennedy, J. F., Dahl, K. R., Graetz, K. A., & Drigotas, S. M. (1992). Individual–group discontinuity from the differing perspectives of Campbell's realistic group conflict theory and Tajfel and Turner's social identity theory. *Social Psychological Quarterly, 55,* 272–291.

Jehn, K. A. (1995). A multimethod examination of the benefits and detriments of intragroup conflict. *Administrative Sciences Quarterly, 40,* 256–282.

Jehn, K. A. (1997). A qualitative analysis of conflict types and dimensions in organizational groups. *Administrative Sciences Quarterly, 42,* 520–557.

Kaplan, H. L., & Sadock, B. J. (Eds.). (1993). *Comprehensive group psychotherapy* (3rd ed.). Baltimore: Williams & Wilkins.

Karau, S. J., & Kelly, J. R. (1992). The effect of time scarcity and time abundance on group performance quality and interaction process. *Journal of Experimental Social Psychology, 28,* 542–571.

Kelly, J. R. (1988). Entrainment in individual and group behavior. In J. E. McGrath (Ed.), *The social psychology of time: New perspectives* (pp. 89–110). Newbury Park, CA: Sage.

Kelly, J. R., & McGrath, J. E. (1985). Effects of time limits and task types on task performance and interaction of four-person groups. *Journal of Personality and Social Psychology, 49,* 395–407.

Kelso, J. A. S. (1995). *Dynamic patterns: The self-organization of brain and behavior.* Cambridge, MA: MIT Press.

Latané, B. (1996). Dynamic social impact: The creation of culture by communication. *Journal of Communication, 46,* 13–25.

Latané, B., & Nowak, A. (1994). Attitudes as catastrophes: From dimensions to categories with increasing involvement. In R. R. Vallacher & A. Nowak (Eds.), *Dynamical systems in social psychology* (pp. 219–249). New York: Academic.

Levine, J. M., & Moreland, R. L. (1990). Progress in small group research. *Annual Review of Psychology, 41,* 585–634.

Lovaglia, M. J. (1994). Relating power to status. *Advances in Group Process, 11,* 87–111.

Månson, P. (1993). What is a group? A multilevel analysis. *Advances in Group Processes, 16,* 253–281.

McGrath, J. E. (1997). Small group research, that once and future field: An interpretation of the past with an eye to the future. *Group Dynamics: Theory, Research, and Practice, 1,* 1–27.

McGrath, J. E., & Altman, I. (1966). *Small group research: A synthesis and critique of the field.* New York: Holt, Rinehart & Winston.

McGrath, J. E., & Argote, L. (in press). Group processes in organizational contexts. In M. Hogg & S. Tindale (Eds.), *Group processes* (Vol. 3). London: Blackwell.

McGrath, J. E., Arrow, H., & Berdahl, J. L. (1999). Cooperation and conflict as manifestations of coordination in small groups. *Polish Psychological Bulletin, 30*(1), 1–14.

McGrath, J. E., Arrow, H., Gruenfeld, D. H, Hollingshead, A. B., & O'Connor, K. M. (1993). Groups, tasks, and technology: The effects of experience and change. *Small Group Research, 24,* 406–420.

McGrath, J. E., & Kelly, J. R. (1986). *Time and human interaction: Toward a social psychology of time.* New York: Guilford.

Moreland, R. L. (1996). Lewin's legacy for small-groups research. *Systems Practice, 9,* 7–26.

Moreland, R. L., Hogg, M. A., & Hains, S. C. (1994). Back to the future: Social psychological research on groups. *Journal of Experimental Social Psychology, 30,* 527–555.

Moreland, R. L., & Levine, J. M. (1982). Socialization in small groups: Temporal changes in individual–group relations. In L. Berkowitz (Eds.), *Advances in experimental social psychology* (pp. 137–192). New York: Academic.

Morgeson, F. P., & Hofmann, D. A. (1999). The structure and function of collective constructs: Implications for multilevel research and theory development. *Academy of Management Review, 24,* 249–265.

Nowak, A., Szamrej, J., & Latané, B. (1990). From private attitude to public opinion: A dynamic theory of social impact. *Psychological Review, 97,* 362–376.

O'Connor, K. M., Gruenfeld, D. H., & McGrath, J. E. (1993). The experience and effects of conflict in continuing work groups. *Small Group Research, 24,* 362–382.

Polley, R. B. (1989). Operationalizing Lewinian field theory. *Advances in Group Processes, 6,* 205–227.

Poole, M. S., & DeSanctis, G. (1989). Understanding the use of decision support systems: The theory of adaptive structuration. In J. Fulk & C. Steinfeld (Eds.), *Organization and communication technology* (pp. 175–195). Newbury Park, CA: Sage.

Prigogine, L., & Stengers, I. (1984). *Order out of chaos.* New York: Bantam.

Ridgeway, C. L., & Berger, J. (1986). Expectations, legitimization, and dominance behavior in groups. *American Sociological Review, 51,* 603–617.

Sanna, L. J., & Parks, C. D. (1997). Group research trends in social and organizational psychology: Whatever happened to intragroup research? *Psychological Science, 8,* 261–267.

Sherif, M. (1936). *The psychology of social norms.* New York: Harper & Row.

Sherif, M., Harvey, O. J., White, B. J., Hood, W. R., & Sherif, C. W. (1961). *Intergroup conflict and cooperation: The Robbers Cave experiment.* Norman, OK: Institute of Social Relations.

Simmel, G. (1902). The number of members as determining the sociological form of the group. *American Journal of Sociology, 8,* 1–46, 158–196.

Stasser, G., & Titus, W. (1985). Pooling of unshared information in group decision making: Biased information sampling during discussion. *Journal of Personality and Social Psychology, 48,* 1467–1478.

Stasser, G., & Titus, W. (1987). Effects of information load and percentages of shared information on the dissemination of unshared information during discussion. *Journal of Personality and Social Psychology, 53,* 81–93.

Steiner, I. D. (1972). *Group process and productivity.* New York: Academic.

Steiner, I. D. (1974). Whatever happened to the group in social psychology? *Journal of Experimental and Social Psychology, 10,* 84–108.

Sundstrom, E., DeMuese, K. P., & Futrell, D. (1990). Work teams: Applications and effectiveness. *American Psychologist, 45,* 129–133.

Triplett, N. (1898). The dynamogenic factors in pace-making and competition. *American Journal of Psychology, 9,* 507–533.

Tuckman, B. W., & Jensen, M. A. C. (1977). Stages of small group development revisited. *Group and Organizational Studies, 2,* 419–427.

VanLear, C. A., & Mabry, E. A. (1999). Testing contrasting interaction models for discriminating between consensual and dissentient decision-making groups. *Small Group Research, 30,* 29–58.

von Bertalanffy, L. (1968). *General systems theory* (Rev. ed.). New York: Braziller.

Warner, R. M. (1979). Periodic rhythms in conversational speech. *Language and Speech, 22,* 381–396.

Worchel, S. (1994). You can go home again: Returning group research to the group context with an eye on developmental issues. *Small Group Research, 25,* 205–223.

Yalom, I. D. (1995). *The theory and practice of group psychotherapy* (4th ed.). New York: Basic Books.

CONTRIBUTOR INFORMATION

CONTENT: *Personality and Social Psychology Review* (*PSPR*) is devoted to publishing original theoretical papers and conceptual review articles in personality and social psychology. As an official publication of the Society for Personality and Social Psychology, *PSPR* (a) supports the society's objectives of advancing personality and social psychology as a science and as a means of promoting human welfare, (b) provides a voice for the field of personality and social psychology worldwide in the sense of tapping important conceptual and empirical developments and new trends, and (c) presents a versatile outlet to accommodate substantive work that does not readily fit the existing publication molds. Our readership includes social, personality, and organizational psychologists and sociologists.

PSPR is intended as a forum for conceptual pieces that initiate new lines of research and theory or provide a coherent framework for existing theory and programs of research. The journal emphasizes theory-based reviews of empirical contributions to a substantive area of research and offers integrative theoretical formulations concerning work in a given area of personality and/or social psychology. Suitable topics for submission include, but are not restricted to, attitudes and social cognition, personality development, personality assessment, interpersonal processes, group behavior, and intergroup relations.

PSPR complements the society's existing journal, *Personality and Social Psychology Bulletin* (*PSPB*), which now focuses exclusively on empirical papers.

MANUSCRIPT PREPARATION: Use a word processor to prepare manuscript. Using 8½- × 11-in. nonsmear paper, type all components (a) double-spaced, (b) 1,800 to 2,000 characters per page (70 to 75 characters per line [including spaces] × 25 to 27 lines per page), (c) on one side of the paper, (d) with each component beginning on a new page, and (e) in the following order—title page (p. 1), abstract (p. 2), text (including quotations), references, appendices, footnotes, tables, and figure captions. Consecutively number all pages (including photocopies of figures). Indent all paragraphs.

Title Page and Abstract: On page 1, type (a) article title, (b) author name(s) and affiliation(s), (c) running head (abbreviated title, no more than 45 characters and spaces), (d) acknowledgments, and (e) name and address of the person to whom requests for reprints should be addressed. On page 2, type an abstract of no more than 150 words.

Editorial Style and References: Prepare manuscripts according to the *Publication Manual of the American Psychological Association* (4th ed., 1994; APA Order Department, P.O. Box 2710, Hyattsville, MD 20784). Follow "Guidelines to Reduce Bias in Language" (*APA Manual*, pp. 46–60).

Double-space references. Compile references alphabetically (see *APA Manual* for multiple-author citations and references). Spell out names of journals. Provide page numbers of chapters in edited books. Text citations must correspond accurately to the references in the reference list.

Tables: Refer to *APA Manual* for format. Double-space. Provide each table with explanatory title; make title intelligible without reference to text. Provide appropriate heading for each column in table. Indicate clearly any units of measurement used in table. If table is reprinted or adapted from another source, include credit line. Consecutively number all tables.

Figures and Figure Captions: Figures should be (a) high-resolution illustrations or (b) glossy, high-contrast black-and-white photographs.

Do not clip, staple, or write on back of figures; instead, write article title, figure number, and *TOP* (of figure) on label and apply label to back of each figure. Consecutively number figures. Attach photocopies of all figures to manuscript.

Consecutively number captions with Arabic numerals corresponding to the figure numbers; make captions intelligible without reference to text; if figure is reprinted or adapted from another source, include credit line.

COVER LETTER, PERMISSIONS, CREDIT LINES: In cover letter, include contact author's postal and e-mail addresses and phone and fax numbers.

Only original manuscripts submitted to *PSPR* will be considered for publication. The cover letter should include a statement that the findings reported in the manuscript have not been previously published and that the manuscript is not being simultaneously submitted elsewhere.

Authors are responsible for all statements made in their work and for obtaining permission to reprint or adapt a copyrighted table or figure or to quote at length from a copyrighted work. Authors should write to original author(s) and original publisher to request nonexclusive world rights in all languages to use the material in the article and in future editions. Include copies of all permissions and credit lines with the manuscript. (See p. 140 of *APA Manual* for sample credit lines.)

MANUSCRIPT SUBMISSION: Submit four (4) high-quality manuscript printouts to the Editor:

Eliot R. Smith
Department of Psychological Sciences
Purdue University
West Lafayette, IN 47907–1364

MANUSCRIPT REVIEW AND ACCEPTANCE: All manuscripts are peer reviewed.

Authors of accepted manuscripts submit (a) disk containing two files (word-processor and ASCII versions of final, postreview version of manuscript), (b) printout of final, postreview version of manuscript, (c) camera-ready figures, (d) copies of all permissions obtained to reprint or adapt material from other sources, and (e) copyright-transfer agreement signed by all co-authors.

It is the responsibility of the contact author to ascertain that all co-authors approve the accepted manuscript and concur with its publication in the journal.

Content of files must exactly match that of manuscript printout, or there will be a delay in publication. Manuscripts and disk are not returned.

PRODUCTION NOTES: Authors' files are copyedited and typeset into page proofs. Authors read proofs to correct errors and answer editors' queries.

www.ingramcontent.com/pod-product-compliance
Ingram Content Group UK Ltd.
Pitfield, Milton Keynes, MK11 3LW, UK
UKHW012331270225
455677UK00027B/809